GLOBALIZATION, POVERTY, AND INCOME INEQUALITY

The Asia Pacific Legal Culture and Globalization series explores intersecting themes that revolve around the impact of globalization in countries on the Asia Pacific Rim and examines the significance of legal culture as a mediator of that impact. The emphasis is on a broad understanding of legal culture that extends beyond traditional legal institutions and actors to normative frameworks and the legal consciousness of ordinary people. Books in the series reflect international scholarship from a wide variety of disciplines, including law, political science, economics, sociology, and history.

Other volumes in the series are:

Pitman B. Potter, *Exporting Virtue? China's International Human Rights Activism in the Age of Xi Jinping*

Sarah Biddulph and Ljiljana Biuković, *Good Governance in Economic Development: International Norms and Chinese Perspectives*

Moshe Hirsch, Ashok Kotwal, and Bharat Ramaswami, eds., *A Human Rights Based Approach to Development in India*

Daniel Drache and Lesley A. Jacobs, eds., *Grey Zones in International Economic Law and Global Governance*

Sarah Biddulph, *The Stability Imperative: Human Rights and Law in China*

Pitman B. Potter, *Assessing Treaty Performance in China: Trade and Human Rights*

Pitman B. Potter and Ljiljana Biuković, eds., *Globalization and Local Adaptation in International Trade Law*

GLOBALIZATION, POVERTY, AND INCOME INEQUALITY

INSIGHTS FROM INDONESIA

Edited by Richard Barichello,
Arianto A. Patunru, and
Richard Schwindt

UBCPress
1971–2021

30 29 28 27 26 25 24 23 22 21   5 4 3 2 1

Printed in Canada on FSC-certified ancient-forest-free paper (100% post-consumer recycled) that is processed chlorine- and acid-free.

Library and Archives Canada Cataloguing in Publication

Title: Globalization, poverty, and income inequality : insights from Indonesia / edited by Richard Barichello, Arianto Patunru, and Richard Schwindt.
Names: Barichello, Richard R., editor. | Patunru, Arianto Arif, editor. | Schwindt, Richard, editor.
Series: Asia Pacific legal culture and globalization (Series)
Description: Series statement: Asia Pacific legal culture and globalization, 1925-0320 | Includes bibliographical references and index.
Identifiers: Canadiana (print) 20210247134 | Canadiana (ebook) 2021024738X | ISBN 9780774865616 (hardcover) | ISBN 9780774865623 (paperback) | ISBN 9780774865630 (PDF) | ISBN 9780774865647 (EPUB)
Subjects: LCSH: Globalization — Indonesia. | LCSH: Poverty — Indonesia. | LCSH: Income distribution — Indonesia. | LCSH: Indonesia — Economic conditions. | LCSH: Indonesia — Social conditions. | LCSH: Indonesia — Foreign economic relations.
Classification: LCC HC447 .G56 2021 | DDC 338.9598 — dc23

Canadä

UBC Press gratefully acknowledges the financial support for our publishing program of the Government of Canada (through the Canada Book Fund) and the British Columbia Arts Council.

This book has been published with the help of a grant from the Canadian Federation for the Humanities and Social Sciences, through the Awards to Scholarly Publications Program, using funds provided by the Social Sciences and Humanities Research Council of Canada.

Printed and bound in Canada
Set in Segoe and Warnock by Artegraphica Design Co.
Copy editor: Deborah Kerr
Proofreader: Jonathan Dore
Indexer: Noeline Bridge
Cover designer: Alexa Love

UBC Press
The University of British Columbia
2029 West Mall
Vancouver, BC V6T 1Z2
www.ubcpress.ca

Contents

Figures and Tables

Figures

Tables

Foreword

PITMAN B. POTTER

This volume examines the conditions of policy development and implementation on issues of human rights and trade in Indonesia, with particular attention to poverty and inequality under globalization. The collected essays discuss trade-related human rights issues such as poverty and income inequality, child well-being, food security, and property rights in local context. Exploring the coordination of trade policy and poverty alleviation in Indonesia, the chapters provide invaluable knowledge on the challenges and opportunities attending relationships between trade and human rights more broadly.

Coordinating local development with international trade and human rights standards is a critical issue for the globalized world. International, regional, and subnational disputes over issues of trade and human rights present increasingly serious obstacles to international cooperation on local development. Resolving and where possible preventing such disagreements will benefit the course of international cooperation in areas of trade and human rights. Such efforts will also help reduce transactional, operational, and opportunity costs resulting from international disputes that make existing relationships more complex and expensive, require significant management costs, and distract public- and private-sector leaders from other more productive pursuits.

Coordinating local performance of human rights standards under conditions of globalization has been difficult in part because of conceptual differences and assumed trade-offs between human rights ideals and trade and development policies. All too often, human rights standards are seen as inconsistent with economic goals of efficiency, growth, and private property rights. Conversely, trade and development policy is often seen as an obstacle to human development goals in areas such as health, education, and food security. As well, coordinating performance of human rights and trade and development standards has been elusive because the officials and specialists who manage local interpretation and implementation of these regimes often have few opportunities for institutional collaboration. The human rights discourse of the right to development offers a potential bridge between these two solitudes.

This volume is supported by the Asia Pacific Dispute Resolution (APDR) Project at the Peter A. Allard School of Law and the Institute of Asian Research at the University of British Columbia (UBC). The theme of the APDR program is "Understanding Integrated Compliance with International Trade and Human Rights Standards from a Comparative Perspective." The project works to build knowledge and policy support for coordinating local performance of international trade and human rights standards in ways that are mutually sustaining rather than conflicted. Since 2009, it has supported policy research in the Asia-Pacific region, with particular attention to Canada, China, India, Indonesia, and Japan. The APDR Project involves a collaborative network of colleagues from UBC and from partner institutions in North America, Asia, and Australia. The project has generated policy proposals for building treaty compliance programs, processes, and institutions that are more responsive to cross-cultural differences and aim to resolve and where possible prevent disputes over trade and human rights. The results of the research are enabling interdisciplinary scholars and policy makers to understand better the requirements for coordinated performance and have the potential to reduce and forestall conflict over trade and human rights, thus benefiting international cooperation.

This book is part of a group of five new edited volumes examining various aspects of local human rights performance presented by the APDR Project and published in the UBC Press Asia Pacific Legal Culture and Globalization series. The volume topics involve the interaction of trade policy with human rights in labour; human rights in health; the right to development; dilemmas of poverty and income inequality; and government accountability and transparency. The work is characterized by a high degree of interdisciplinarity though focused on questions of legal culture, international law, and globalization in the countries that compose the Asia-Pacific region.

The books are grounded in original empirical research as well as qualitative and quantitative analysis relating to international trade and human rights.

Research for this volume and the APDR Project has been supported by the Social Sciences and Humanities Research Council of Canada under its Major Collaborative Research Initiatives program, for which my colleagues and I are deeply thankful. The APDR Project has benefited immensely from input and advice from an International Advisory Board comprised as follows:

The Honourable Jack Austin (former Government Leader in the Senate of
    Canada, former President Canada China Business Council),
Joseph Caron (former Canadian High Commissioner to India, Ambassador
    to China, and Ambassador to Japan),
The Honourable Irwin Cotler (former Member of Parliament and Minister of
    Justice Canada),
Professor Thomas Cottier (former Managing Director, World Trade Institute,
    Berne, Switzerland),
Jonathan Fried (Senior Associate, Center for International and Strategic Stud-
    ies; formerly Coordinator for International Economic Relations, Global
    Affairs Canada; former Ambassador and Permanent Representative of
    Canada to the World Trade Organization, Geneva, Switzerland)
Professor John Hogarth (Professor Emeritus, Peter A. Allard School of Law,
    University of British Columbia), and
Professor Hans-Ulrich Petersmann (European University, Florence ITA).

This project has included a wide range of graduate students and post-doctoral research fellows, who contributed as researchers, analysts, and writers. The work on this volume was greatly enhanced by the input of Wisnu Adiwijoyo, Abby Kendrick, and Alison Yule.

I have been privileged to serve as principal investigator for the APDR Project. I am grateful to the many colleagues from across our research network who have contributed their time and expertise to strengthen the work we have done together. Particular thanks go to Project Manager Rozalia Mate for her stellar contributions to the operational details of the project.

GLOBALIZATION, POVERTY, AND INCOME INEQUALITY

1

Indonesia

Economic History, Growth, Poverty, Income Inequality, and Trade

RICHARD BARICHELLO

Whatever one's views about globalization, whether it is good or bad, diminishing or being sustained, the topic generates ongoing debate about its effects on various human rights. This volume contributes to that important discussion with a set of eleven largely empirical chapters focused on the country of Indonesia.

The two main human rights areas examined here, poverty and income inequality, are highly important and, if anything, growing in significance as public policy issues around the world. Poverty has always been a high-priority topic, especially in developing countries and to major international aid agencies such as the World Bank. But income inequality vaulted back into prominence after the publication of Thomas Piketty's *Capital in the Twenty-First Century* (2013) with new data showing rapid increases in inequality around the globe. With respect to both poverty and inequality, much debate persists about the extent of the problems, their causes, and the best public policy responses to address them. Moreover, there is increasing interest from both academic and public policy perspectives regarding the causal links between growing inequality in rich countries and other social problems such as suicide and substance abuse (most recently, see "Mourning in America" 2020).

For globalization, the other main topic in this volume, we primarily focus on international trade, but we also include globalized standards, such as those associated with an expansion of trade and markets. The impact of international trade on these two human rights concerns has become one of the most debated topics in international and domestic politics. This increased attention is particularly encouraged through the trade policies of the Trump administration but is also evident in the Brexit referendum and the new Brexit-related policies of the United Kingdom. Aside from the costly uncertainty these trade policies have created for all countries, they have reignited a long-standing dispute about the merits of freer trade in a wide range of countries, not just the United States and Britain. This book addresses both these highly topical subject areas directly.

A developing country, Indonesia has attained some success in moving into the lower reaches of the "middle income" category. However, its poverty-reduction achievements of the 1980s and 1990s have not been matched since then, a lack of success that is broadly attributed to Acemoglu and Robinson's (2012) "middle income trap." This has prompted much debate within Indonesia as to whether the populist policies of the current president, Joko Widodo ("Jokowi"), to restrict trade have actually reduced or increased poverty since he came to power in 2014. Similarly, given that inequality is worsening in Indonesia, there is disagreement over whether his recent policies have helped or hindered its amelioration.

These questions are addressed empirically in the current volume. The analyses use local data and related evidence, making this book a useful country case study for international researchers who are interested in these popular topics and eager for additional country data and experiences, especially from such a large country. And, importantly, it is highly topical *within* Indonesia in the context of the lively policy debates noted above, and can contribute to those discussions.

Another feature of this volume is that some chapters do not simply use aggregate data to probe the issues. Half of them delve into micro circumstances (case studies), where the standard conclusions appear not to hold. Therefore, the reader can recognize nuances that must be kept in mind in addressing the effects of freer trade on poverty or inequality in specific regional or sectoral/commodity areas in Indonesia. This serves to remind researchers that results are often dependent on local situations, something that can be lost when only aggregate data are used. By contrast, many chapters in this book, and indeed many volumes in the Asia Pacific Legal Culture and Globalization series, place a premium on local circumstances. This means attention to local institutions, local technologies, and micro-data that condition or impose constraints on decisions by firms and individuals.

To provide context for this book, we turn first to a description of Indonesia, with specific attention to its economic history and data on four important variables of this volume: economic growth, poverty, income inequality, and trade. Finally, we give a detailed overview of the component studies and their findings.

Background to Indonesia

Straddling the equator and spread across an archipelago of thousands of islands, Indonesia is a large, diverse middle-income country. It possesses many distinctions: it has the fourth-largest population in the world (258 million in 2015), the world's largest Muslim population, the tenth-largest economy in purchasing power parity terms (and the largest in Southeast Asia), membership in the G-20, and more than three hundred ethnic groups. Given its large population, it is also characterized by high density, especially on the island of Java, a feature that has posed challenges for food production and poverty reduction, especially prior to the mid-1980s (World Bank 2017).

In 1998, it became a lively democracy and has had direct elections for the president since 2004. It also shifted from highly centralized political decision-making during the era of President Soeharto (1967–98), becoming one of the most decentralized states in the world. Unexpected as this was, it generated praise in light of Indonesia's geographical context and history. As Walden (2017) puts it: "While its neighbours in Southeast Asia have become increasingly autocratic, Indonesia continues to quietly consolidate its democratic institutions and run successful elections for numerous levels of government." However, more recently than 2017 a different perspective has gained traction, that democracy in Indonesia has been declining in quality: "The Jokowi government has taken an 'authoritarian turn' ahead of the 2019 elections, highlighting its manipulation of powerful law enforcement and security institutions for narrow, partisan purposes, as well as the administration's concerted efforts to undermine and repress democratic opposition" (Power 2018, 307).

The country has experienced relatively rapid economic growth and a moderate degree of trade openness at 43 percent of GDP (2018 data), up from 24 percent in 1960. But for comparison, this is only two-thirds the level of trade openness found in Canada today. As part of the post-1998 democratization, local populism has taken the form of demands for more protectionist policies in a variety of economic sectors. One result is that this measure of trade openness has fallen significantly from 96 percent in 1998 back to the levels from the late 1970s to the early 1990s (World Bank 2019b).

These substantial changes in economic policy, performance, trade, and democracy make Indonesia very attractive for doing quantitative research on related economic topics. It has generated high levels of variability in those factors, which make it a valuable case study for measuring statistically how changes in trade openness affect other variables of importance, such as poverty and income inequality. To give some background on the nature of the Indonesian economy and how it has performed in a selection of economic spheres, we review detailed data on economic growth, poverty, and income inequality.

Economic Growth Performance

During the 1960s, some influential development economists (such as Gunnar Myrdal) believed that Indonesia would never achieve rising incomes, but since the late 1960s they have grown quickly by any standard. The most rapid increase occurred from 1970 to the Asian Financial Crisis that began in 1997, during which Indonesia averaged 6.6 percent real growth in GDP per year. This performance would rank the country among the top ten performing economies in the world over this period (Germany, Korea, and China, for example, grew at 9.0, 8.9, and 8.7 percent each year, respectively). It would also put Indonesia ahead of Chile, Brazil, Japan, and Turkey, vaulting the country upward in terms of almost all indicators of economic and social development (World Bank 2019a).

From 2001 to 2015, its growth slowed notably, but it still remained in the narrow range of 4.9 to 6.2 percent per year. Whereas 5.5 percent annual compound growth in real GDP during this period did not match China's Olympian record, it nonetheless meant that Indonesia has grown sufficiently to double average incomes every thirteen years. This has moved it well up into the World Bank's "middle income" tier, with a per capita income above US$3,500 since 2010. This places Indonesia almost at the top of the "lower middle income" category. To put this trend in terms of actual levels, GDP per capita rose from US$857 in 2000 to US$3,603 by 2016. It has also had strong positive effects in reducing poverty, in both urban and rural areas.

Indonesia's economy pursued the following trajectory: it grew at 7.4 percent per year during the 1970s, 5.5 percent in the 1980s, 6.9 percent from 1990 to 1997, but only 4.1 percent from 1990 to 2000 (adding in the significant recession, –13 percent in 1998, of the Asian Financial Crisis), 5.2 percent in the 2000s, and 5.5 percent from 2010 to 2018. The performance of those last nine years is equal to the average growth rate of the entire forty-eight years from 1971 to 2018 (5.6 percent per year). It is normal for a country's growth rate to decline as incomes increase, but Indonesia's performance was probably strongly influenced by its changing stance on trade policy. To put this differently, the slowdown in growth rates since the Asian Financial Crisis shows signs that Indonesia is falling into the "middle income trap," described so convincingly by Acemoglu and Robinson (2012). This economic growth experience is given attention here because of its strong influence on other economic and social well-being variables of interest to our topic.

Poverty

Diminishing poverty has been a major objective of the Indonesian government. Although this goal does not particularly distinguish Indonesia from other developing countries, its success in this regard does. Few countries can show as much poverty reduction as Indonesia has achieved since about 1970, especially during certain subperiods. In other words, across several administrations, Indonesia appears to be serious about attaining this objective.

This commitment has its origins in the so-called *orde baru* (new order) period of President Soeharto, from 1967 to 1998. Not only did the government adopt poverty reduction as a relatively explicit policy, it also achieved commendable success. This claim is not meant to whitewash other policy and performance characteristics of the period. Indeed, Soeharto's policies increasingly favoured his family and cronies, corruption and rent seeking were commonplace, and human rights were given a low priority. But an objective review of the period must note the many-pronged policy attention to poverty, especially in rural areas where it is most severe, and the commitment to realize success here from the very top. Even Soeharto's attention to poverty can be seen as rooted in a traditional and fundamental Indonesian value, captured in the Indonesian term *gotong royong,* "mutual assistance" or "mutual self-help." As Prawiro (1998, 85) describes it,

> *Gotong royong* grew over centuries of Indonesia history and cannot be attributed to any particular government or individual. If, for example, a villager finds himself in distress, be it financial, physical, or even emotional, according to *gotong royong* it is the duty of the other villagers to help solve the problem.

In holding this value, Indonesia can be contrasted with countries that value the individualism of unfettered laissez-faire capitalism.

Over the period from 2000 to 2016, Indonesia has experienced considerable success in lowering its poverty rate. Using Indonesia's official poverty ("headcount") line as the metric, poverty has fallen from affecting 19 percent of the population in the year 2000 to 10 percent in 2018. This decline has been remarkably sustained, except for a brief 2 percentage point increase in 2006. From 2006 to 2013, the poverty rate fell relatively rapidly, by 0.9 percentage points per year. Although it has continued to fall each subsequent year to 2018, the downward trajectory in the poverty rate has flattened.

However, as for the economic growth rate, these gains are dwarfed by those from the 1970s to the 1990s. The data from that period use a lower threshold for the poverty line, so they are not entirely comparable to the more recent data cited above, but in 1976, the share of the population below that poverty line was 41 percent. This figure had fallen to 29 percent by 1980, to 18 percent by 1987, and to 11 percent by 1996. These improvements were quite spectacular, showing remarkable success relative to most countries, even if many people by the mid-1990s remained not far above that poverty line. Current World Bank data using a different poverty line threshold indicate somewhat higher poverty rates, showing them at 17.5 percent in 1996, rising to 23 percent in 1999 (following the Asian Financial Crisis), then declining quite steadily, as noted above, to the 2018 value of 10 percent (World Bank 2018).

This success was accomplished by a great variety of policy instruments, in addition to the kind of economic growth mentioned above. That growth, especially when it exceeded roughly 6 percent a year, appeared to have a particularly strong effect in reducing poverty. In addition, government macro-economic policy was always sound and kept inflation at moderate levels (below 10 percent a year). Food prices were also kept relatively low in the 1970s, although this policy was replaced from the 1990s onward by measures that raised prices, especially that of rice, arguably to assist farmers.

A number of policies were more effective in helping rural residents by supporting rural areas differentially, especially in the 1970s and 1980s, including supplying cash grants to otherwise poor local governments and investing in infrastructure, health care centres, and schools. Broad support for agriculture was undertaken to increase food crop production through protectionist border policies (tariffs and import quotas) as well as large fertilizer subsidies. During the 1980s and 1990s, Indonesia favoured programs of low-priced rice, and since about 2000 has favoured cash grants, both targeting families designated as "poor."

Finally, unlike that of some other Asian countries, the government refrained from imposing restrictions on rural-to-urban migration. This perhaps unplanned "policy" may have been one of the most effective rural anti-poverty strategies. Relocating from the countryside to the city is a well-established trend in Indonesia. It is propelled by many factors but is aided by both high population density, especially on Java, and moderate levels of education that enable rural residents to be competitive in finding city jobs, in addition to the aforementioned lack of migration restrictions.

Income Inequality

Indonesia has long had the social objective of trying to ensure that its economic progress would be widely shared among citizens. Even during the Soeharto era, a wide distribution of the fruits of economic growth was clearly promoted by certain economics-related cabinet ministers, known collectively as the "Berkeley mafia," a name derived from the University of California campus where a number of these "technocrat" ministers received their PhDs. One could argue that this unstated "policy" had its origins in gotong royong, mutual assistance, as was the case for poverty reduction. This objective was seen as desirable even though a number of government policies had regressive effects, as is common in virtually all countries. Furthermore, in any policy analysis it was considered a requirement for the analyst to undertake a detailed evaluation of a policy's distributional effects.

The most widely used measure of inequality is the Gini coefficient, which ranges from 0 to 100 percent, with lower values indicating more equality and higher values showing greater inequality.[1] Back in the 1980s, Indonesia's Gini was in the upper twenties to lower thirties percent, considered internationally to be a relatively equal distribution of income. However, as in most countries, the Indonesian Gini coefficient rose after 2000. It was at 30 percent in 2000, rising to about 35 in 2005, to 40–41 in 2012–13, and falling slightly since then. In March 2016, it dropped 1.1 points to 39.7 percent, which was the first time since 2011 that it had dipped below 40. This decline is due to income gains by the middle 40 percent of households, largely at the expense of the top 20 percent of households. On the whole, Indonesia's Gini coefficient has resembled that of Canada, and the two measures have moved similarly during this period. Indonesia has also been quite successful in avoiding Gini coefficient increases to the 45–55 range. Coefficients in this range indicate high levels of income inequality and are associated with Singapore, Brazil, China, and the United States.

Government policies have played a role in this accomplishment. Although Indonesia has a relatively low average rate for income tax, with modest progressivity in rates, it has various government programs whose purpose is to increase incomes or lower the prices of basic consumption items for the poor. For example, a conditional cash transfer program was expanded in 2015 to include 3.5 million households. The World Bank estimates that this change contributed possibly 0.1 percentage points of reduction in poverty, almost one-third of the observed decline in the poverty rate in 2016. Although one could argue that most redistributive programs in Indonesia focus on reducing poverty rather than on introducing progressive taxation of higher-income households, these measures still have some effect on lowering Gini coefficients because they raise the incomes of the poorest groups.

Elsewhere in this volume, empirical studies measure the effects of other policy variables in lowering the Gini coefficient, such as increasing trade openness. Another set of policies, used both to reduce poverty and income inequality, have aimed to increase the domestic supply of rice and make it more available to poor people. But in fact, rice prices on balance have increased substantially since the mid-1980s, showing that policy objectives other than poverty reduction are at work, such as supporting farmer incomes. And the latter objective appears to dominate the desire to lower rice prices to consumers. The chosen government rhetoric is that raising rice prices will diminish poverty among rice *farmers*, and this too is examined in Chapters 6 and 7.

Trade

As noted earlier, Indonesia had a moderate level of trade openness at 43 percent of GDP in 2018 (World Bank 2019b). For comparison, both the world average and the average across East Asia and the Pacific (the World Bank region that contains Indonesia and its Southeast Asian [i.e., Asian] neighbours) sit at 58 percent. But this measure has fluctuated greatly over the past sixty years. It bounced between 10 and 35 percent during the unstable 1960s, climbed steadily from 29 percent to 54 percent in the 1970s, and largely flattened for the next eighteen years, from 53 percent in 1980 to 56 percent in 1997. This masked a decline in trade openness during a protectionist period in the first half of the 1980s (to 40 percent), followed by a rising share of trade in a unique interlude of unilateral trade deregulation that occurred in the late 1980s and early 1990s. The result was an export boom that increased openness from 40 percent to 56 percent over the decade until the country was hit with the 1997 Asian Financial Crisis.

But after a 1998 spike, trade openness declined quite steadily from about 70 percent to its current low level of around 40 percent. Data on trade in services show that it has dropped even more significantly than trade in goods. In 2000, services trade accounted for 12.5 percent of GDP, but by 2010 its share had fallen to 6.0 percent. These declines are a reflection, in part, of the increasing tendency toward protectionism in Parliament and among political leaders since the 1998 instigation of free elections. The advent of democracy has seen an explosion in industry lobbying, which has commonly pushed for higher trade barriers. Politicians have largely complied. It is as if politicians and policy makers have become increasingly doubtful of the benefits of trade openness for economic growth and poverty reduction. Some of the chapters in this volume address this question empirically.

The end result of these political pressures, policy decisions, and other factors is that trade has grown more slowly in Indonesia than in most of its neighbours, such as China, India, Malaysia, and Vietnam. In 2015, their measures of trade openness were 40 percent, 42 percent, 134 percent, and 179 percent, respectively, compared with Indonesia's 42 percent. But since 1980, China's trade openness has increased by 226 percent, India's by 179 percent, Malaysia's by 19 percent, and Vietnam's by a whopping 670 percent (since 1986 only). In Indonesia, by contrast, trade openness actually *declined* by 20 percent after 1980.

Recently, in the four years from 2012 to 2015, Indonesian adoption of trade-restricting measures surpassed its adoption of trade-liberalizing measures. During that period, Indonesia was among the world's top users of trade barriers (World Bank 2016), mostly in the form of non-tariff measures. However, a reversal of these actions occurred in 2016, with trade-liberalizing measures dominating for three consecutive quarters, even though non-tariff measures continue to proliferate. Given the volatility of trade policy measures over the years, it is unclear if 2016 signals a change in policy direction. In any case, it will not affect the work in this volume, virtually all of which involves data from earlier years. What is clear is that whenever trade restrictions increase, as they have often done since 2000, they almost always result in higher consumer prices and, to some degree, more poverty.

The Chapters in This Volume

This volume consists of eleven chapters. Although Chapter 2 reviews the literature on income inequality that is not specific to Indonesia, the others focus on Indonesian data and institutions, and most are authored or co-authored by Indonesians. They show the impacts of economic globalization, largely focused on trade but also examining foreign direct investment (FDI, now often included in trade agreements), standards, land rights, and markets, on the two dimensions of human rights, poverty and income inequality. The chapters do not primarily discuss how national institutions or policies function. They do, however, pay substantial attention to the policy implications or options arising from their findings, even if those policies did not enter directly into their work.

Poverty is defined as an absolute level of income, with several widely used numeraires. For the distribution of incomes, the focus is on how widely incomes are spread at the bottom and top of the distribution as measured by Gini coefficients.

The chapters are a mix of a) overall measured relationships between poverty or income inequality and increased globalization, especially trade, and b) micro case studies that explore disaggregated results by region, commodity, population subgroups, or unique regulatory circumstances such as property rights. Combining aggregate data results and micro perspectives in the same study is somewhat unusual.

Aggregate data at the level of the country, province, or county give broad relationships, which are important for choosing policy directions. But micro studies are also essential in showing that populations are not homogeneous, that numerous exceptions to standard results do arise, and that the distribution effects across subgroups are significant. Subgroup experiences can generate opposition to policies that favour the general good, and *that* opposition can derail policies that are in the overall public interest. Identification of such subgroups can suggest where special policy support could be devised to compensate those who lose due to the policy. Policies that reduce trade barriers or circumstances that arise from increased globalization are good examples. The research in this book illustrates a variety of cases in which overall benefits occur, though with some localized losses or disadvantaged groups.

Across the chapters, we show support using Indonesian data for the relationship between increased trade and reduced poverty, but that findings are mixed for the effect of increased trade on inequality levels. This is broadly consistent with studies conducted elsewhere. A majority of the chapters also reveal that when one disaggregates in some fashion, exceptions occur. For example, some globalization measures have no quantifiable effect on the incomes of farmers. Although globalization reduces poverty overall, the well-being of children can be diminished in certain circumstances. Similarly, there are mixed health outcomes from globalization.

In Chapter 2, James Dean and Colin McLean examine the global evidence on whether economic growth increases or decreases inequality. They also outline the existing policy options that address inequality. The authors find broad empirical evidence that income inequality has *increased* across countries over the last thirty years but contradictory evidence to support the widespread view that a trade-off inevitably occurs between growth and inequality. In looking at national policy options to deal with growing inequality, they argue that public investment is preferable to cash transfers. But they also draw out the point that international trade agreements could exacerbate income inequality unless appropriate mechanisms counter it.

Chapter 3, by Teguh Dartanto, Yusuf Sofiyandi, and Nia Kurnia Sholihah, employs trade openness (total trade/GDP) as a variable to explain poverty levels and income inequality. The authors use a panel of eleven years of data drawn from thirty-three Indonesian provinces. The results show that trade openness significantly increases economic growth, and although it reduces poverty, the effect is small. It also worsens income inequality, but here too with a very small effect. These findings for Indonesia mirror the general literature review presented in Chapter 2.

In Chapter 4, Yessi Vadila and Budy Resosudarmo seek to explain regional expenditure inequality. In this chapter, the effect of globalization, measured by trade openness and foreign direct investment, on inequality is examined through a panel of eight years and twenty-two provinces. During the period under study, all three variables rose in most provinces. But when the model was estimated with a larger set of explanatory variables, the effects were mixed: FDI in a province lowered its inequality, trade openness increased it, and inequality in higher education resulted in greater income disparity. The authors also found support for a Kuznets effect on growth versus inequality, in that as incomes grew, inequality rose but then fell.

Chapter 5, written by Santi Kusumaningrum and her colleagues, deals with a particular dimension of poverty – children in low-income families. The chapter discusses many elements of child well-being (health, nutrition, education, and birth registration) and how children suffer disproportionately from both inequality of incomes and poverty. The authors build on the results from Chapter 2 by showing that even with expanded trade and the resulting aggregate poverty reduction, child poverty can rise due to poverty-inequality interactions. Policy and programs are discussed at length to show how children can best achieve their potential and to ensure that the benefits of increased trade and incomes can trickle down to poor kids.

In Chapter 6, Richard Barichello and Faisal Harahap focus on rural poverty by examining the effects of rice prices (in effect, trade policy through import tariffs) on farm wage rates. Standard political rhetoric argues that higher rice prices are needed to raise the incomes of poor rice farmers, meaning that robust trade barriers will help the poor. However, the results of this chapter contradict this common claim. They show that, in fact, higher rice prices have very small positive effects on farm wage rates, a trend that is strongly offset by their negative impact on rice consumers. The latter category includes the many farms that produce rice but are still *net* rice buyers. These results indicate that *reducing* trade barriers in rice actually helps to lessen overall poverty, both rural and urban. They also demonstrate that ongoing increases in the non-farm wage rates have had almost ten times the positive effect on farm wage rates than higher rice prices, which were introduced in 2000. The policy implication here is that, where reducing rural poverty is concerned, non-farm economic growth is a more effective tool than raising rice prices, which is consistent with the findings of the next chapter.

Chapter 7, by Arianto Patunru, is a case study of rice, taking access to food as a human right. The author reveals that a disaggregated approach at the commodity level is valuable to understand the distributional effects of trade policy. Offering a comprehensive review of the data, he shows that trade restrictions on rice have raised the domestic price far above comparable international examples. Restricting access to globalized rice markets has hurt all rice consumers, but because this staple food is so important in Indonesia, it has particularly harmed the poorest segment of society while benefiting only a small group of wealthier people. These results support those of Chapter 6 by concluding that reducing rice trade barriers will help decrease poverty in Indonesia.

In Chapter 8, Bustanul Arifin examines the impact of new global export standards on the well-being of coffee farmers. This applies specifically to eco-certification, in which certain environmental standards must be followed in growing this crop. It is effectively a product-branding measure that is consumer-driven but is expected to help coffee growers. The data for Indonesia appear to indicate that eco-certification has had little influence on farm-gate prices for coffee producers. But it does provide other benefits of a social nature, including improvements in community-cooperative governance, coordinating the work of farmer organizations, and encouraging other methods to enhance coffee quality.

Chapter 9, by Evi Nurvidya Arifin and Aris Ananta, describes how globalized adoption of digital technologies has placed people with visual disabilities at an even greater disadvantage, due to the heightened demand for good eyesight. In fact, this demand has exposed the substantial neglect of vision problems in Indonesia. What is even more frustrating is that thanks to global improvements in eye care, many of the conditions mentioned in the chapter are relatively inexpensive to treat. Unlike the examples in earlier chapters, this case largely revolves around technologically driven aspects of globalization, rather than government policy such as trade protection. But here the new technologies present both problems and cures. Nevertheless, serious attention to this increasingly critical problem calls for a set of government policy responses.

In Chapter 10, Michael Leaf discusses urban property rights. In effectively managing globalization, one element of public policy is getting the institutions right, such as the institutions that support international trade. This typically includes establishing some form of freehold ownership in land to provide tenure security for local economic investment, as the prevailing global standard in property rights. But this is too simple in the case of Jakarta, where there has been a rearticulation of the colonial-era land law that underpins the so-called informal market in land and emphasizes the traditional role of territorial land claims as a collective right. The result is a dualism, with traditional collective rights sitting alongside a modern (globalized) set of individual property rights, officially registered by the corporate development sector. This chapter shows how these two often conflict. The private trade and investment sector can claim formal rights to the city, but the collective political right of those who are excluded from this growth of the formal economy is also voiced, creating tension and conflict. New institutions to resolve this situation are needed but not yet in evidence.

In the final chapter, Richard Schwindt reflects on the ties between what is written in the economics and human rights literatures on the interface between globalization and compliance with international human rights. He notes the close correspondence between the two in terms of poverty. But economic inequality can be separated into horizontal and vertical inequality. Here, the economics and human rights communities are quite aligned on horizontal inequality but much less so on vertical inequality. Economists have increased their attention to economic inequality in recent years, but unlike freedom from extreme poverty, economic equality is not yet clearly recognized as a human right. The author reviews the chapters in the volume, drawing out the lessons they provide.

Note

1 A Gini coefficient of 0 (or 0 percent) indicates perfect equality where all incomes are equal, and a value of 1 (or 100 percent) shows maximum inequality, such as where one person has all the income and everyone else has no income. In practice, a value of 20–30 percent shows a very high level of income equality (as in the Scandinavian countries), whereas values above 50 percent characterize countries with the most unequal income distribution.

References

Acemoglu, Daron, and James A. Robinson. 2012. *Why Nations Fail: The Origins of Power, Prosperity, and Poverty.* New York: Crown.

"Mourning in America." 2020. *Economist,* January 11, 64.

Piketty, Thomas. 2014 (English). *Capital in the Twenty-First Century.* Cambridge, MA: Harvard University Press.

Power, Thomas P. 2018. "Jokowi's Authoritarian Turn and Indonesia's Democratic Decline." *Bulletin of Indonesian Economic Studies* 54, 3: 307–38. DOI: 10.1080/00074918.2018.1549918.

Prawiro, Radius. 1998. *Indonesia's Struggle for Economic Development: Pragmatism in Action.* New York: Oxford University Press.

Walden, Max. 2017. "Democracy in Indonesia: A Cause for Celebration." *The Interpreter,* February 20. https://www.lowyinstitute.org/the-interpreter/democracy-indonesia-cause-celebration.

World Bank. 2016. "Indonesia Economic Quarterly, June 2016: Resilience through Reforms." http://www.worldbank.org/en/country/indonesia/publication/indonesia-economic-quarterly-june-2016-resilience-through-reforms.

–. 2017. "Indonesia Overview." http://www.worldbank.org/en/country/indonesia/overview.

–. 2018. "Poverty headcount ratio at national poverty lines (% of Population)-Indonesia." https://data.worldbank.org/indicator/SI.POV.NAHC?locations=ID.

–. 2019a. "GDP growth (annual %) – Indonesia." Constant 2010 US$. https://data.worldbank.org/indicator/NY.GDP.MKTP.KD.ZG?locations=ID

–. 2019b. "Trade (% of GDP)-Indonesia." https://data.worldbank.org/indicator/NE.TRD.GNFS.ZS?locations=ID.

2

Globalization and Inequality

Causes, Consequences, and Cures

JAMES W. DEAN and COLIN McLEAN

Most economists agree that globalization encourages growth. Most also agree that growth reduces absolute poverty: "a rising tide lifts all boats." But whether growth increases or decreases income inequality is the subject of fierce debate. This essay looks at that disagreement.

We consider both theory and evidence but concentrate on evidence. We also ask whether and how public policy might intervene to reduce inequality. In theory, free market growth in the absence of redistributive taxes and transfers will inevitably benefit some more than others, since both talent and opportunity are unequally endowed. Public policy can intervene by redistributing income to compensate for disparities in talent but also by increasing equality of opportunity.

Much of the debate about policies to reduce inequality is rooted in disagreement about which kind of intervention to emphasize. Options include not just income redistribution but wealth redistribution, the most extreme version of which advocates ownership of the means of production by the population at large: communism.

Why Benefits from Globalization Are Unequally Distributed

We take it as given that globalization leads to growth and ask instead whether such growth necessarily leads to inequality. We also ask, later in the essay, whether inequality is necessary to engender growth. These issues require careful distinctions between types of inequality. Following Milanovic (2016), we distinguish between three:

1 Intra-national inequality: between individuals in a given country
2 International inequality: between countries, based on a representative income
3 Global inequality: between all individuals in the world.

The relationship between inequality and growth must be considered through each of these lenses. By "globalization" we mean increased flows of goods, services, capital, technology, finance, and people between countries. It is tempting to assume that such flows, if they are voluntary, necessarily cause countries to grow. After all, voluntary trade between individuals is almost by definition mutually beneficial to buyers and sellers. Buyers will not purchase goods or services unless they believe they will be better off, and sellers will not do business with them unless they believe they will be better off. The same is true of voluntary borrowing and lending of money: I will not borrow unless I believe I benefit; neither will you lend unless you believe you benefit. These are the "mutual gains from trade" on which much economic theory is premised.

However, this argument runs into difficulties when it is scaled up to the international level. A central paradox of globalization is that trade between countries does not necessarily benefit everyone in those countries. Exporters and importers benefit, but producers of import-competing goods and services do not. Nor does borrowing and lending between countries necessarily advantage both parties. Sovereign states that borrow act as agents for present and future populations who may or may not benefit, depending on whether their governments squander the money or invest it for the general social good. And foreign lenders to sovereign states may not benefit either: they have no collateral other than the tax base of the borrowing country, and they risk losses due to unilateral default.

In short, there are potential losers and gainers from international trade and finance because the agents who make the contracts – typically governments, international organizations, or banks – do not and cannot represent the interests of all individuals and groups within the nation-states or the organizations they represent. Hence, the benefits from globalization may not be equally distributed both within and between countries, which implies that globalization may increase income inequality at either level of analysis.[1] But globalization may also decrease income inequality if, as is common, the pre-globalized economy had considerable underemployment, monopolistic returns to previously protected domestic producers, or a host of other distortions generated by an uncompetitive environment. We must move beyond theory to empirical evidence.

Evidence of Growing Inequality

The evolution of income inequality over the last quarter-century differs depending on which concept of income inequality we use. Milanovic (2016) presents evidence that income inequality between nations has increased in absolute terms, but weighting countries by their population sizes shows that income inequality between them has decreased. This drop is due almost entirely to China, which is home to roughly one-fifth of the world's population and has seen double-digit average income growth rates for twenty-five years, far higher than any other large country. If China is removed from the data set, inequality *between countries* rises, even if population size is taken into account. On the other hand, *global* inequality – the distribution of income across the world's entire population including China – remains very high, with no clear trend over the last half of the twentieth century.[2]

The evidence also indicates that income inequality has increased in the majority of globalized countries since the late 1970s, in some cases quite substantially – notably in four of the most populous, China, India, the United States, and the United Kingdom (Figure 2.1). These trends appear even when we consider net rather than market inequality, taking taxes and transfers into account (Figure 2.2).[3] Because developed countries have more significant redistributive programs than developing ones, net inequality tends to be substantially lower than market inequality in the former. However, as Ostry, Berg, and Tsangarides (2014) note, redistribution programs in most developed countries have not kept pace with rising market inequality, resulting in worsening inequality even where these programs are in place. One curious exception to this overall picture of market and net inequality is China, whose net inequality has exceeded its market inequality since 2007. This appears to indicate a significant amount of regressive redistribution, transferring income from the poor to the rich, although the exact causes are currently not clear.

In determining the effect of globalization on inequality, it is difficult to disentangle inequality that is a by-product of domestically driven growth from that which is a by-product of internationally driven growth: growth that is driven by exports of goods and services, foreign investment, imports

FIGURE 2.1
Market Gini for selected countries, 1980–2012

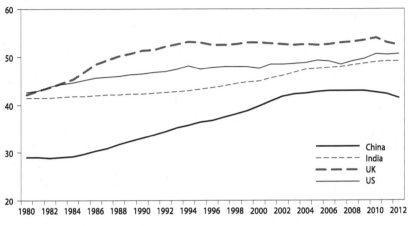

Source: Solt (2020).

of technology and ideas, and imports and exports of people. This is particularly true in "developing" or "emerging" economies (we use the two terms interchangeably), since rapid growth is typically driven by globalization rather than domestic economic drivers.

This raises two fundamental policy issues. The first is whether domestic as opposed to global drivers of growth should be prioritized. For example, four of the largest players in our globalized world – the United States, China, Japan, and Germany – all face demand-side policy choices: between stimulating their economies via spending that originates at home (with domestic consumers, domestic investors, and domestic governments), as opposed to stimulating via spending that originates abroad (with foreign consumers and foreign investors). Second, countries face supply-side policy choices: for example, between investing in infrastructure such as health and education, which enhances human capital but may or may not lead to export income, or investing in physical capital such as resource extraction or ports and airports, which enhances productivity of the export sector more directly.

OUR CONCERN IN this essay is with policy choices that are likely to improve income equality. But also our concern is with trade-offs between income equality and growth: ideally, we would like to identify policies that enhance equality without reducing growth. Our premises are that growth

FIGURE 2.2
Net Gini for selected countries, 1980–2012

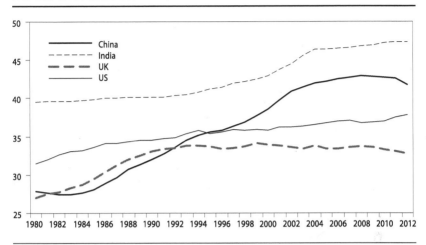

Source: Solt (2020).

per se is a good thing and that increased income equality per se is also a good thing. More precisely, we assume that growth that does not increase income inequality is good, as is improved income equality that does not decrease growth. We will cite new evidence that such policy options exist. They could be called "Pareto optimal" options, in the sense that they increase income for most, without reducing the income of others. Of course, in the real world no macro-economic policy can be truly Pareto optimal, since some in the macro-economy will be hurt; but we will argue that some policies come close.

Why Is Growth Good?

Some would argue that growth generates negative externalities, such as pollution, congestion, and even obsession with work versus leisure. An early advocate of this position was Mishan (1967). We share these concerns but argue that a necessary (though by no means sufficient) condition to ameliorate these externalities is increasing income; that is, growth makes it possible to tax and transfer to deter or to compensate for the harms done. We also suggest that modern technology often enables more sustainable growth and that pricing policies, such as mobility taxes or carbon taxes, can incentivize behavioural and technological change, ultimately reducing negative externalities.

OVER AND ABOVE the fact that growth makes compensating losers more affordable, our central argument in its favour is that in principle, a larger pie enables all segments of society, be they rich or poor, powerful or powerless, to increase their incomes without displacing the incomes of others. In other words, stagnant or shrinking economies are more prone to conflict than are growing economies. One of the most persuasive advocates of this position is Benjamin Friedman (2005), who provides historical evidence from the United States, Britain, France, and Germany. A corollary of the argument is that in principle, growth can reduce absolute poverty. In practice, this seems to have been the case: the number of people in the world who live on under $1.25 per day declined from 1.93 billion in 1981 to just over 1 billion in 2011, a drop of roughly 52 percent (World Bank 2014). In short, we contend that although growth is not unconditionally good, it has the potential to generate enormous benefits when issues of unequal distribution and negative externalities are properly taken into account.

Why Is Inequality Bad?

Conventional economics sometimes simply assumes that people as individuals prefer higher absolute incomes to lower ones, irrespective of what other people's incomes may be. By that standard, people would be equally as content with a society where, for instance, the top 1 percent received 90 percent of national income as they would with a society where the top 1 percent received just 1 percent, as long as they themselves received the same absolute income in either case. This is an extreme example, but it is undoubtedly true that up to a point, most people care more about levels of, and expected increases in, their absolute incomes than they do about how much better off others are. In China, for instance, incomes of even the bottom 10 percent are now much higher than they were before the early 1980s, and it seems plausible that the Chinese prefer the current economic environment to the previous autarkic one, despite the fact that income distribution today is much more unequal.

Nevertheless, there are powerful reasons to object to extreme and persistent income inequality, whether on moral or ethical grounds (inequality is "unfair"), or with respect to the growing literature on happiness. In recent decades, economists have weighed in on this literature alongside psychologists and philosophers, and have attempted to measure what makes people happy. A very readable example is Richard Layard (2005).

A pervasive finding in the economics literature on happiness is that relative income is important. People compare themselves with their peers –

with neighbours, co-workers, and fellow citizens – and up to a point are happier if they are either equal to or relatively better off than those around them. People also like to believe that they live in a society where upward income mobility is possible: an economy of absolutely equal incomes offers no such hope. But after income differences become too great, overall subjective well-being tends to decrease – both because people see the situation as unfair and because the gap is so large as to seem insurmountable (Dean 2007).

Beyond the impact of inequality on personal unhappiness, there are societal effects due to negative externalities. Anthropologists Wilkinson and Pickett (2009) document the damage that inequality can do to societies. They begin by ranking a sample of twenty-five rich, developed countries in order of income equality, ranging from Japan, the most equal, to the United States, the most unequal. They then relate this ranking to a wide range of societal disorders, including suicide, depression, teenage pregnancy, crime and violence, and even cancer. Consistently, the incidence of these disorders rises with income inequality. Notably, they claim, the incidence of each disorder in each country is independent of whether the individual is upper, middle, or lower income. A plausible implication is that the stresses associated with inequality, rather than poverty per se, cause the disorders. For example, the United States has the highest incidence of disorders in their sample as well as the greatest inequality, despite the fact that its average income is also the highest.

New Evidence on the "Trade-Off" between Inequality and Growth

For forty years, conventional wisdom about growth and inequality has relied on the logic and evidence in Arthur Okun's classic book *Equality and Efficiency: The Big Trade-Off* (1975). Okun's logic is based on the assumption that inequality is an incentive to work harder. Conventional wisdom has also relied on the famous Kuznets curve (Figure 2.3), according to which inequality first rises and then declines as income per capita grows (Kuznets 1955).

Yet, surely this cannot be the whole story. Depending on its source, inequality can be correlated with either high growth or low growth: If, for example, it is due to an increase in the relative demand for skilled versus unskilled labour, it reflects higher productivity in the workforce and thus higher average incomes. But if inequality is due to an increase in the relative supply of unskilled versus skilled labour, it reflects lower productivity and income is lower (Rodrik 2014).

FIGURE 2.3
Hypothetical Kuznets curve

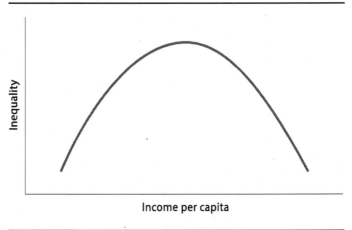

Income per capita

Note: Empirically observed curves aren't smooth or symmetrical.

In most countries, inequality is due to a combination of the two: high and rising demand for skilled versus unskilled labour, in combination with an oversupply of unskilled relative to skilled labour. Given this unfortunate starting point, and assuming agreement that high inequality is detrimental to both individual and societal welfare, most countries face a policy challenge: how best to reduce inequality without reducing economic growth. Until recently, policy makers have implicitly accepted the wisdom received from economists of a generation ago – that growth in developing countries unavoidably engenders inequality (Kuznets), and inequality in all countries incentivizes growth (Okun).

Remarkably, however, an extensive sample study by the International Monetary Fund (IMF) (Ostry, Berg, and Tsangarides 2014, 26) concludes otherwise. The study states,

> there is surprisingly little evidence for the growth-destroying effects of fiscal redistribution at a macroeconomic level. We do find some mixed evidence that very large redistributions may have direct negative effects on growth duration, such that the overall effect – including the positive effect on growth through lower inequality – may be roughly growth-neutral. But for non-extreme redistributions, there is no evidence of any adverse direct effect. The average redistribution, and the associated reduction in inequality, is thus associated with higher and more durable growth.

Their analysis is the first to use a recently compiled cross-country dataset that distinguishes market (before taxes and transfers) inequality from net (after taxes and transfers) inequality. The main findings are as follows (Ostry, Berg, and Tsangarides 2014, 4):

> First, more unequal societies tend to redistribute more. It is thus important in understanding the growth-inequality relationship to distinguish between market and net inequality ... Second, lower net inequality is robustly correlated with faster and more durable growth, for a given level of redistribution. These results are highly supportive of our earlier work ... Third, redistribution appears generally benign in terms of its impact on growth; only in extreme cases is there some evidence that it may have direct negative effects on growth. Thus the combined direct and indirect effects of redistribution – including the growth effects of the resulting lower inequality – are on average pro-growth.

These findings are supported by a broad evaluation of research on the connection between growth and inequality performed by the United Nations Development Programme (UNDP 2013). Regarding the inequality-growth connection, the authors conclude from the empirical literature that "beyond a certain threshold, inequality harms growth and poverty reduction, the quality of public relations in the public and political spheres of life and individuals' sense of fulfilment and self-worth" (UNDP 2013, 3). Regarding the growth-inequality connection, they conclude that "there is nothing inevitable about growing income inequality; several countries managed to contain or reduce income inequality while achieving strong growth performance" (UNDP 2013, 3).

In short, the IMF and UNDP results suggest that except in extreme cases, redistribution via taxes and transfers is growth inducing. Moreover, ample evidence from other studies, which show that growth reduces poverty, implies a positive feedback that reinforces the immediate redistributive impact of taxes and transfers (for example, Alesina and Rodrik 1994; Easterly 2007; Dollar, Kleineberg, and Kraay 2013). And finally, there is ample evidence of reverse causation: inequality reduces growth. Researchers who have looked at rates of growth over long periods of time (for example, Alesina and Rodrik 1994; Perrson and Tabellini 1994; Perotti 1996), the level of income across countries (Easterly 2007), and the duration of growth spells (Berg, Ostry, and Zettelmeyer 2012), have found that inequality is associated with slower and less durable growth.

Domestic Policy

If redistribution via taxes and transfers is growth inducing, and growth is good, and inequality is bad, does it follow that most countries should tax and transfer more than they do at present? The answer, as so often the case in the real world, is neither an unqualified "yes" nor an unqualified "no." Rather, "it depends."

It depends first on how much redistribution has already taken place. "Developed" countries typically have a longer history of affluence than "developing" countries. Western Europe, North America, and Japan industrialized in the nineteenth century, with high growth rates and concomitant concentrations of income and wealth at the top. At the beginning of the twentieth century, the income distributions of these countries were more unequal than they are today. To varying degrees, this was remedied by legislating progressive income taxes and social welfare systems, such as state pensions, unemployment insurance, and welfare payments for the poor. Industrialization also encouraged the rise of unions, which acted to advance and protect labour's share of national income versus capital's, though the strength of these measures in many developed countries has undergone significant erosion since the 1970s.

Developing countries such as China and now India have industrialized more recently, and have not yet adopted redistribution schemes on the scale of most developed countries. Neither have the post-communist countries of the former Soviet Union, where capitalist-style industrialization and growth took off only after 1990. In these countries, tax-and-transfer schemes will probably have greater per-dollar equity and growth impacts than in developed countries, where a basic standard of living is already for the most part guaranteed.

Inequality-targeting policies also depend on culture, a concept typically eschewed by economists. But economists are comfortable with analyzing tastes for leisure versus work, as well as the tastes for risk versus security. Countries with differing cultures and histories have very different appetites for leisure and for risk. Notably, North Americans demonstrably choose to work longer hours and take more risks than do Western Europeans: their work weeks are longer, holiday periods are shorter, social insurance is skimpier, and venture capitalists are more abundant. These habits have become institutionalized, but they were democratically chosen.

Arguably, Asian cultures embody even longer work hours and in some countries more tolerance for risk than those in North America, though generalization across dozens of Asian countries is dangerous to say the least. The Asian experience with industrialization and high growth is relatively recent, although Japan is an interesting exception: It was the earliest in Asia to industrialize in the modern sense, and it was forced to reindustrialize after its capital was dissipated and destroyed by the Second World War. For perhaps fifty years after the end of the war, the Japanese worked longer hours than Europeans or Americans. But traditional Japanese culture is also relatively risk averse. Hence, as the country rebuilt its affluence, extensive and expensive corporate and state welfare schemes were established, and work weeks were shortened. These developments are less evident in much of the rest of Asia, partly because industrialization occurred later than in Japan but perhaps also because some Asian countries may be less risk averse. Japan's industrial structure, dominated by large vertically integrated conglomerates (*zaibatsu*) that often offer jobs and security for life, has influenced Korea's (the *chaebol* being their version of Japan's *zaibatsu*) and Indonesia's, but its influence is not so evident in, for example, Vietnam.[4]

China and India also diverge from the Japanese model. Modern Chinese firms, including foreign-controlled examples, demand long hours and typically no longer offer social safety nets, such as housing, pensions, job security, and enterprise-run schools, although some of these perks survive in the remaining state-owned enterprises, which account for about one-quarter of GDP. Income distribution in the new China has become more unequal than in the United States or any other developed economy. Redistribution via taxes and transfers, as well as universal government-funded social safety nets for unemployment, retirement, and even health care, are still in their infancy. India has a longer history of redistribution, especially to poor farmers (reinforced by protection against agricultural imports), but it has yet to develop a major manufacturing export sector. This in turn means that the kind of paternalist security and welfare offered by Japan's *zaibatsu,* Korea's *chaebol,* or China's state-owned enterprises is absent.

In short, most of developing Asia redistributes less than most of the developed world, with the caveat that Japan is, of course, highly developed: in fact, its after-tax-and-transfer income distribution is one of the developed world's most equal. Thus, there is more room for redistributive policies in developing countries than in developed countries (Figure 2.4). Moreover, if we accept the results of Ostry, Berg, and Tsangarides (2014), higher taxes and transfers for developing countries should be pro-growth, or at worst growth-neutral.

FIGURE 2.4
Net and market Gini for OECD and non-OECD countries, 2011

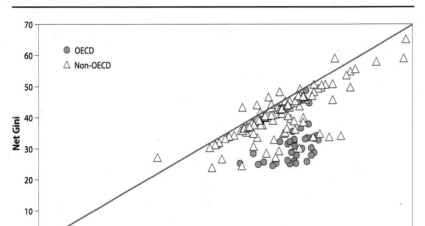

Note: The 45-degree line indicates where market Gini equals net Gini and represents the absence of income redistribution. Points that fall close to this line denote countries with weak redistribution systems, whereas points below the line denote countries that have more robust systems. This figure is a partial recreation of Figure 7 in Ostrey, Berg, and Tsangarides (2014, 23).
Source: Solt (2016) and authors' calculations.

However, the devil is in the details. First, is it better to bias redistribution toward taxes or toward transfers? If the latter, do deficits matter? Standard Keynesian theory and evidence suggest that when resources – labour and capital – are un- or underemployed, and when money markets are slack (the supply of loanable funds is greater than the demand for them), deficits are likely to stimulate growth in real output. But with full employment, "real" crowding out causes the excess spending associated with deficits to result in inflation rather than real growth. Moreover, if money markets are tight, interest rates rise and "financial" crowding out occurs: declines in investment and consumer spending offset the increases in government spending associated with the deficit.

A second crucial detail is the sustainability of deficits. Annual deficit flows (borrowing) cumulate to ever-larger stocks of debt, on which interest must be paid. The simple rule of thumb is that the debt-to-GDP ratio is "sustainable" as long as debt grows no more rapidly than GDP – in other words, as long as the growth rate is larger than the interest rate. The presumption is that the government spends the proceeds of its deficit on growth – producing capital goods.

This brings us to the third crucial detail: the composition of government spending. If the deficit is simply spent on transfer payments such as welfare for the poor, unemployment insurance, and retirement pensions, the impact on future growth is likely to be minimal if not negative. But if it is spent on appropriate infrastructure, such as bridges, roads, railroads, airports, plumbing for clean water, medical care – and, not least, education – the impact on growth can be substantial.

In other words, government spending on transfer payments typically amounts in effect to spending on consumption (alleviating the plight of the poor in the short run), whereas government spending on appropriate infrastructure amounts in effect to spending on investment (facilitating growth and thus consumption – by both poor and rich – in the future). This choice – between redistributive transfers and growth-enhancing infrastructure investment – is particularly stark for poor developing countries. For example, it is at the crux of the economic choices that were placed before India in its 2014 election: Prime Minister Modi's victory can be interpreted in part as a vote to move on the margin from consumption transfers to infrastructure investment.[5]

In summary,

1 Redistributive policies, though they may be justified solely on ethical grounds, do not normally hinder growth, even if they are simply of the tax-and-transfer variety. We assert this based on recent analysis by Ostry, Berg, and Tsangarides (2014), using the data from the Standardized World Income Inequality Database (Solt 2016), which includes 173 countries, including 37 developed (OECD) and 113 developing (non-OECD) countries.

2 If redistribution generates a deficit, this will create real growth for as long as resources remain unemployed, assuming that monetary policy accommodates fiscal policy.

3 To the extent that the proceeds of the deficit are spent on public investment rather than consumption, growth will be enhanced.

4 As long as GDP growth is greater than the interest rate paid to service debt, a country's debt load will decrease, leaving room to run continued deficits without increasing the debt load. Hence, high-growth countries can run deficits without amplifying their debt load as long as the proceeds are sufficiently growth enhancing.

International Policy

Intra-country policy is normally designed and enforced by national governments. International policy is designed by international organizations such as the World Bank, the IMF, and the World Trade Organization (WTO). Strictly speaking, these bodies have no enforcement power. The role of the World Bank is to make long-term development loans, whereas that of the IMF is to make short-term emergency loans. The World Bank may attach conditions to its loans: for example, about working conditions, human rights, or environmental issues.

The IMF almost always attaches conditions of a different kind, having to do with economic reforms whose purpose is to remedy the mismanagement that got the country into trouble in the first place. Such reforms often involve stopping subsidies that are important to the poor: these might include subsidies on cooking or heating oil, rice, grain, transportation, gasoline, electricity, or simply cash welfare payments. In developing countries, the poor often outnumber the rich, so the withdrawal of such subsidies is unpopular with most of the citizenry. If the country is democratic, the government may be voted out of office (as happened in Greece in January 2015); if it is not democratic, street protests and violence may force the government from power.

The WTO has no enforcement power either, but countries that do not wish to conform face the stark choice between not joining or withdrawing ex post (and hence forgoing the benefits of multilateral free trade and investment). Compared to its predecessor, the GATT (General Agreement on Tariffs and Trade, 1947–95), the WTO imposes much more stringent regulatory rules on trade and investment – so-called harmonization that is designed to make international trade and investment simpler. This process has been called "hyper-globalization" (Rodrik 2012), and it may well run against the interests of all but the rich and/or importers, exporters, and foreign investors.

One example of WTO-sponsored harmonization measures that move well beyond the GATT concerns patents and copyrights; developing countries are required to bring their domestic laws into alignment with intellectual property laws in developed countries (Rodrik 2012). Conflict in recent years between pharmaceutical companies and the Indian government over the cost of life-saving medicines for impoverished consumers has underscored the negative impact of these regulations on developing countries.

Another example concerns ongoing WTO negotiations to eliminate agricultural subsidies and increase market access in both developed and developing member countries, as these issues were largely untouched by the GATT. Since at least the 2001 Doha Round, there has been widespread recognition that the impacts of such trade liberalization measures will be very different in developing as opposed to developed countries (Stewart and Bell 2015). Although subsidy cuts to agribusinesses in the latter would be balanced by increased international market access, in the former these cuts could directly affect the affordability and availability of food for poor or impoverished populations.

Similar concerns about international inequality have been raised with respect to the Trans-Pacific Partnership (TPP).[6] The current form of the agreement proposes significantly stronger regulations than found in the WTO, with respect to issues of intellectual property rights, copyright, patenting, trade secrets, domestic health and safety regulations, foreign investment rules, labour and environmental laws, international data flows, and market access and competition laws. Furthermore, the TPP ventures into regulatory territory that is not covered under the WTO, including provisions on international regulatory coherence and the operation of state-owned enterprises.[7]

Critics of the TPP argue that the race to reduce "non-tariff barriers to trade" risks constraining the domestic policy-making abilities of participating countries in ways that could exacerbate income inequality. Investor-state arbitration provisions, for example, would allow corporations to take legal action against governments by alleging that regulations created by the latter reduced expected returns on investments (Sinclair 2013). The arbitration provisions could conceivably apply to a developing country that attempts to raise minimum wages, on the grounds that they increase labour costs and reduce expected profits for foreign investors. Given that international income inequality has increased over the lifetime of existing WTO agreements, there is little reason to expect that it will decline under the TPP.

Conclusions

Several conclusions follow from our discussion. *Does globalization cause inequality?* We have seen that this cannot be determined a priori, as there are strong theoretical reasons for holding that globalization can create both more and less inequality. Similarly, empirical evidence is ambiguous. Depending on the level of analysis, globalization since the 1980s has either increased inequality (within-country and between-country, excluding China) or decreased it (between-country, including China).

Does growth cause inequality? Although it is evident that globalization generates growth, the relationship between growth and inequality is complex. Distinguishing cause and effect is crucial. Whereas there is considerable evidence that inequality, particularly extreme inequality, reduces growth, there is also evidence that growth can diminish inequality. Economists have traditionally held, largely on theoretical grounds, that there is an inevitable trade-off between growth and equality, but a mounting body of empirical evidence suggests that this is not the case. Growth need not lead to heightened inequality, as several Latin American countries have demonstrated beginning in the mid-1990s. Nor is increased inequality a necessary condition for robust growth. Long-term growth, in fact, appears to be stronger when high levels of inequality are absent.

Can national policy intervention decrease inequality while facilitating growth? Strong new evidence from the IMF suggests that it can. The appropriate policies depend on a variety of factors, including the magnitude and nature of redistributive programs, existing debt burdens and growth rates, and the fit between monetary and fiscal policies. Crucially, redistribution in and of itself is insufficient: government spending on health, education, programs to encourage women to work, and physical infrastructure is crucial. So also is tax and regulatory policy that boosts employment and small-scale enterprise.

Can international policy intervention decrease inequality? Although international organizations such as the IMF, World Bank, and WTO ostensibly exist to facilitate growth and development internationally, and so decrease inter-country inequality, there are few policy mechanisms at the international level to mitigate worsening intra-country inequality. International trade agreements have helped to lift millions out of poverty in the late twentieth and early twenty-first centuries, and average incomes have risen, but there is evidence that these agreements have also exacerbated inequality. In short, national, not international, policies must be relied on to mitigate inequality. This may become more difficult in future as multilateral agreements progressively seek to constrain domestic policies in an effort to reduce non-tariff barriers to trade.

Relevance to Indonesia

As a number of chapters in this volume demonstrate, these observations are consistent with the patterns of globalization and income inequality in Indonesia. For example, in Chapter 4, Yessi Vadila and Budy Resosudarmo use province-level data and find that opening of capital markets via increased foreign direct investment was associated with a reduction in expenditure inequality in Indonesia from 2003 to 2010. In Chapter 5, Santi Kusumaningrum and her colleagues obtain a related result in their focus on children. They find that child poverty and inequality interact to reduce child well-being in terms of health, nutrition, education, and birth registration. In Chapter 3, Teguh Dartanto, Yusuf Sofiyandi, and Nia Kurnia Sholihah find that increased trade openness exacerbated inequality, but the effect, though statistically significant, was very small. And in Chapter 6, Richard Barichello and Faisal Harahap show that increased protection (reduced trade openness) via higher rice prices has worsened poverty and, through higher rice land prices, has probably done the same for inequality. These chapters reflect the ambiguous links between more trade or globalization and the level of inequality that we found in our review of the broader literature on this subject.

Notes

1 This suggests that unconditionally scaling up the logic of the "mutual gains from trade" argument from individuals to nations commits the fallacy of composition.

2 As Milanovic (2016) notes, uncertainty over the trend in global inequality is due to a lack of reliable household survey data in many countries.

3 Net income inequality means inequality after taking taxes and transfers into account.

4 Of the largest 100 companies in the Association of Southeast Asian Nations, by market capitalization, 27 are in Malaysia, 21 in Singapore, 21 in Thailand, 16 in Indonesia, 13 in the Philippines, and 2 in Vietnam.

5 See Ravallion (2009) for an overview of India's subsidy-focused transfer policies since the 1990s. Contrast with speculation over the focus of the 2015 federal budget, as discussed in Rastello (2015).

6 Currently involved nations include Australia, Brunei, Canada, Chile, Japan, Malaysia, Mexico, New Zealand, Peru, Singapore, the United States, and Vietnam.

7 See Fergusson, McMinimy, and Williams (2015) for a concise, if US-centric, overview of the TPP.

References

Alesina, Alberto, and Dani Rodrik. 1994. "Distributive Politics and Economic Growth." *Quarterly Journal of Economics* 109, 2: 465–90.

Berg, Andrew, Jonathan D. Ostry, and Jeromin Zettelmeyer. 2012. "What Makes Growth Sustained?" *Journal of Development Economics* 98, 2: 149–66.

Dean, James W. 2007. "National Welfare and Individual Happiness: Income Distribution and Beyond." *Journal of Policy Modeling* 29, 4: 567–75.

Dollar, David, Tatjana Kleineberg, and Aart Kraay. 2013. "Growth Is Still Good for the Poor." Policy Research Working Paper No. 6568. Washington, DC: World Bank.

Easterly, William. 2007. "Inequality Does Cause Underdevelopment: Insights from a New Instrument." *Journal of Development Economics* 84, 2: 755–76.

Fergusson, Ian F., Mark A. McMinimy, and Brock R. Williams. 2015. *The Trans-Pacific Partnership (TPP): Negotiations and Issues for Congress.* Washington, DC: Congressional Research Service.

Friedman, Benjamin M. 2005. *The Moral Consequences of Economic Growth.* New York: Knopf.

Kuznets, Simon. 1955. "Economic Growth and Income Inequality." *American Economic Review* 45 (March): 1–28.

Layard, Richard. 2005. *Happiness: Lessons from a New Science.* New York: Penguin.

Milanovic, Branko. 2016. *Global Inequality: A New Approach for the Age of Globalization.* Cambridge, MA: The Belknap Press of Harvard University Press.

Mishan, Ezra J. 1967. *The Costs of Economic Growth.* New York: Praeger.

Okun, Arthur M. 1975. *Equality and Efficiency: The Big Trade-Off.* Washington, DC: Brookings Institution Press.

Ostry, Jonathan D., Andrew Berg, and Charalambos G. Tsangarides. 2014. *Redistribution, Inequality, and Growth.* Staff Discussion Notes No. 14/2. Washington, DC: International Monetary Fund.

Perotti, Roberto. 1996. "Growth, Income Distribution, and Democracy: What the Data Say." *Journal of Economic Growth* 1, 2: 149–87.

Perrson, Torsten, and Guido Tabellini. 1994. "Is Inequality Harmful for Growth?" *American Economic Review* 84, 3: 600–21.

Rastello, Sandrine. 2015. "Infrastructure vs Subsidies: What Will It Be in Modi's Budget?" *Bloomberg News,* February 26. http://www.bloomberg.com/news/articles/2015-02-27/infrastructure-vs-subsidies-what-will-it-be-in-modi-s-budget.

Ravallion, Martin. 2009. "A Comparative Perspective on Poverty Reduction in Brazil, China, and India." *World Bank Research Observer* 26, 1: 71–104.

Rodrik, Dani. 2012. *The Globalization Paradox: Why Global Markets, States, and Democracy Can't Coexist.* Oxford, UK: Oxford University Press.

–. 2014. "Good and Bad Inequality." Project Syndicate, December 11. http://www.project-syndicate.org/commentary/equality-economic-growth-tradeoff-by-dani-rodrik-2014-12.

Sinclair, Scott. 2013. "Opening Remarks on Canada and the Trans-Pacific Partnership (TPP): Presentation to the House of Commons Standing Committee on International Trade, May 27, 2013." Ottawa. Canadian Centre for Policy Alternatives. http://www.policyalternatives.ca/sites/default/files/uploads/publications/National%20Office/2013/06/Canada_and_the_Trans_Pacific_Partnership.pdf.

Solt, Frederick. 2020. "Measuring Income Inequality Across Countries and Over Time: The Standardized World Income Inequality Database." *Social Science Quarterly* 101(3): 1183–99. SWIID Version 9.0, October 2020.

–. 2016. "The Standardized World Income Inequality Database." *Social Science Quarterly* 97, 5: 1267–81. SWIID Version 3.1, December 2011.

Stewart, Terence P., and Stephanie M. Bell. 2015. "Global Hunger and the World Trade Organization: How the International Trade Rules Address Food Security." *Penn State Journal of Law and International Affairs* 3, 2: 113–55.

UNDP (United Nations Development Programme). 2013. *Humanity Divided: Confronting Inequality in Developing Countries.* New York: UN Bureau for Development Policy.

Wilkinson, Richard, and Kate Pickett. 2009. *The Spirit Level: Why Greater Equality Makes Societies Stronger.* New York: Bloomsbury Press.

World Bank. 2014. "Poverty Overview." http://www.worldbank.org/en/topic/poverty/overview.

3

Trade Expansion in Indonesia

The Impact on Poverty and Income Inequality

TEGUH DARTANTO, YUSUF SOFIYANDI,
and NIA KURNIA SHOLIHAH

Since 1980, Indonesia has proven a remarkable success in tackling poverty, despite challenges such as the 1997 Asian Financial Crisis. Sustained economic growth and macro-economic stability have been the primary driving factors in reducing its poverty (Dartanto and Otsubo 2016; Miranti 2010; Suryahadi, Suryadarma, and Sumarto 2009). Also during this period, its socio-economic conditions rapidly improved. Since the 1980s, its per capita GDP has increased three-fold (Dartanto and Otsubo 2016). The World Bank (2017) reported that the per capita GDP (purchasing power parity, 2005 US$) of Indonesia had jumped from $1,323 in 1983 to $4,271 in 2012. Absolute poverty has significantly decreased from 28.6 percent in 1980 to 12.0 percent in 2012, according to headcount ratios (measured by the national poverty line) (BPS 2017).

Despite impressive progress in the reduction of extreme poverty, economic growth in Indonesia has not always aided the members of lower socio-economic groups (Dartanto and Patunru 2015). As the rate of poverty reduction starts to slow, inequality continues to rise significantly. For example, the Gini coefficient, which represents the income distribution of a nation's residents, and is the most commonly used measure of inequality, increased from roughly 0.33 in 2002 to 0.413 in 2013 (BPS 2014). As of 2009, almost 100 million Indonesians were living in absolute poverty and in vulnerable conditions. In fact, the average growth rate of household income per capita was 26.5 percent during 2006–12, varying from 9.0 percent for the lowest quintile to 29.0 percent for the highest. If we look at who holds the greatest wealth in this distribution, the wealth of the forty-three thousand richest Indonesians (who represent only 0.02 percent of the population) is equivalent to 25 percent of Indonesia's GDP (De Silva and Sumarto 2014), indicating a highly disproportionate rate of income growth that has favoured the most wealthy.

At the provincial level, statistics show diverse socio-economic progress during 2003–13 (BPS 2017). In that time, the provincial poverty rate significantly decreased, varying from a 2.8 percentage point drop in Bali to a 13.4 percentage point fall in Maluku. Although income inequality steadily diminished in most provinces during this ten-year period, East Java and DKI Jakarta were outliers, experiencing a rise of Gini index ranging from 0.003 in the former (2013) to 0.159 in the latter (2013). It is our theory that a decrease in income equality and wealth distribution, at both the national and the provincial level, will lead to greater social polarization and thus exacerbate social tensions, undermining economic progress (Lee, Wong, and Law 2007). It has already been demonstrated that growth in income inequality overall (both national and provincial) impedes the growth elasticity of poverty reduction (Banerjee and Duflo 2003), generating a detrimental impact on the growth prospects of a developing economy such as Indonesia's.

The exposure of the Indonesian economy to the international economy continued to grow until the Global Financial Crisis of 2008, after which it began to shrink. Its highest exposure occurred in 2005, when the trade openness index (a ratio between total trade – export and import – compared to total GDP) reached almost 64 percent.[1] This ratio fell below 50 percent in 2013. Despite this recent decline, the exposure of regional Indonesian economies (at the provincial level) to the international trade market grew markedly between 2000 and 2013, becoming more integrated into the global market (shown by the ratio of trade to GDP: see Figure 3.1). Figure 3.1 charts the correlation between trade openness, poverty, and inequality in Indonesia, showing that as trade openness rose since 2010, poverty decreased and inequality (Gini index) increased. Thus, international trade provides opportunities for local producers to access a wider market and for low-income populations to have cheaper products, but it appears to worsen income inequality at the same time.

Evidently, the impact of trade openness on the poverty-growth-inequality triangle is theoretically conflicted and empirically ambiguous. Musila and Yiheyis (2015) and Trejos and Barboza (2015) confirm that the relationship between trade openness and economic growth is straightforward, in that

FIGURE 3.1

Trade openness index, poverty rate, and Gini index, 2000–13

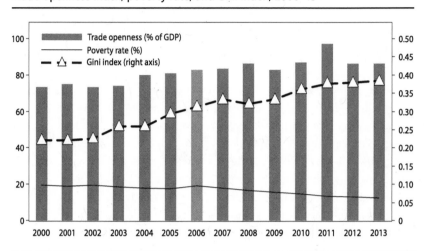

Source: Indonesia Database for Policy and Economic Research, 2016.

countries with a higher degree of trade openness may experience faster per capita economic growth. Similarly Bergh and Nilsson (2011) and Niimi, Vasudeva Dutta, and Winters (2007) show that globalization indicated by trade openness is good for poverty reduction. However, Castilho, Menéndez, and Sztulman (2012) confirm the opposite effect. Additionally, Rivas (2007) finds that trade openness increases regional inequality. Therefore, the relationship between trade openness and poverty/inequality is still inconclusive, both theoretically and empirically.

Literature Review

Impact of Trade Openness on Economic Growth

There is a general consensus in the literature that trade liberalization, or trade openness, does appear to have a simple and straightforward connection with economic growth (Figure 3.2). The theory is that as trade openness increases, more rapid economic growth will be achieved. Here, more trade openness means more capital inflows (foreign direct investment) or more import/export international trade activity. An abundance of data on the global economy from 1960 to 1990 shows that countries with higher openness in trade have experienced faster productivity growth (see Deme and Homaifar 2001; Musila and Yiheyis 2015; Rodríguez and Rodrik

FIGURE 3.2
Relationship between poverty, growth, and inequality (PGI triangle)

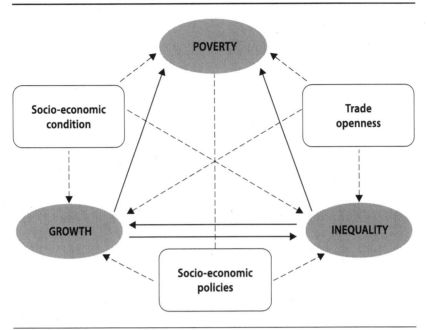

Source: Dartanto and Patunru (2015).

2000; Sachs and Warner 1995; and Trejos and Barboza 2015). Musila and Yiheyis (2015) find that trade openness positively affects the level of investment and the rate of economic growth, although the impact on the latter is statistically insignificant. In the long term, a change in trade openness influences economic growth through the interaction with physical capital growth.

Employing various estimation methods for a sample of twenty-three Asian countries, Trejos and Barboza (2015) analyze the relationship between trade openness and output growth, using both a static ordinary least squares (OLS) technique and a dynamic error correction model (ECM) estimation. At the country-specific level, the results provide robust empirical evidence, indicating that higher trade openness is not the main engine of economic growth.

Correspondingly, a study from Japan shows that the growth of imports rather than exports has a long-run positive relationship with economic expansion (Deme and Homaifar 2001). Sachs and Warner (1995) mention that open developed economies grew at 2.29 percent per year. Rodríguez and

Rodrik (2000) also find that the effect of trade reform on GDP growth is positive and significant.

Trade openness and growth have a positive correlation in some developing countries, including in southeastern Europe (Fetahi-Vehapi, Sadiku, and Petkovski 2015). A study across developing countries shows that trade promotes growth through a number of channels such as technology transfers, scale economies, and comparative advantage (Yanikkaya 2003). Other studies on developing countries conclude that trade openness generally has a positive relationship with GDP and economic growth (Harrison 1996), including in East Asia and Latin America (Chen 1999) and some African countries (Yeboah et al. 2012).

Impact of Trade Openness on Poverty

Trade openness is broadly accepted as a crucial factor in generating successful economic growth, especially when policy-driven initiatives are sustained over time. Tsai and Huang (2007) show that sustained economic growth is the major driving force for poverty reduction in Taiwan. Although inward foreign direct investment (FDI) has no significant impact on the mean income of the poor, outward FDI from Taiwan since 1987 seems to have adversely affected the poorest 20 percent of Taiwanese. Examining data from 114 countries (1983–2007), Bergh and Nilsson (2011) investigate the relationship between globalization and World Bank absolute poverty estimates, finding a significant negative correlation between globalization and poverty. Similarly, a study of Vietnam shows that trade liberalization substantially reduced poverty over the period 1993–98 (Niimi, Vasudeva Dutta, and Winters 2007).

Further, a study using detailed micro-data across Brazilian states from 1987 to 2005 (Castilho, Menéndez, and Sztulman 2012) suggests that trade liberalization contributes to growth in urban poverty and inequality and may be linked to reductions in rural inequality (possibly poverty). On the other hand, Winters, McCulloch, and McKay (2004) find that there can be no simple general conclusion about the relationship between trade liberalization and poverty. For her part, Harrison (2005) confirms that trade openness improves access to the markets of developed countries, thus helping to ensure that poor countries benefit from it. In examining the impact of the US-Vietnam bilateral trade agreement, McCaig (2011) concludes that trade openness increases Vietnam's access to the markets of developed countries, with a positive effect on its wages and poverty rates.

Impact of Trade Openness on Inequality

Most time-series studies (Anderson 2005; Milanovic 2005; Rivas 2007) find that greater trade openness increases the relative demand for skilled labour, but most cross-country studies find that it has little influence on overall income inequality. In developing countries, trade openness may affect income inequalities through several channels: factor price ratios, asset inequalities, spatial inequalities, gender inequalities, and the amount of income redistribution (Anderson 2005). Rivas (2007) finds that trade openness has a dual impact: it benefits regions that have low levels of education, thereby tending to reduce regional inequality, but it also benefits regions with high levels of income and infrastructure, thereby tending to increase regional inequality, but it also benefits regions with high levels of income and infrastructure, thereby tending to increase regional inequality. This latter effect tends to be greater than the former, so that trade openness ultimately exacerbates regional inequality.

Using data from household budget surveys, Milanovic (2005) finds that globalization makes income distribution worse in very poor countries and better in developed countries. In addition, Aradhyula, Rahman, and Seenivasan (2007), through analyzing a panel of country-level data, reveal that trade openness increases income inequality in developing countries but reduces it in developed countries (though the coefficient is not statistically significant).

In looking at a sample of 106 developing countries during the period 1980–2010, Trabelsi and Liouane (2013) conclude that trade openness contributed to intensifying wage inequality in such countries. However, in contrast, another study employs the Heckscher-Ohlin-Samuelson theorem to confirm that trade openness favours unskilled workers, permits faster growth, and slows down income inequality in developing countries (Wood 1994). In contrast, using a dynamic specification to estimate the impact of trade on within-country income inequality in a sample of seventy developing countries from 1980 to 1999, Meschi and Vivarelli (2007) suggest that total aggregate trade flows are weakly related with income inequality. Daumal (2013) determines that Brazil's trade openness tends to contribute to inequality *reduction*, whereas the opposite results occur in India, where trade openness plays a major role in aggravating income inequality among states. Several studies that examine the relationship between trade openness and inequality produce various results since they use different methodology, data and regional coverage.

Socio-Economic Conditions and Policies

As revealed in the discussion above, theory alone cannot predict how much poor people in developing countries will benefit from trade openness. Nonetheless, the academic literature does provide an important framework for directing trade policy reform, to ensure that policies align with the overall economic development goals of reducing poverty and inequality. One way to accomplish this is to better understand the socio-economic conditions that affect economic development amid trade reform.

For example, Ravallion (2007) suggests the importance of combining trade reforms with well-designed social protection policies. Lee (2005) emphasizes that trade liberalization has a particularly significant impact on employment. Furthermore, one positive effect of trade liberalization in developing countries, related to socio-economic status, is the increased participation of women in the labour market (Santos-Paulino 2012).

Overall, we therefore learn that in understanding the social impact of trade policy on poverty and inequality, one should *not* look solely at income poverty as it is conventionally measured or as operating in a vacuum apart from the socio-economic conditions (such as gender and employment) that are integral to its positive development over time.

Trade Openness, Growth, Inequality, and Poverty in Indonesia

General Conditions

In a diverse society such as that of Indonesia, which is characterized by a great deal of regional disparity, there is an urgent need to analyze the statistical facts and interrelationship of trade openness, growth, inequality, and poverty at the provincial level. Table 3.1 compares averages of trade openness (percentage of GDP), the economic growth rate, inequality (Gini index), and the poverty rate among all Indonesian provinces from 2000 to 2013. Although the national poverty rate was 11.96 percent in 2012, it was almost triple that in eastern provinces such as Maluku, Papua, and West Papua. In contrast, the rate in provinces such as DKI Jakarta, Bali, North Sulawesi, and Bangka-Belitung was less than half of the national average.

Provinces whose trade openness index was higher than the national average (about 0.94 times to GDP) experienced relatively high economic growth. The relevant provinces here were East Kalimantan, West Papua, Riau, and Riau Islands. Similarly, in provinces where the trade openness index was lower than the national average, economic growth was relatively

TABLE 3.1
Average of trade openness, growth, inequality, and poverty at the
provincial level, 2000–13

Province	Average trade openness (% of GDP)	Average growth rate (%)	Delta Gini index	Delta poverty rate (%)
Aceh	51	4.2	0.22	−8.7
North Sumatra	70	5.7	0.08	−3.2
West Sumatra	30	5.5	0.10	−5.4
Riau	75	8.0	0.12	−2.4
Jambi	89	6.5	0.10	−4.5
South Sumatra	71	6.2	0.11	−11.1
Bengkulu	45	5.6	0.14	−6.2
Lampung	73	5.3	0.09	−2.8
Bangka-Belitung	126	5.3	0.19	−3.1
Riau Islands	181	6.8	0.36	−3.5
DKI Jakarta	109	5.8	0.11	−5.6
West Java	83	5.5	0.12	−1.9
Central Java	97	5.1	0.12	−8.0
DI Yogyakarta	87	4.6	0.09	−3.1
East Java	93	5.5	0.06	−5.8
Banten	133	6.9	0.24	−5.0
Bali	139	5.4	0.12	−4.0
West Nusa Tenggara	60	4.4	0.10	−13.6
East Nusa Tenggara	59	4.9	0.07	−3.2
West Kalimantan	54	4.7	0.12	−4.4
Central Kalimantan	85	5.6	0.11	−2.4
South Kalimantan	97	5.4	0.09	−1.2
East Kalimantan	153	8.6	0.08	−7.1
North Sulawesi	71	5.7	0.15	−3.4
Central Sulawesi	30	7.4	0.13	−8.7
South Sulawesi	57	6.3	0.13	−7.2
South East Sulawesi	48	7.4	0.16	−14.5
Gorontalo	33	7.1	0.32	−16.8
West Sulawesi	37	7.0	0.35	−6.6
Maluku	60	4.6	0.25	−16.9
North Maluku	61	5.1	0.32	−5.8
West Papua	118	7.9	0.43	−13.5
Papua	121	2.5	0.26	−11.9

Source: Compiled from the database of Badan Pusat Statistik (BPS) (Statistics Indonesia), 2016, March 28.

low, below the national average. Among others, Bengkulu, West Sumatra, West Kalimantan, West Nusa Tenggara, and East Nusa Tenggara were included in this category.

However, this positive relationship between trade openness and the economic growth rate did not occur in every province. For example, Papua and Bangka-Belitung had a high trade openness index but a low economic growth rate. In contrast, Central Sulawesi, West Sulawesi, and Gorontalo had low trade openness but a relatively high economic growth rate. This shows that a high average of trade openness does not necessarily ensure the achievement of a high economic growth rate (Table 3.1).

High trade openness is associated with a quick reduction of poverty rates. Provinces with a relatively high trade openness index, namely West Papua and Papua at 118 and 121, respectively, significantly decreased their poverty rate between 2000 and 2013. Even in West Papua, the rate dropped significantly to 13.5 percent, whereas that of Papua diminished to 11.9 percent. These numbers are above the national average for poverty reduction, which reaches only 6.72 percent.

Each province's achievement in reducing the poverty rate did not necessarily rely on its high trade openness index. This can be understood by comparing the 2000 poverty rate with that of 2013. In Bali, the rate dropped only 4 percent even though the average trade openness index was 139 percent of the GDP (the third-highest in Indonesia). A similar situation occurred in Banten and South Kalimantan, where the rate dropped by 5.0 percent and 1.2 percent, respectively, whereas average trade openness reached 133 and 97 percent of the GDP.

Table 3.1 and Figure 3.3 reveal that higher trade openness is associated with higher economic growth as well as a lower poverty rate. Unfortunately, it is also linked with greater inequality. Rising income inequality (as seen on the Gini index) in provinces with relatively high trade openness suggests that their economic growth is less inclusive than before. The benefit of economic growth generated by trade openness is disproportionally distributed in society. This was true for the Riau Islands and North Sulawesi, where the change in income inequality between 2000 and 2013 was relatively high, respectively by 0.15 and 0.36 points, although both had economic growth of over 5.5 percent a year, with a respective trade openness index at 1.81 and 0.7 times the GDP. This change in inequality is high compared with the change at the national level, which reached only 0.05. One factor in the very rapid rise of inequality in North Sulawesi was a commodity price boom during 2000–13. Because North Sulawesi is an agriculture-based province, its

FIGURE 3.3
Trade openness and economic growth, 2000–13

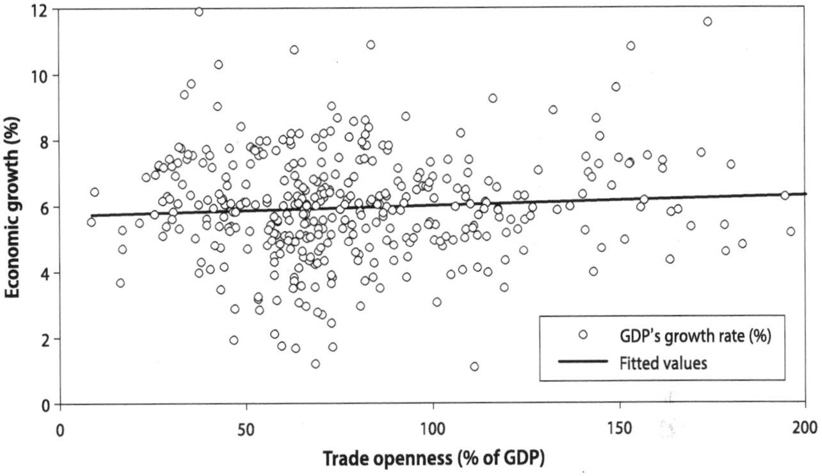

Source: Compiled from the database of BPS, 2016, March 28.

landowners enjoyed most of the benefit of the price boom, via high agricultural prices.

Correlation Analysis of Poverty-Growth-Inequality

This section shows how trade openness relates to poverty, economic growth, and inequality (PGI), based on Indonesian provincial data for 2000–13, as depicted in Figures 3.4 to 3.7. All figures show a simple correlation and plot between two variables. Figure 3.4 depicts the correlation between provincial trade openness, measured by the trade openness index, the sum of exports and imports divided by GDP, and economic growth, measured by GDP growth rates at the provincial level. Figure 3.5 displays the correlation between trade openness and poverty. Figure 3.6 shows the correlation between trade openness and inequality – the latter represented by the Gini coefficient. For each figure, we separated the data population into two groups (i.e., provinces whose mining sector did or did not make a large contribution to GDP), to investigate whether differing patterns existed.

Figure 3.3 confirms the economic theory that there is a positive correlation between trade openness and economic growth. A simple linear regression confirms that provinces having higher trade openness tend to have significantly higher rates of growth.[2] This positive correlation between trade

FIGURE 3.4

Trade openness and economic growth, 2000–13: Mining provinces

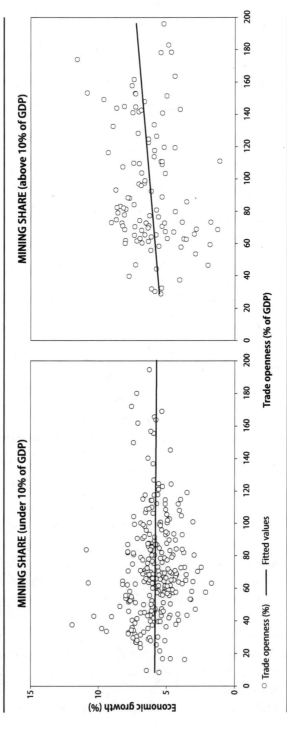

Source: Compiled from the database of BPS, 2016, March 28.

FIGURE 3.5
Trade openness and poverty rate, 2000–13

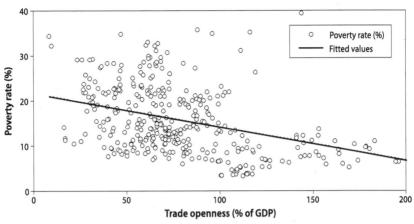

Source: Compiled from the database of BPS, 2016, March 28.

openness and economic growth is even stronger for the "mining-sector" provinces.

The positive correlation graph for mining provinces as a group (in Figure 3.7) indicates the benefits of "inclusive growth" that this sector potentially has on other economic sectors in Indonesia.[3] Figure 3.7 perhaps suggests that the Indonesian mining sector is able to create a strong multiplier-effect for other economic sectors, significantly boosting the total GDP rate of growth.

Figure 3.5 suggests that higher trade openness may have helped alleviate the poverty rate in Indonesia between 2000 and 2013. In addition, the simple linear correlation confirms that provinces with higher trade openness tend to have significantly lower poverty rates. Moreover, Figure 3.6 suggests that there is a weak positive correlation between trade openness and inequality. In general, this result is as expected for Indonesia (with the exception of a few provinces mentioned above), as it is consistent with the broader literature on this subject.

If the population data is separated into "mining" and "non-mining" provinces, the correlations between trade openness and rising inequality can be seen to differ between the two groups (Figure 3.7). For the non-mining provinces, the correlation appears to be weakly positive and significant, whereas it is stronger for the mining provinces. This result indicates that an

FIGURE 3.6

Trade openness and Gini index in all Indonesian provinces, 2000–13

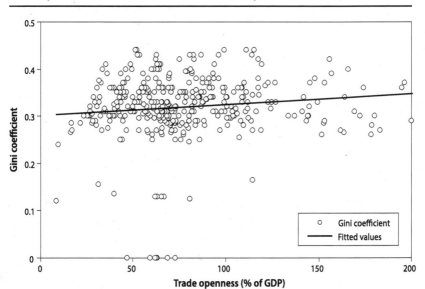

Source: Compiled from the database of BPS, 2016, March 28.

increase in income levels from the mining sector as trade openness expands is likely to benefit the richest, generating a larger gap in inequality between the rich and the poor. In the non-mining provinces, this relationship is less pronounced.

Contribution of Government Institutions and Regulations to Promoting Trade Openness

When analyzing the relationship between trade openness and the PGI triangle in Indonesia, we also need to consider the development of the former in terms of institutions and regulations. It is important to see whether and how they influence changes in trade openness. Institutional factors, such as policy planning, can help provide a clear road map for improving trade openness in the future. Furthermore, gaining a better understanding of regulatory factors can help to create an equitable trade and investment climate in which to support mounting trade openness.

Ideally, institutions that operate within a country or region and are tasked with managing key aspects of its international trade sector must have a road map for equitable open development of that sector. Some countries draw up

FIGURE 3.7

Trade openness and Gini index, 2000–13: Mining provinces

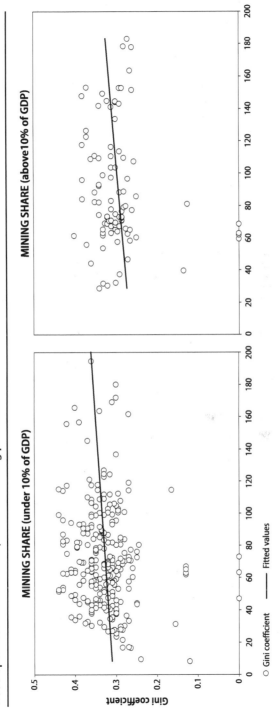

Source: Compiled from the database of BPS, 2016, March 28.

FIGURE 3.8

Indonesian government strategies to promote trade openness

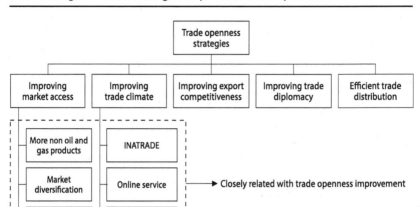

Source: Strategic Plan Ministry of Trade Republic of Indonesia (various years), 2016, March 30.

road maps to enhance bilateral cooperation with other countries. For example, Pakistan established a bilateral trade road map with Britain (UKFCO 2014) and India. Some developing countries have already concerned themselves with a similar issue: for example, Comoros created a trade road map that is integrated into its national development plan and focused on investment policy and institutional trade reform. Comparably, the EU produced a Road Map for EU Trade Policy (FTA 2014), whose mission supports both free and sustainable trade.

Although Indonesia has not generated a specific road map of policy directions for increasing trade openness, the Ministry of Trade has designed and implemented programs and policies with this end in mind (see Figure 3.8). For example, the ministry's strategic policy plan includes the objectives of optimizing bureaucratic reform and improving non-oil export performance (Ministry of Trade 2015).

Significant growth in mining sector across Indonesia tends to benefit primarily the richest population group. For this reason, the Ministry of Trade developed a policy road map to improve market access and economic growth in the non–oil-and-gas sectors, to enhance the performance of their exports. Focusing on market diversification is anticipated to benefit a wider range of the population, not solely the richest percentile.

Indonesia has also embarked on bureaucratic reform by improving its licensing procedure for foreign trade sectors. For example, the number of licence applications that can be completed online has been expanded to fifty-five types, and their processing time has been limited to three days. Making operations move more efficiently through regulatory improvement can promote faster and more efficient growth for the non–oil-and-gas businesses that operate within the foreign trade sector.

As a developing country that is still reforming its trade sector, Indonesia has not been able to make manufacturing goods its main driver of exports. Generally, this has not changed much since about 1990, which means that Indonesia's foreign trade still relies on raw materials from natural resources (see Table 3.2). This phenomenon is due to the relatively weak ability of domestic producers to compete with high-output/low-cost producers in the foreign market. The situation is aggravated by the poor quality of the domestic logistical system, which boosts the cost of transporting goods. Nevertheless, some changes have occurred in respect of certain types of exports.

Employing historical data on Indonesian foreign trade, we found that the picture for non-oil exports changed considerably from 2000 to 2013 (see Table 3.2). For instance, exports of manufacturing goods (SITC 6 and SITC 8) decreased by 4.3 percent and 3.3 percent, respectively. In contrast, export in raw materials (SITC 2) and machinery, equipment, and transportation (SITC 7) increased by 1.7 percent and 2.2 percent, respectively.[4] There was a very marked rise in the export of beverages and tobacco products (SITC 1). Growing more rapidly than all other sectors, it increased its share by 10.3 percent, which moved it into the top three sectors. The share of oil and gas products (SITC 3) also increased, by 2.2 percent, whereas that of chemical goods (SITC 5) fell.

Along with the absence of a specific road map for the development of trade openness, regulations from lower-level institutions in the Indonesian trade sector have not been widely implemented. One exception involves participation in free trade agreements and the establishment of special economic zones. As of 2016, Indonesia had joined at least four regional agreements: the ASEAN-ANZ Free Trade Agreement, ASEAN-China Free Trade Agreement, ASEAN-Korea Free Trade Agreement, and ASEAN-India Free Trade Agreement. However, regulations are still limited to a commitment to free trade and do not substantially or directly relate to trade and investment activities. An example of a missing substantial regulation is one that provides incentives for domestic businesses to improve the competitiveness of their products in foreign markets.

TABLE 3.2
Average growth rate and share of Indonesia's exported goods
by SITC classification

		Share of total exports (%)		Average growth (%)
SITC	Exported goods	2000	2013	2000–13
0	Food and live animals	4.05	3.44	8.3
1	Beverages and tobacco	3.91	14.23	23.1
2	Crude materials, inedible, except fuels	32.23	33.96	11.2
3	Mineral fuels, lubricants, and related materials	3.49	5.66	14.2
4	Animal and vegetable oils, fats, and waxes	13.60	9.77	8.3
5	Chemicals and related products	5.39	2.80	4.4
6	Manufactured goods classified chiefly by material	11.60	7.26	5.8
7	Machinery and transport equipment	4.67	6.88	15.1
8	Miscellaneous manufactured articles	16.87	13.61	7.9
9	Commodities and transactions not classified elsewhere in the SITC	4.12	2.36	4.8

Source: Trade Map (authors' estimation), 2016, March 20.

Trade openness in Indonesia has been indirectly encouraged by regulatory changes issued by non-trading institutions, such as those tied to taxation and employment. Therefore, the Indonesian government deregulated some trade-sector rules through its Economic Policy Package (Paket Kebijakan Ekonomi) in 2015 and 2016. The deregulation provisions included in that package are summarized in Tables 3.3a and 3.3b.

TABLE 3.3A
Deregulated import policies

No.	Regulation on import (as of March 28, 2016)	Status
1	Tire import	Withdrawn
2	Importer identification number (Angka Pengenal Importir)	Simplified
3	Sugar trading between islands	Eased

▶

No.	Regulation on import (as of March 28, 2016)	Status
4	Optical disc import	Withdrawn
5	B3 waste import	In process
6	Alcoholic drink trading	In process
7	Modern shop licensing	In process
8	Used capital good import	In process
9	STTP (Surat Tanda Terima Pemberitahuan/payment confirmation receipt letter) import	Withdrawn
10	SNI (Standar Nasional Indonesia/Indonesian national standardization)	Withdrawn (SPB/Surat Perintah Pengeluaran Barang/Release Order)
11	Bahasa label	SKPLBI (Surat Keterangan Pencantuman Label dalam Bahasa Indonesia/Certification and Labelling in Indonesian Language) deleted
12	Horticulture commodity import	Withdrawn
13	The Spice import	Withdrawn
14	Cooling-system-based goods import	Simplified provision
15	Ozone-depleting substances import	Simplified provision
16	Special imported product	Simplified provision
17	TPT (textile and product of textile) import	Simplified provision
18	Batik-themed textile import	Simplified provision
19	Forestry product import	In process
20	Sugar import	In process
21	Iron-steel import	In process
22	Pearl import	In process
23	Colour printer/photocopy device import	In process
24	Salt import	In process

Source: Ministry of Trade (2015).

TABLE 3.3B
Deregulated export policies

No.	Regulation on export	Status
1	Wood export	In process
2	Rice export	In process
3	Non-pharmacy precursor export	In process
4	CPO export	In process
5	Mineral refining product export	In process
6	Rice export-import	In process
7	Oil and gas export	In process

Source: Ministry of Trade (2015).

Interestingly, this deregulation has concentrated more on imports than on exports. This might be due to existing deregulation whose focus is on improving the competitiveness of the domestic industry through the provision of cheap raw materials. The Economic Policy Package is intended to create more value added domestically, and then it is expected to create job opportunities and more benefit sharing in society. It would directly affect the pattern of provincial trade flow and provincial economic growth. For instance, banning mineral exports in the short run will slow down regional economic growth, such as in Papua.

Estimating the Impact of Trade Openness on the PGI Triangle

Econometric Approach

This section focuses on measuring the impact of trade openness on the PGI triangle. Within a model that includes the role of socio-economic variables, we test whether trade policy changes affected poverty, growth, and inequality. A series of panel regression analyses on trade openness and the PGI triangle was estimated, using a provincial data set and the following three equations:

Trade openness – poverty equation

$$\Delta P_{it} = \alpha_i + \beta \cdot TO_{it} + \lambda \cdot \Delta Y_{it} + \varphi \cdot \Delta G_{it} + \gamma Z_{it} + \varepsilon_{it} \qquad (1)$$

Trade openness – growth equation

$$\Delta Y_{it} = \alpha_i + \beta \cdot TO_{it} + \lambda \cdot \Delta Y_{it} + \varphi \cdot lnG_{it} + \varphi \cdot lnP_{it-1} \qquad (2)$$
$$+ \gamma Z_{it} + \chi \cdot GP_{it} + \varepsilon_{it}$$

Trade openness – inequality equation

$$\Delta G_{it} = \alpha_i + \beta \cdot TO_{it} + \varphi \cdot lnY_{it-1} + \varphi \cdot lnG_{it-1} + \varphi \cdot lnP_{it-1} \quad\quad (3)$$
$$+ \gamma Z_{it} + \chi \cdot GP_{it} + \varepsilon_{it}$$

Where Y is income (or expenditure); ΔY is the economic growth rate; TO is the trade openness index; G is the Gini index; ΔG is a change in the Gini index; P is the poverty rate; ΔP is a change in the poverty rate; Z is a vector of socio-economic factors such as economic structure, foreign direct investment, the provincial competitiveness index, and household access to electricity and infrastructure; GP is government policies (such as expenditure on infrastructure); and ε is the error term. Finally, the subscripted $i = 1...33$ indicates provinces and t is the time span, $t = 2000...2013$. Figures 3.3–3.7 show the simple relationship between trade openness and the PGI triangle, but we still needed to determine whether the relationships are significant. The econometric models above would assess whether this were the case. The impact of trade openness on poverty-growth-inequality in a region is also dependent on other variables such as the provincial economic structure and infrastructure readiness. Therefore, by adding several control variables on the regression, we can provide a better specified measure of the relationship between trade openness and PGI in Indonesia.

We used data from multiple sources. Our sample consisted of thirty-three provinces observed from 2000 to 2013. We assumed that no significant changes occurred in Indonesia's macro-economic stability indicators during this period. The basic dataset at the provincial level was obtained from the Indonesia Database for Policy and Economic Research, which is maintained by the World Bank and Badan Pusat Statistik (BPS) (Statistics Indonesia).

Econometric Results: Is Trade Openness Good for Poverty and Inequality?

Trade Openness and Poverty

Table 3.4a (Appendix) shows the results of our poverty, growth, and inequality equations. According to our estimations, trade openness plays a statistically significant role in reducing poverty in three of our seven specifications. This is second only to the income inequality variable in how important trade openness is in diminishing poverty. The elasticity of poverty to trade openness, however, was always low, in the range of 0.001–0.003. These results led us to conclude that, in and of itself, trade openness is not enough to diminish poverty markedly.

A number of variables, in addition to aggregate income per capita and GDP growth rates, can be suggested to further reduce poverty. This list could include policy and regulatory frameworks, infrastructure, and foreign direct investment (FDI), but none is consistently significant in explaining poverty reduction, at least as far as our data set, with its relatively recent time period of 2000–13, is concerned. GDP levels or growth rates are periodically positive and significant (across our seven regressions, each one is significant twice), the infrastructure variable (access to electricity) is positive and also twice significant, and the level of inequality has a negative effect on poverty reduction, significantly so in four regressions.

Other variables (the level of competition, the unemployment rate, asphalt roads, population density, the share of total GDP from the mining sector, and FDI) all have signs that are as predicted or plausible but are never statistically significant. One can speculate about why these variables have a positive (negative for the unemployment rate and the share of mining-sector GDP) effect on poverty reduction, how they could be more narrowly measured (such as with a rural or urban focus), or what other variables might be important (such as access of the poor to financial institutions). But with the use of these rather aggregate provincial observations, measured only over the post-Soeharto years (after 1998), our regressions with these other variables exhibit correlations only, lacking statistical significance. It would be reasonable to conclude that much more than trade openness is needed to reduce poverty and that the list of variables in Table 3.4a can be used as a guide to future estimations with other, possibly more micro, data sets.

Trade Openness and Economic Growth

According to previous empirical studies, such as those discussed above, trade openness should have a positive relationship with economic growth. Our models confirm that it does boost provincial economic growth in Indonesia. The elasticity of economic growth to trade openness was around 0.01 to 0.02 percent (Table 3.4b).

Other variables are also important, as previously discussed in our literature review. For example, pre-2000 GDP, the level of inequality, the level of competition, and the share of mining-sector GDP in total GDP all have significantly positive effects on GDP growth in various regressions, and population density has a negative effect. Interactions across the PGI variables are intriguing: high levels of poverty reduce economic growth, and increased inequality increases growth. The level of manufactured exports has no effect, but their share of total exports has a significantly positive effect. FDI and infrastructure investment variables have no significant impact on the growth rate. Although the former may be unexpected, these results show only a positive, statistically insignificant correlation. Similarly, infrastructure investments would be expected to show positive effects, but they don't appear to do so. This result may indicate that government budgets were not allocated efficiently during the study period and could have been focused on financing more productive investments. Other variables that were expected to increase economic growth rates, such as investments in various forms of education, were not included in these regressions.

Trade Openness and Inequality

Table 3.4c (Appendix) confirms that trade openness has had a significant impact on inequality in Indonesia. The inequality elasticity to trade openness was, however, very small at approximately 0.0001. The possible explanation as to why trade openness led to an increase in inequality is that it expands potential foreign markets for tradable sectors, such as the non-staple agricultural sector (palm oil, coffee, cacao, rubber), the manufacturing sector, and the mining and quarrying sector. During the period 2007–13, these three sectors experienced a price boom, which resulted in a windfall profit since international prices of their commodities exceeded the production cost to a noteworthy extent. Since these three sectors are quite capital-intensive, the upper income group most probably enjoyed the unexpected profit. Consequently, trade openness led to an increase in inequality. This explanation is consistent with what appears in Table 3.4c, that a rise in the mining sector's share of GDP significantly exacerbated inequality.

Other statistically significant determinants of inequality are the first lagged Gini coefficient (negative), economic growth, and the first lagged poverty rate. All intensified inequality. The positive relationship between economic growth and inequality confirms that the former is not particularly inclusive, meaning that the lowest income groups benefit the least from growth. The provinces that are most dependent on mining activity, and thus have an additional degree of inequality, are West Papua, Bangka-Belitung, and East Kalimantan.

Seven other independent variables were used to test for their influence on inequality, but they contributed no significant effect in almost every case. Except for infrastructure investment levels and the previous year's Gini coefficient, they all had positively signed coefficients, meaning that they all increased inequality. But in virtually all cases, the coefficients showed insignificant correlations. They included three dimensions of infrastructure aside from the investment level, the level of competition, population density, and FDI.

Concluding Remarks

During the last thirty years, Indonesia has implemented many pro-growth economic policies while simultaneously generating a number of "pro-poor" policies that attempt to provide benefits to low-income groups. Nonetheless, its moderately rapid economic growth has helped to create significant economic disparity between regions, at least as measured at the provincial level. Income levels tended to expand unevenly, in that the incomes of the "haves" grew faster than those of the "have-nots."

Correspondingly, we need to think about why Indonesia has not managed to realize its expected inclusive economic growth. The link among poverty, economic growth, and inequality (the PGI triangle) illustrates a policy framework that can be used to create a more inclusive economy. Our research shows that trade openness has significantly contributed to economic growth and, more modestly and less significantly, to poverty reduction. It created new opportunities for the private sector to expand its markets as well as new job opportunities, increasing economic growth. However, our findings reveal that some benefits of trade openness are disproportionally distributed throughout society, which could be responsible for heightening inequality.

The Good and the Bad of Trade Openness

Drawing on these findings, we believe that trade openness should be considered more broadly to include the enlarged economic growth and the quite modest poverty reduction it has brought, but also the increase in income inequality, however small that may be. Looking forward for policy means that if higher economic growth but with less inequality is to be achieved, trade openness could increase its focus on growth in the manufacturing sector and decrease reliance on the mining sector. Other studies have found that foreign investment, improved infrastructure (as in transportation and utilities), and a competitive trade and investment climate are important means of accelerating poverty reduction, even if those variables had no such significant effect in our research.

Rethinking These Results and Appropriate Interventions

Even if our results show that trade openness has a modest impact on decreasing poverty and increasing inequality, the literature reviewed above confirms that such effects can be more sizable and significant. Part of this discrepancy may lie in the fact that we employed provincial averages as our unit of observation, possibly concealing the variation that would have provided statistical significance or larger effects. Almost all our results are qualitatively the same as those in prior studies.

Our results do show the complementary relation between economic growth and poverty reduction, and even more clearly the trade-off between economic growth or poverty reduction, on the one hand, and income inequality, on the other. Generating policies that will benefit lower-income groups and minimize the inequality effects is the challenge of the moment. For example, investing in infrastructure in poverty-stricken rural areas may be an effective path to this. Similarly, seaport investment in low-income areas will create greater opportunities, in conjunction with trade openness, to benefit low-income groups, not just the elites on Java. Such investments in the transport sector will be particularly helpful when increased trade openness is pursued.

Lastly, given the recent rise of economic nationalism, this study urges the government to continuously promote "inclusive trade openness" as a policy to encourage economic growth, diminish poverty, and mitigate the adverse impact of inequality. Ultimately, in the face of growing economic nationalism, our findings suggest that policy should be directed toward trade openness but that it should be inclusive: choose policies that promote economic growth and reduce poverty but not at the cost of increasing inequality in Indonesia.

Appendix

TABLE 3.4A
Effects of trade openness in poverty reduction

Poverty rate (in differences)	(1)	(2)	(3)	(4)	(5)	(6)	(7)
Trade openness (in % of GDP)	0.00354* (2.49)	0.00273* (2.10)	0.00147 (1.54)	0.00145 (1.54)	0.00147 (1.53)	0.00172** (1.86)	0.00118 (1.21)
Economic growth	0.0472** (1.92)	0.0290 (1.22)	0.0252 (1.04)	0.0252 (1.04)	0.0249 (1.01)	0.0239 (0.95)	0.0639* (2.11)
Gini coefficient	-5.601** (-1.66)	-3.868 (-1.23)	-4.921** (-1.69)	-4.889** (-1.66)	-4.839 (-1.40)	-4.820 (-1.39)	-6.481** (-1.71)
Households access to electricity		0.00875 (1.60)	0.00820* (2.44)	0.00846* (2.36)	0.00541 (1.19)	0.00597 (1.25)	0.00775 (1.52)
Competitiveness index (province)			0.0725 (1.06)	0.0762 (1.11)	0.0294 (0.33)	0.0246 (0.28)	0.0147 (0.15)
GDP per capita			0.0939 (1.62)	0.0953 (1.63)	0.103** (1.72)	0.113** (1.79)	0.0835 (1.22)
Unemployment rate				-0.00430 (-0.27)	-0.0000968 (-0.01)	-0.000940 (-0.05)	-0.00738 (-0.37)
Villages with asphalt					0.00170 (0.57)	0.00155 (0.47)	0.00115 (0.34)

	(1)	(2)	(3)	(4)	(5)	(6)	(7)
Population density					0.0248 (0.50)	0.0173 (0.30)	0.0415 (0.68)
Share of mining sector to GDP						−0.0573 (−0.52)	−0.0281 (−0.24)
Foreign direct investment							0.000914 (0.04)
Observations	377	372	317	317	315	315	278
Adjusted R^2	0.162	0.222	0.437	0.435	0.427	0.424	0.441
F	15.44	15.15	17.11	15.99	14.05	12.77	10.31

Notes: t statistics in parentheses.

* $p<0.05$

** $p<0.10$

TABLE 3.4B

Effects of trade openness in economic growth

Economic growth (in differences)	(1)	(2)	(3)	(4)	(5)	(6)
Trade openness (in % of GDP)	0.0159*	0.0157*	0.0115**	0.00658	0.00814***	0.00931***
	(3.74)	(3.70)	(2.33)	(1.46)	(1.74)	(1.68)
GDP (t-1)	0.254	0.188	0.0766	0.319***	0.312	0.628***
	(1.57)	(0.87)	(0.42)	(1.75)	(1.40)	(1.80)
Gini coefficient (t-1)	5.868**	5.856**	6.271**	7.140**	6.269*	4.381
	(2.07)	(2.00)	(2.14)	(2.32)	(2.69)	(1.19)
Poverty rate (t-1)	-0.0781	-0.0476	-0.0653	-0.496**	-0.396***	-0.738**
	(-0.37)	(-0.20)	(-0.28)	(-2.07)	(-1.75)	(-2.53)
Export manufactured goods (t-1)	0.0376	0.0353	0.0502	-0.0225	-0.0313	-0.192
	(0.60)	(0.56)	(0.85)	(-0.37)	(-0.41)	(-1.34)
Infrastructure expenditure		0.138	0.154	-0.00432	-0.0276	0.0656
		(0.84)	(0.98)	(-0.02)	(-0.13)	(0.30)
Share of mining sector to GDP			0.623**	0.670**	0.615**	0.433
			(2.01)	(2.32)	(2.13)	(1.49)
Provincial competitive index				1.694*	1.688*	1.077**
				(4.28)	(3.59)	(2.15)

Population density				-0.860*	-0.870*	-0.965*
				(-6.28)	(-6.31)	(-6.17)
Foreign direct investment					0.0439	0.0337
					(0.96)	(0.62)
Share of manufactured goods in export (%)						0.0277***
						(1.77)
Observations	244	220	220	194	163	142
Adjusted R^2	0.401	0.375	0.387	0.447	0.443	0.431
F	12.33	9.956	11.99	13.18	10.99	9.835

Notes: t statistics in parentheses.
* $p < 0.010$
** $p < 0.05$
*** $p < 0.10$

TABLE 3.4C
Effects of trade openness in increasing inequality

Gini coefficient (in differences)	(1)	(2)	(3)	(4)	(5)	(6)	(7)
Trade openness (in % of GDP)	0.0000947**	0.0000892**	0.0000860**	0.000016**	0.000115**	0.000121*	0.000112**
	(2.30)	(2.16)	(2.07)	(2.54)	(2.44)	(2.62)	(2.26)
Gini coefficient (t-1)	−0.193*	−0.195*	−0.184*	−0.201*	−0.203*	−0.206*	−0.225**
	(−4.65)	(−4.67)	(−3.16)	(−3.42)	(−3.44)	(−3.42)	(−2.26)
Economic growth	0.00235*	0.00237*	0.00213*	0.00213*	0.00205**	0.00203**	0.00231**
	(3.68)	(3.72)	(2.68)	(2.62)	(2.47)	(2.37)	(1.98)
Poverty rate (t-1)	0.000852*	0.000897*	0.000935*	0.000935*	0.000945*	0.000928*	0.00115*
	(3.37)	(3.49)	(3.30)	(3.34)	(3.26)	(3.13)	(3.37)
Competitiveness index (province)		0.00317	0.00497***	0.00231	0.00488	0.00452	0.00308
		(1.58)	(1.77)	(0.84)	(1.31)	(1.21)	(0.80)
Infrastructure expenditure			−0.00160	−0.0000511	−0.00141	−0.00113	−0.00108
			(−1.07)	(−0.03)	(−0.85)	(−0.68)	(−0.64)
Households access to electricity			−0.0000443	−0.000113	−0.000149	−0.000145	−0.0000403
			(−0.37)	(−0.91)	(−1.10)	(−1.06)	(−0.31)
Villages with asphalt			0.0000385	0.0000721	0.0000387	0.0000277	0.00000407
			(0.55)	(1.06)	(0.41)	(0.28)	(0.04)

	(1)	(2)	(3)	(4)	(5)	(6)	(7)
Share of mining sector to GDP				0.00860*	0.00760**	0.00782**	0.00690***
				(2.78)	(2.14)	(2.20)	(1.87)
Population density					0.000627	0.000742	0.00119
					(0.37)	(0.43)	(0.62)
Number of accessed main seaport						−0.00198	−0.00461
						(−0.65)	(−1.38)
Foreign direct investment							0.000344
							(0.43)
Observations	384	384	303	303	279	279	240
Adjusted R^2	0.297	0.298	0.309	0.324	0.339	0.338	0.336
F	6.775	6.039	4.120	3.969	3.783	3.589	2.696

Notes: t statistics in parentheses.

* $p<0.010$

** $p<0.05$

*** $p<0.10$

Notes

1 Authors' compilation from the Indonesia Database for Policy and Economic Research.
2 A simple linear regression explores the relationship between an outcome (GDP growth rate) and an explanatory variable (trade openness as defined above). The p-value for the slope, $\beta 1$, is a test of whether or not changes in the explanatory variable are really associated with changes in the outcome. The interpretation of the confidence interval for $\beta 1$ is usually the best way to convey what has been learned from the regression. No interpretations should be given if the basic statistical assumptions are violated.
3 The World Bank refers to "inclusive growth" to denote both the pace and pattern of economic growth, which are interlinked and assessed together. The United Nations Development Programme sees inclusive growth as both an outcome and a process. On the one hand, it ensures that everyone can be involved in the growth process, in terms of both decision-making and participating in growth itself. On the other hand, inclusive growth is one whose benefits are shared equitably. Inclusive growth thus implies participation and benefit sharing (OECD 2014).
4 The Standard international trade classification, abbreviated as SITC, is a product classification of the United Nations (UN) used for external trade statistics (export and import values and volumes of goods), allowing for international comparisons of commodities and manufactured goods.

References

Anderson, Edward. 2005. "Openness and Inequality in Developing Countries: A Review of Theory and Recent Evidence." *World Development* 33, 7: 1045–63.

Aradhyula, Satheesh V., Tauhidur Rahman, and Kumaran Seenivasan. 2007. "Impact of International Trade on Income and Income Inequality." Paper presented at the American Agricultural Economics Association annual meeting, Portland, OR, July 29–August 1.

Badan Pusat Statistik (BPS) (Statistics Indonesia). 2014. "Data on Gini Ratio by Province." https://www.bps.go.id/indicator/23/98/1/gini-rasio.html.

–. 2016. "Compilation Data on Trade Openness, Growth, Inequality, and Poverty at the Provincial Level." https://www.bps.go.id.

–. 2017. "Garis Kemiskinan Menurut Provinsi, 2013–2020." https://www.bps.go.id/linkTableDinamis/view/id/1120.

Banerjee, Abhijit V., and Esther Duflo. 2003. "Inequality and Growth: What Can the Data Say?" *Journal of Economic Growth* 8, 3: 267–99.

Bergh, Andreas, and Therese Nilsson. 2011. "Globalization and Absolute Poverty: A Panel Data Study." IFN Working Paper 862. Research Institute of Industrial Economics. https://dx.doi.org/10.2139/ssrn.2363784.

Castilho, Marta, Marta Menéndez, and Aude Sztulman. 2012. "Trade Liberalization, Inequality and Poverty in Brazilian States." *World Development* 40, 4: 821–35.

Chen, Been-Lon. 1999. "Trade Openness and Economic Growth: Evidence in East Asia and Latin America." *Journal of Economic Integration* 14, 2: 265–95.

Dartanto, Teguh, and Shigeru Otsubo. 2016. "Intrageneration Poverty Dynamics in Indonesia: Households' Welfare Mobility before, during, and after the Asian

Financial Crisis." JICA Research Institute Working Paper No. 117. https://www.jica.go.jp/jica-ri/publication/workingpaper/wp_117.html.

Dartanto, Teguh, and Arianto Patunru. 2015. "Examining the Nexus of the Poverty-Growth-Inequality Triangle in Indonesia: Empirical Evidence from Province-Level." In *Data Globalization and Development*, Vol. 2, *Country Experience*, ed. Shigeru Thomas Otsubo, 64–82. London: Routledge.

Daumal, Marie. 2013. "The Impact of Trade Openness on Regional Inequality: The Cases of India and Brazil." *International Trade Journal* 27, 3: 243–80.

De Silva, Indunil, and Sudarno Sumarto. 2014. "Does Economic Growth Really Benefit the Poor? Income Distribution Dynamics and Pro-Poor Growth in Indonesia." *Bulletin of Indonesian Economic Studies* 50, 2: 227–42.

Deme, Mamit, and Ghassem A. Homaifar. 2001. "Openness and Economic Growth in Japan and South Korea: An Empirical Investigation." *Economia Internazionale/International Economics, Camera di Commercio di Genova* 54, 2: 163–75.

Fetahi-Vehapi, Merale, Luljeta Sadiku, and Mihail Petkovski. 2015. "Empirical Analysis of the Effects of Trade Openness on Economic Growth: An Evidence for South East European Countries." *Procedia Economics and Finance* 19: 17–26.

FTA. 2014. "Road Map for EU Trade Policy, 2014–2019: Develop the Full Potential of EU Trade." Accessed June 16, 2021. http://www.fta-intl.org/sites/default/files/FTA%20Road%20Map%20for%20EU%20Trade%20Policy.pdf.

Harrison, Ann. 1996. "Openness and Growth: A Time-Series, Cross-Country Analysis for Developing Countries." *Journal of Development Economics* 48, 2: 419–47.

–. 2005. "The Impact of Trade Liberalization on Poverty." Summary of conference procedings, Woodrow Wilson International Center for Scholars, Washington, DC, April 15.

Indonesia Database for Policy and Economic Research, 2016, April 29. https://databank.worldbank.org/source/indonesia-database-for-policy-and-economic-research.

Lee, Eddy. 2005. "Trade Liberalization and Employment." DESA Working Paper No. 5, ST/ESA/2005/DWP/5. https://www.un.org/esa/desa/papers/2005/wp5_2005.pdf.

Lee, Kim-ming, Hung Wong, and Kam-yee Law. 2007. "Social Polarisation and Poverty in the Global City: The Case of Hong Kong." *China Report* 43, 1: 1–30.

McCaig, Brian. 2011. "Exporting Out of Poverty: Provincial Poverty in Vietnam and U.S. Market Access." *Journal of International Economics* 85, 1: 102–13.

Meschi, Elena, and Marco Vivarelli. 2007. "Trade Openness and Income Inequality in Developing Countries." University of Warwick, Centre for the Study of Globalisation and Regionalisation, Working Paper No. 232. https://www.researchgate.net/publication/39960499_Trade_Openness_and_Income_Inequality_in_Developing_Countries.

Milanovic, Branko. 2005. "Can We Discern the Effect of Globalization on Income Distribution? Evidence from Household Budget Surveys." *World Bank Economic Review* 19, 1: 21–44.

Ministry of Trade. 2015. "Strategic Plan of the Ministry of Trade, 2015–2019." https://www.kemendag.go.id/en/about-us/strategic-planning/2015–2019-strategic-plan.

Miranti, Riyana. 2010. "Poverty in Indonesia 1984–2002: The Impact of Growth and Changes in Inequality." *Bulletin of Indonesian Economic Studies* 46, 1: 79–97.

Musila, Jacob W., and Zelealem Yiheyis. 2015. "The Impact of Trade Openness on Growth: The Case of Kenya." *Journal of Policy Modeling* 37, 2: 342–54.

Niimi, Yoko, Puja Vasudeva Dutta, and L. Alan Winters. 2007. "Trade Liberalisation and Poverty Dynamics in Vietnam." *Journal of Economic Integration* 22, 4: 819–51.

OECD. 2014. "Report on the OECD Framework for Inclusive Growth." https://www.oecd.org/mcm/IG_MCM_ENG.pdf.

Ravallion, Martin. 2007. "Inequality Is Bad for the Poor." In *Inequality and Poverty Re-examined,* ed. Stephen P. Jenkins and John Micklewright, 37–61. Oxford: Oxford University Press.

Rivas, Marcela González. 2007. "The Effects of Trade Openness on Regional Inequality in Mexico." *Annals of Regional Science* 41, 3: 545–61.

Rodríguez, Francisco, and Dani Rodrik. 2000. "Trade Policy and Economic Growth: A Skeptic's Guide to the Cross-National Evidence." *NBER Macroeconomics Annual 2000* 15: 261–338.

Sachs, Jeffrey D., and Andrew Warner. 1995. "Economic Reform and the Process of Global Integration." *Brookings Papers on Economic Activity* 1995, 1: 1–118.

Santos-Paulino, Amelia U. 2012. "Trade, Income Distribution and Poverty in Developing Countries: A Survey." United Nations Conference on Trade and Development, UN Doc. UNCTAD/OSG/DP/2012/1. https://unctad.org/en/Publications Library/osgdp20121_en.pdf.

Suryahadi, Asep, Daniel Suryadarma, and Sudarno Sumarto. 2009. "The Effects of Location and Sectoral Components of Economic Growth on Poverty: Evidence from Indonesia." *Journal of Development Economics* 89, 1: 109–17.

Trabelsi, Mohamed Ali, and Naoufel Liouane. 2013. "Trade Liberalization and Fight against Poverty." *International Journal of Economics and Financial Issues* 3, 2: 370–75.

Trade Map. 2016. https://www.trademap.org/.

Trejos, Sandra, and Gustavo Barboza. 2015. "Dynamic Estimation of the Relationship between Trade Openness and Output Growth in Asia." *Journal of Asian Economics* 36: 110–25.

Tsai, Pan-Long, and Chao-Hsi Huang. 2007. "Openness, Growth and Poverty: The Case of Taiwan." *World Development* 35, 11: 1858–71.

UKFCO. 2014. "UK-Pakistan Trade and Investment Roadmap." https://www.gov.uk/government/publications/uk-pakistan-trade-and-investment-roadmap.

Winters, L. Alan, Neil McCulloch, and Andrew McKay. 2004. "Trade Liberalization and Poverty: The Evidence So Far." *Journal of Economic Literature* 42, 1: 72–115.

Wood, Adrian. 1994. "Globalisation and the Rise in Labour Market Inequalities." *Economic Journal* 108, 450: 1463–82.

World Bank. 2017. "GDP per capita (current US$) – Indonesia." Accessed 2017. https://data.worldbank.org/indicator/NY.GDP.PCAP.CD?locations=ID.

Yanikkaya, Halit. 2003. "Trade Openness and Economic Growth: A Cross-Country Empirical Investigation." *Journal of Development Economics* 72, 1: 57–89.

Yeboah, Osei-Agyean, Cephas B. Naanwaab, Shaik Saleem, and Akua S. Akuffo. 2012. "Effects of Trade Openness on Economic Growth: The Case of African Countries." Paper presented at the Southern Agricultural Economics Association annual meeting, Birmingham, AL, February 4–7.

4

Is Globalization Associated with Income Inequality?

The Case of Indonesia

YESSI VADILA and BUDY P. RESOSUDARMO

Globalization is the result of growing interdependence between countries due to increases in shared trade, finance, and ideas in a global marketplace. International trade and cross-border investment flows are the core elements of this integration (Soubbotina and Sheram 2000). "Globalization" refers to greater mobility in production factors (such as capital and labour) and a greater world market integration, facilitated through increases in trade and foreign investment (Milanovic 2002).

In recent decades, more and more countries, including those in the developing world, are globalizing their economy, whereby their economic activities are increasingly integrated into that of the world (OECD 2010). Arguably, developing countries take this step to expand economic growth, raise national income levels, and in doing so, provide the poor with more opportunities to improve their lives (Dollar and Kraay 2002). However, it remains debatable whether the benefits of globalization are equally distributed across households in developing countries, so as not to *worsen* income disparities (Soubbotina and Sheram 2000). Most countries, particularly those in the developing world, aim to avoid this outcome (Todaro 1999).[1]

Globalization is typically measured by observing increasing levels of foreign direct investment (FDI) and/or of trade openness. Some studies have attempted to establish a clear nexus between globalization and inequality. For example, using multi-country data, Tsai (1995) reveals that FDI increases income inequality in the host country. Using a specific-country case study, Zhang and Zhang (2003) show that globalization is an important contributor to regional inequality. In contrast, Sato and Fukushige (2009) argue that trade openness reduces income inequality in South Korea, whereas FDI increases income inequality. However, Mah (2002) contends that in Korea neither changes in trade openness nor in FDI inflow significantly affect the Gini coefficient.[2] It is clear from these studies that no definitive conclusion has been reached on this subject. This is exacerbated by the dearth of empirical studies in developing countries on the issue.

Studying the association between globalization and income inequality in Indonesia is important for at least four reasons: First, Indonesia is the world's largest island country, with a population of more than 258 million people, making it the fourth-most populous country on the planet. Thus, with its significant population, Indonesia offers an interesting developing country case study. Second, since the 1980s Indonesia has adopted policies to liberalize its trade and to encourage more FDI, giving rise to its noteworthy place in the globalization of the developing world. Third, since the 1980s, it has achieved reasonably solid rates of economic development (approximately 5.5 percent growth annually), which is significant when contrasted with continuing increases in income inequality (Yusuf and Sumner 2015). Finally, the notable issue of worsening income inequality in Indonesia is becoming a critical global policy agenda.[3]

Despite the importance of this much-needed research, studies on the impact of globalization on income inequality in Indonesia have been relatively limited. A number examine the determinants of inequality (Hughes and Islam 1981; Asra 1989; Hill 2008; Leigh and Van der Eng 2009; Akita, Kurniawan, and Miyata 2011; Nugraha and Lewis 2013; Tadjoeddin 2013; Gordon and Resosudarmo 2019; Vadila and Resosudarmo 2020). Although most of these studies include trade openness as part of their discussion, they do not specifically address the link between globalization and inequality.

In this chapter, we tackle this empirical gap and build on previous studies by examining the correlation between globalization and regional income inequalities in Indonesia, as a specific developing country case study. We do this by measuring provincial flows of FDI and trade openness, and their relationships with provincial income inequalities, represented by provincial household expenditure inequalities. Initially, however, we review a number of studies on globalization and income inequality.

A Literature Review

The two main channels through which developing countries benefit from globalization have been relatively well established (Milanovic 2002). The first is through trade openness, whereby, according to the Heckscher-Ohlin theorem, a higher intensity of export and import increases a country's economy through higher intensity in using its relative abundant factor inputs. The second channel is through increasing FDI and portfolio investments by capital-rich countries, which enables the recipient country to augment their economic output. In the following, we discuss the nexus between trade openness and income inequality as well as between FDI and income inequality and then unpack the situation in Indonesia.

Trade Openness and Income Inequality

Literature that supports the idea that trade openness reduces income inequality typically applies the following logic: Trade openness encourages labour-rich countries, which are mostly developing countries, to export relatively labour-intensive goods and import relatively capital-intensive ones (Salvatore 2007). Hence, for developing countries, trade openness is expected to increase the output of labour-intensive sectors and to reduce that of capital-intensive sectors. If the output of labour-intensive sectors increases, the real incomes of unskilled labourers, comprised mostly of the poor, rises (Bhagwati and Srinivasan 2002). Meanwhile, the declining output of capital-intensive sectors reduces the real income of capital owners, who are typically among the rich. Thus, for developing countries, trade openness would diminish income inequality.

In contrast, literature that takes the opposite view maintains that capital owners and highly skilled labourers in labour-intensive sectors make much higher capital gains than their unskilled labourer counterparts (Spilimbergo, Londoño, and Székely 1999; Stiglitz 2002). Also, some believe that greater trade openness weakens the ability of governments to redistribute income (Anderson 2005).

FDI and Income Inequality

In addressing globalization and inequality, the literature often suggests that an influx of FDI, typically accelerating the process of industrialization and benefiting more capital owners and skilled workers, tends to amplify income inequality in developing countries. Authors who espouse this conclusion adhere to the modernization theory – the supposition that inequality is considered a necessary prerequisite for modernizing the economy, i.e., industrialization, which then increases incomes of all people (Tsai 1995). This argument is represented in the Inverted U-Curve Hypothesis of Simon Kuznets (1955), which explains that income inequality generally increases in the early stages of a country's economic development and then declines progressively until its development goals are achieved (Adelman and Morris 1973). Thus, despite its income inequality consequences, modernization theory posits that FDI remains relevant for developing countries since an increasing influx of FDI is a key driver for development.

Authors who hold that FDI tends to exacerbate income inequality champion the Dependency Theory (Prebisch 1949; Singer 1949). According to this theory, the greatest benefits of FDI usually accrue to a country's elite, who are stereotyped as caring only about their own interests and the welfare of people in their own socio-economic group, instead of the public at large. Here, resources flow from a poor and undeveloped lower-working-class periphery to a core of wealthy elites, enriching the latter at the expense of the former (Prebisch 1962).

Contemporary dependency theorists hence claim that international economic dependence on foreign capital produces a "development of underdevelopment" on the periphery of society (Chase-Dunn 1975), whereby political and economic forces, which attempt to mobilize and distribute national development, are suppressed (Rubinson 1976; Bornschier 1983).

Although a wealth of literature supports the hypothesis that FDI heightens income inequality, this does not necessarily preclude the opposite hypothesis that FDI could, in fact, *reduce* it. This could mainly be the case in countries where FDI flows primarily into labour-intensive sectors, and the development of those sectors then benefits unskilled workers.

Trade, FDI, and Income Inequality in Indonesia

From independence until the mid-1960s, Indonesia partially closed its economy by disengaging the country from the international economy as well as from most international organizations and by nationalizing foreign properties in the country. From 1967 onward, the new order government led by the then President Soeharto gradually opened up the economy to international trade and commerce. Despite this, a swing back to protectionism occurred in the 1970s. The trade and investment policies of Indonesia have changed significantly since the 1980s, shifting it to a much more open economy. Since then, the economy has remained relatively open (Basri and Hill 2008). By about the mid-2010s, Indonesia had the most open economic regime of all Southeast Asian countries.

As it had undergone comprehensive trade liberalization since the 1980s, its exports and imports increased until 2010 (Figure 4.1), even though several anti-trade-liberalization movements cropped up from time to time. It is generally argued that this upsurge in trade openness, indicated by an increase in total exports and imports, facilitated the continued growth of the country's gross domestic product (GDP) in the 1990s and 2000s (Figure 4.2).

FIGURE 4.1
Indonesia's exports and imports, 1981–2010

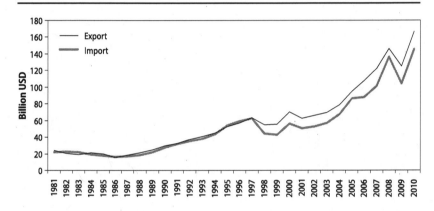

Source: BPS, via CEIC Dataset (2019a).

FIGURE 4.2
Total trade and gross domestic product of Indonesia, 1981–2010

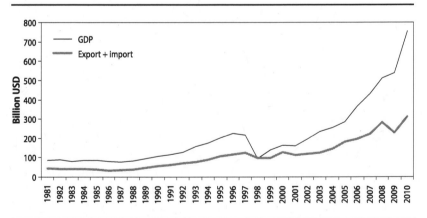

Source: BPS, via CEIC Dataset (2019a, 2019b).

Since the early 2010s, Indonesia had adopted three strategies for international trade: supporting the agenda of the World Trade Organization (WTO), encouraging regional economic integration through free trade agreements, and developing bilateral agreements along with economic cooperation.

Nevertheless, McGuire (2004) argued that Indonesia has never had a comprehensive foreign trade policy. Its current trade policy emerged as a result of reactive and ad hoc political agendas, rather than intentionally as a well-planned road map. The government has adjusted tariff and non-tariff levels in some sectors, mostly in reaction to international pressures. Though commitments to the WTO and other trade agreements do help to maintain an open economy, pressures from domestic anti-trade-liberalization movements continually challenge its ability to keep the economy open (Basri and Patunru 2012).

Since the mid-1960s, Indonesia has also paid particular attention to attracting FDI, realizing that it is an important driver for economic growth. Policies simplifying investment procedure and infrastructure development, as well as the relaxation of policies on the share of firms' foreign ownership, have been gradually implemented, inducing the annual amount of FDI realization to grow since then. Figure 4.3 shows the annual FDI from 1995 to 2011.

FIGURE 4.3
Realized Foreign Direct Investment (FDI) in Indonesia, 1995–2011

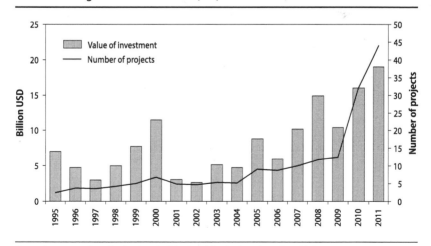

Source: Investment Coordinating Board of the Republic of Indonesia (BKPM), 2019.

By the early 2010s, it can be seen that the highest realization of FDI was located in the Java corridor, followed by Sumatra, Maluku, Papua, Sulawesi, Kalimantan, Bali, and the Nusa Tenggara corridor (BKPM 2013). The realization of FDI in 2013 can be seen in Figure 4.4.

FIGURE 4.4
FDI realization across Indonesian regions, 2013

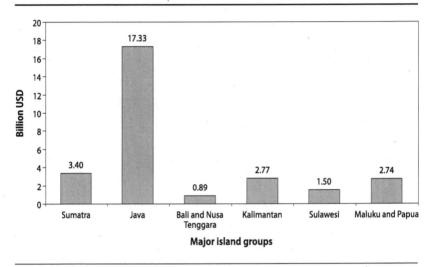

Source: Investment Coordinating Board of the Republic of Indonesia (2019).

FIGURE 4.5
Level of expenditure inequality (Gini Coefficient) in Indonesia, 2000–10
(percentage points)

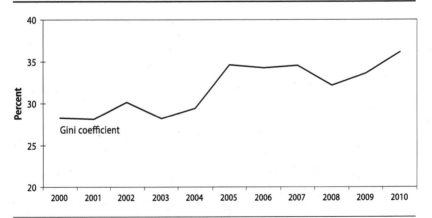

Source: SUSENAS Data (2000–2010), BPS (2019c).

While levels of trade openness and FDI have increased, income inequality in Indonesia, as measured by the Gini coefficient for individual consumption expenditure, rose as well. Figure 4.5 shows Gini coefficients for the period 2000–10, and Table 4.1 provides the average Gini coefficients for twenty-two provinces from 2000 to 2010. Table 4.1 shows that the five provinces with the highest levels of inequality were Yogyakarta, South Sulawesi, Banten, DKI Jakarta, and East Kalimantan, whereas Jambi and Central Kalimantan had the least inequality. It is, hence, important to understand whether or not this increase with income inequality is associated with the increasing intensity of trade and FDI.

TABLE 4.1

Average level of expenditure inequality in 22 provinces, 2000–10 (percentage points)

No.	Province	Average Gini	No.	Province	Average Gini
1	North Sumatra	32.41	12	Banten	36.10
2	West Sumatra	30.08	13	Bali	32.30
3	Riau	32.32	14	West Kalimantan	30.78
4	Jambi	28.05	15	Central Kalimantan	27.22
5	South Sumatra	30.00	16	South Kalimantan	33.85
6	Lampung	30.37	17	East Kalimantan	35.16
7	DKI Jakarta	35.30	18	North Sulawesi	32.66
8	West Java	34.26	19	Central Sulawesi	33.36
9	Central Java	31.10	20	South Sulawesi	36.92
10	Yogyakarta	39.10	21	West Nusa Tenggara	33.77
11	East Java	32.97	22	East Nusa Tenggara	34.86

Source: SUSENAS Data (2000, 2010), BPS (2019c).

Empirical Study

This chapter is an attempt to provide evidence regarding whether globalization is associated with increased income inequality in Indonesia by examining the relationships between provincial trade and FDI values and provincial Gini coefficients.

The Basic Model

The main variables of interest in our basic model are trade openness, measured by total trade intensity over provincial gross domestic product (GDP), and FDI, measured by the ratio between provincial FDI realization and provincial GDP. Other control variables determining provincial income inequality include provincial government spending as a share of provincial GDP (which we assumed was an intervention to reduce income inequalities), agricultural labour share, and human capital as well as short-term economic growth.

To examine the association of globalization with inequality, we adopt the empirical model developed by Tsai (1995):[4]

$$gni_{i,t} = \beta_0 + \beta_1. trade_{i,t} + \beta_2. fdi_{i,\bar{t}} + \beta_3. gdpp_{i,\bar{t}} + \tag{1}$$
$$\beta_4. gdpp_{i,\bar{t}}^2 + \beta_5. gov_{i,\bar{t}} + \beta_6. agri_{i,\bar{t}} + \beta_7. gro_{i,\bar{t}} +$$
$$\beta_8. lit_{i,t-3} + \beta_9. ed_{i,t-3} + \varepsilon_{i,t}$$

where:
i = index for province
t = index for year
$\bar{t}$ = index for three-year average (t, t–1 and t–2)
$gini_{i,t}$ = provincial Gini coefficient × 100
$trade_{i,i}$ = (provincial exports + provincial imports)/provincial GDP × 100
$fdi_{i,\bar{t}}$ = provincial FDI flow/provincial GDP × 100
$gdpp_{i,\bar{t}}$ = logarithm of real provincial GDP per capita
$gov_{i,\bar{t}}$ = provincial government spending/provincial GDP × 100
$agri_{i,i}$ = provincial agricultural labour force/total labour force × 100
$gro_{i,\bar{t}}$ = annual growth rate of real provincial GDP per capita
$lit_{i,t-3}$ = provincial literacy rate
$ed_{i,t-3}$ = total completed secondary school/total population in each province
$\varepsilon_{i,t}$ = normally distributed disturbance term.

Please note that the dependent variable (provincial Gini coefficient) is measured in year t. All explanatory variables, except provincial literacy rate and proportion of population finishing secondary school, are the three-year average of their time values in years t, $t-1$, and $t-2$. The literacy rate and proportion of population finishing secondary school indicator uses a three-year time lag ($t-3$) before the year of Gini (t). This strategy is chosen to reduce the short-term dynamics of the variables. We estimate the relationship in equation (1) with several different estimation strategies, described in the empirical results section, to get a reliable estimation result.

Data Sources and Variables
We employed annual data covering the period 2003–10 for twenty-two Indonesian provinces for which data on FDI and trade are available. This

data on FDI and trade comes from the Ministry of Trade and the Investment Coordinating Board of the Republic of Indonesia (BKPM), respectively. Other data utilized is from Badan Pusat Statistik (BPS) (Statistics Indonesia). The main BPS information is taken from BPS publications or derived from Indonesia's National Socio-Economic Household Survey (SUSENAS). We used the following eight variables (1–8) in our econometric model to generate empirical results:

1 Provincial expenditure inequality ($gini_{i,t}$): The Gini coefficient is a measure of aggregate income inequality ranging from zero (perfect equality) to one (perfect inequality). The Gini coefficient used in this chapter is derived from individual consumption expenditure data, on the basis that expenditure data are more reliable than income data. Data on Gini is obtained from BPS publications.

2 Provincial export-import share of provincial GDP ($trade_{i,\bar{t}}$): This share is an indicator of the level of trade openness, which is an important indicator of globalization. Data for this variable is obtained from the Ministry of Trade annual data set recording the ratio of exports plus imports to GDP of province i in year $\bar{t}$.

3 Ratio of provincial FDI to provincial GDP ($fdi_{i,\bar{t}}$): The flow of provincial FDI is the value of realized foreign direct investment in a province, obtained from the BKPM. Data on FDI is in US dollars. We multiply with the real exchange rate to transfer this information into Indonesian rupiah.

4 Provincial real GDP per capita ($gdpp_{i,\bar{t}}$): This variable is a proxy for the average welfare of each resident in a province during a given period. This is a typical measure used to represent levels of economic development. Information on this variable is taken from BPS publications. We use the natural logarithm form of this variable and the quadratic of this natural logarithm form to represent the Kuznets hypotheses, which predicts that the coefficient of this variable will be positive and that of the natural logarithm form will be negative. This would mean that income inequality increases during the early stages of a country's development and then declines progressively as the optimum level of development is achieved.

5 Ratio of provincial government spending and provincial GDP ($gov_{i,\bar{t}}$): This variable is a proxy for the quality or effectiveness of provincial government. In general, we expect that the sign would be positive. Higher government spending would lead to more equal income distribution. However, what could be considered to be the sign of this variable is debatable.

6 Provincial share of agricultural workers ($agri_{i,\bar{t}}$): This variable is defined as the ratio of the number of agricultural workers to the total number of workers in province i for period $\bar{t}$. The core data were obtained from SUSENAS. In general, it is expected that the higher the ratio of agricultural labour to the total labour force, the higher the income equality in that province (Tsai 1995).

7 Literacy rate ($lit_{i,t-3}$): The literacy rate is intended to measure the basic educational level of the general population (Tsai 1995). Data for this is obtained from BPS publications. It is expected that the sign of this variable would be positive.

8 Proportion of population that has finished secondary school ($ed_{i,t-3}$): This variable is the proportion of the population that has at least completed a secondary level of education, which captures the higher degree of human capital beyond the primary level of education (Ahluwalia 1976). Whereas Tsai uses a ten-year lag for both human capital indicators, we employed only a three-year lag due to data limitations. We used year lags because we assumed that workers with good human capital development would make an impact on inequality in future years. This is based on the common knowledge that education has a long-term effect. The hypothesis is that the accumulation of general human capital improvements, such as education and literacy, will reduce inequality in income (Ram 1984).

Empirical Results

We first use the ordinary least squares (OLS) estimation technique on the model in equation (1). After conducting several post-estimation tests on our OLS results, we further implement the fixed effects (FE) estimation technique on the model in equation (1). Discussion of these estimates is as follows.

Table 4.2 provides the coefficient estimates of the model in equation (1) using a pooled OLS with several different approaches. Column (1) is the result from a plain pool OLS estimation. Columns (2), (3), (4), and (5) are the results of estimating the pooled OLS using the White, Rogers, Newey-West, and Driscoll-Kraay approaches, respectively, ensuring that we obtain an estimation with robust standard errors. Overall, results in columns 1 to 5 are roughly similar. Standard errors do not drastically change among all procedures. Thus, this finding suggests that cross-dependence in the residuals might not be present here.

TABLE 4.2

Pooled OLS estimation for provincial globalization and provincial income inequality

	OLS (1)	White (2)	Rogers (3)	Newey-West (4)	Driscoll-Kraay (5)
Constant	42.366***	42.366***	42.366**	42.366***	42.266**
	(12.400)	(10.272)	(15.227)	(11.415)	(14.829)
trade	0.042***	0.042***	0.042**	0.041***	−0.054***
	(0.107)	(0.009)	(0.015)	(0.011)	(0.014)
fdi	−0.054**	−0.054***	−0.054***	−0.054***	0.042***
	(0.026)	(0.016)	(0.013)	(0.016)	(0.009)
gdpp	56.265***	56.265**	56.265***	56.265**	56.265
	(18.345)	(22.616)	(19.175)	(22.987)	(39.189)
gdpp^2	−28.671***	−28.671**	−28.671***	−28.671**	−28.671
	(9.007)	(11.174)	(9.373)	(11.347)	(19.414)
gov	0.009	0.009	0.009	0.009	0.009
	(0.078)	(0.076)	(0.103)	(0.083)	(0.072)
agri	0.032	0.032	0.032	0.032	0.032
	(0.032)	(0.030)	(0.033)	(0.035)	(0.018)
gro	−0.025	−0.025	−0.025	−0.025	−0.025
	(0.024)	(0.022)	(0.024)	(0.023)	(0.018)
lit	−0.067	−0.067	−0.068	−0.067	−0.068
	(0.063)	(0.068)	(0.090)	(0.077)	(0.114)
ed	0.234***	0.234***	0.234***	0.234***	0.234**
	(0.061)	(0.049)	(0.074)	(0.058)	(0.082)
N	176	176	176	176	176
F-stat.	6.77	9.74	8.16	8.25	2167.8
R^2-adj.	0.228	0.268	0.268		0.268

Notes:

* = significantly different from zero at 10% level

** = significantly different from zero at 5% level

*** = significantly different from zero at 1% level.

Numbers in parentheses are standard errors.

Table 4.3 shows results using different techniques to obtain estimated standard errors for the fixed effects (FE) estimation technique. The Hausman test comparing the results from pooled OLS estimates and FE estimates indicates that the coefficient estimates from pooled OLS estimations are not consistent; thus, we concentrated our analysis based on the results obtained from using the FE estimation techniques. Column (6) shows the results from a plain FE estimation. Columns (7), (8), (9), (10), and (11) are results from FE estimations with White, Rogers, Parks-Kmenta, Beck and Katz, and Driscoll-Kraay procedures. The first four columns in Table 4.3 (columns (6)–(9)) show a somewhat similar result. Whereas columns (10) and (11) produce rather distinctive results.

The expansion from column (6) into columns (7) and (8) is intended to deal with any heteroskedasticity problem in general, while the expansion to column (9) is to deal with cross-sectional dependence issues. The fact that results from these three columns are relatively similar indicates that there is no serious heteroskedasticity problem.

The expansion to columns (10) and (11) aims to deal with temporal and spatial dependence issues in the residuals of time-series cross-section models, as well as an auto-correlation issue. These Parks-Kmenta and Beck and Katz procedures addressing any possible auto-correlation issue produce better, more robust results; as can be seen from the relatively lower standard errors and from the fact that coefficients of trade openness as well as share of secondary school graduates become significantly different from zero. Thus, we focus on the results from columns (10) and (11).

The interesting results, as seen in columns (10) and (11), are the correlation between globalization and inequality. On one hand, both columns (10) and (11) show that FDI is negatively and significantly associated with income inequality. Thus, the higher the level of FDI, the lower the provincial income inequality. In other words, increases in FDI are beneficial for income inequality. This finding is important as it differs from some other studies, for example that of Tsai (1995).

On the other hand, our results show that variable trade openness is associated with a significant increase in income inequality; i.e., the more open to trade the province, the worse the provincial income inequality. These results support Rubinson's (1976) argument that the more a country depends on external markets, the higher its degree of income inequality. Our results, however, are contrary to that of Tsai (1995), in which the estimated coefficient of trade openness is positive and significant.

TABLE 4.3

Fixed effects estimation for provincial globalization and provincial income inequality

	FE (6)	White (7)	Rogers (8)	Driscoll-Kraay (9)	Parks-Kmenta (10)	Beck and Katz (11)
Constant	−107.296***	−107.296***	−107.296***	−107.297**	42.366***	44.129***
	(41.354)	(36.714)	(36.713)	(43.683)	(12.043)	(13.742)
trade	0.020	0.020	0.020	0.020*	0.042***	0.054***
	(0.022)	(0.026)	(0.026)	(0.008)	(0.010)	(0.010)
fdi	−0.062**	−0.062*	−0.062*	−0.062*	−0.054**	−0.070***
	(0.031)	(0.032)	(0.032)	(0.030)	(0.025)	(0.018)
gdpp	40.807**	40.807**	40.807**	40.807	56.265***	32.468*
	(17.683)	(15.314)	(15.314)	(23.637)	(17.816)	(17.453)
gdpp^2	−16.618*	−16.618**	−16.617**	−16.618	−28.671***	−17.134**
	(8.345)	(6.673)	(6.673)	(10.871)	(8.748)	(8.565)
gov	0.215	0.215	0.215	0.215**	0.009	−0.040
	(0.299)	(0.348)	(0.348)	(0.075)	(0.075)	(0.074)
agri	−0.007	−0.007	−0.007	−0.007	0.032	0.05
	(0.066)	(0.058)	(0.058)	(0.045)	(0.031)	(0.049)
gro	−0.006	−0.006	−0.006	−0.006	−0.025	−0.020
	(0.020)	(0.016)	(0.016)	(0.015)	(0.023)	(0.020)
lit	0.129	0.129	0.129	0.129	−0.068	0.005
	(0.112)	(0.107)	(0.107)	(0.081)	(0.234)	(0.090)
ed	0.174	0.174	0.174	0.174	0.059***	0.275***
	(0.136)	(0.152)	(0.152)	(0.162)	(0.060)	(0.079)
N	176	176	176	176	176	176
F-stat.	10.18	19.12	19.12	2167.8		
R^2	0.0776	0.0776	0.0776	0.268		0.2685
Wald chi^2					64.61	109.61

Notes:

* = significantly different from zero at 10% level

** = significantly different from zero at 5% level

*** = significantly different from zero at 1% level.

Numbers in parentheses are standard errors.

It is important to note that our results do not imply that trade openness is bad for the poor. It might be that all household incomes expand with trade openness, as indicated by the decline in the provincial portion of poor people during the period of our data set. However, at the same time the income of the rich rises by more than that of the poor, resulting in more income disparity despite an improvement in income for the poor.

The results in columns (10) and (11) support the Kuznets hypothesis; i.e., they provide evidence of an inverted U-curve between economic growth and inequality at the provincial level. The coefficient of LNGRDPP is positive and significant, and that of LNGRDPPS is negative and significant.

Literacy rate is not significant but the share of secondary school graduates is. It proves to be significant in all estimations, and the coefficients are all positive. This means that the development of human capital in terms of higher education attainment is linked with worsening income inequality in a province. This result supports Glomm and Ravikumar's (1992) argument that higher education may not be an equalizer of income inequality in the short run. This might not be because higher education is bad for development, as it is undoubtedly important. Nevertheless, the finding in our study, as well as those of Glomm and Ravikumar (1992) and of Gregorio and Lee (2002), argues that, given many people do not graduate from secondary school in Indonesia, an increasing share of secondary school graduates could produce a markedly unequal distribution of educational attainment; thus ultimately contributing to worsening income inequality.

Furthermore, Lopez, Thomas, and Wang (1998) claim that although higher education by itself does not guarantee successful development of the overall society, the distribution of higher education, or who gets educated, matters a great deal. Higher education can have big impact on the overall economic development of a society if all members of its population are presented with the same opportunities to access it. It is hence possible that the benefits of higher education are skewed toward more advantaged people only, which could then have an enormously significant impact on income inequality.

As regards to the other variables (government spending, share of agricultural labour, and growth), none are significantly different from zero. Hence, they are not the important covariates of provincial income inequality in Indonesia.

Conclusion

In this chapter, we analyzed the relationship between globalization and provincial income inequality in twenty-two Indonesian provinces for the period 2003 to 2010. We measured globalization by trade openness and foreign direct investment.

Admittedly, our research method had several weaknesses. First, using data from only twenty-two of Indonesia's thirty-three provinces might induce a selection bias problem. Second, the lack of a long-term data series greatly reduced the reliability and robustness of our results. Third, a reverse causality problem might exist in our estimations. Income inequality might be a cause of the levels of FDI and trade openness. Fourth, 2003–10 was a commodity boom period, in which exports and imports related to the mining and plantation sectors significantly increased (Burke and Resosudarmo 2012). Varying structures of sectoral exports and imports could produce different results. Hence, taking into account these weaknesses, we are very cautious in drawing conclusions from our empirical analysis. We do not argue that we find causal relations from globalization to income inequality. We do, however, find some evidence that there is a significant association between the two during the period of our analysis. Furthermore, we also argue that our results could provide some insight into the relationship between globalization and income inequality in Indonesia, therefore contributing to the debate on the issue.

Our results show that globalization might have a complex association with income inequality at the provincial level. On the one hand, the higher the FDI in a province, the lower the income inequality in that province. This disparity indicates that increasing the amount of FDI might have been supporting the development of unskilled, labour-intensive sectors. Hence, higher benefits accrue to unskilled labourers, most of whom are poor.

On the other hand, our data reveal that trade openness exhibits a significant and positive association with income inequality. Therefore, according to this result, although liberalizing trade might increase the income of everyone in the province, it might benefit the rich more than the poor.

The present chapter also concludes that levels of economic development are important covariates of income inequality. Our results demonstrate that an inverted U-curve relationship does exist between provincial economic development and income inequality. Another important aspect of income inequality is human capital, particularly when measured by the share of people who have graduated from secondary schools. In Indonesia, a large segment of the population has not entered secondary school, so an increase in the share of people who have graduated from secondary school might induce greater levels of educational inequality. Overall, greater educational inequality could thus ultimately induce greater income inequality.

Further research is certainly needed to confirm our findings. This chapter hopefully would encourage more research on this subject in Indonesia.

Notes

1 Although there are many reasons for seeing an increase in income inequality as harmful, we do not debate them in detail here, as the subject falls beyond the scope of this chapter.

2 A Gini coefficient (also called a ratio or an index) measures, through statistical dispersion, the income distribution of a country's residents and is often used as a yardstick for economic inequality.

3 Conducted in Bali, 2013, the last High-Level Panel of Eminent Persons meeting paid special attention to this issue.

4 The basic model might exhibit endogeneity problems if there are any uncontrolled variables that are related to FDI, trade, and Gini. We deal with this possible problem of uncontrolled variables by using the provincial fixed-effect model. Another source of endogeneity is reverse causality, which we address by using an average of three years' values or three years' lag for all of the right-hand-side variables. That way the Gini is less likely to significantly determine the right-hand-side variables. We understand that perhaps our methods of dealing with possible endogeneity may not be the most effective. However, because our intention is to give a broad picture of the association between globalization and income inequality, the issue of endogeneity does not need to be perfectly resolved at this time.

References

Adelman, I., and C.T. Morris. 1973. *Economic Growth and Social Equity in Developing Countries.* Stanford: Stanford University Press.

Ahluwalia, M.S. 1976. "Income Distribution and Development: Some Stylized Facts." *American Economic Review* 66, 2: 128–35.

Akita, T., P.A. Kurniawan, and S. Miyata. 2011. "Structural Changes and Regional Income Inequality in Indonesia: A Bidimensional Decomposition Analysis." *Asian Economic Journal* 25, 1: 55–77.

Anderson, E. 2005. "Openness and Inequality in Developing Countries: A Review of Theory and Recent Evidence." *World Development* 33, 7: 1045–63.

Asra, Abuzar. 1989. "Inequality Trends in Indonesia, 1969–1981: A Re-Examination." *Bulletin of Indonesian Economic Studies* 25, 2: 100–10.

Badan Pusat Statistik (BPS) (Statistics Indonesia). 2019a. Provincial Export-Import Table. Available at: www.bps.go.id/subject/8/eksporimpor.html#subjekViewTab3.

–. 2019b. Provincial Product Domestic Bruto Table. Available at: www.bps.go.id/subject/169/produk-domestik-bruto--pengeluaran-.html#subjekViewTab3.

–. 2019c. National Social Economic Survey (SUSENAS) 2000–2010, Statistical Publication, Jakarta.

Basri, M.C., and H. Hill. 2008. "Indonesia–Trade Policy Review 2007." *World Economy* 31, 11: 1393–1408.

Basri, M.C., and A.A. Patunru. 2012. "How to Keep Trade Policy Open: The Case of Indonesia." *Bulletin of Indonesian Economic Studies* 48, 2: 191–208.

Bhagwati, J., and T.N. Srinivasan. 2002. "Trade and Poverty in the Poor Countries." *American Economic Review* 92, 2: 180–83.

Bornschier, V. 1983. "World Economy, Level Development and Income Distribution: An Integration of Different Approaches to the Explanation of Income Inequality." *World Development* 11, 1: 11–20.

Burke, P., and B.P. Resosudarmo. 2012. "Survey of Recent Developments." *Bulletin of Indonesian Economic Studies* 48, 3: 299–324.

Chase-Dunn, C. 1975. "The Effects of International Economic Dependence on Development and Inequality: A Cross-National Study." *American Sociological Review* 40, 6: 720–38.

Dollar, D., and A. Kraay. 2002. "Spreading the Wealth." *Foreign Affairs* 81, 1: 120–33.

Glomm, G., and B. Ravikumar. 1992. "Public versus Private Investment in Human Capital: Endogenous Growth and Income Inequality." *Journal of Political Economy* 100, 4: 818–34.

Gordon, I.G., and B.P. Resosudarmo. 2019. "A Sectoral Growth-Income Inequality Nexus in Indonesia." *Regional Science Policy and Practice* 11, 1: 123–39.

Gregorio, J.D., and J.W. Lee. 2002. "Education and Income Inequality: New Evidence from Cross-Country Data." *Review of Income and Wealth* 48, 3: 395–416.

Hill, H. 2008. "Globalization, Inequality, and Local Level Dynamics: Indonesia and the Philippines." *Asian Economic Policy Review* 3, 1: 42–61.

Hughes, G.A., and I. Islam. 1981. "Inequality in Indonesia: A decomposition analysis." *Bulletin of Indonesian Economic Studies* 17, 2: 42–71.

Investment Coordinating Board of the Republic of Indonesia. 2019. Investment Realization: Foreign Direct Investment (FDI) www.bkpm.go.id/en/statistic/foreign-direct-investment-fdi.

Kuznets, S. 1955. "Economic Growth and Income Inequality." *American Economic Review* 45, 1: 1–28.

Leigh, A., and P. Van der Eng. 2009. "Inequality in Indonesia: What Can We Learn from Top Incomes?." *Journal of Public Economics* 93, 1–2: 209–12.

Lopez, R., V. Thomas, and Y. Wang. 1998. *Addressing the Education Puzzle: The Distribution of Education and Economic Reform.* Washington, DC: World Bank.

Mah, J.S. 2002. "The Impact of Globalization on Income Distribution: The Korean Experience." *Applied Economics Letters* 9, 15: 1007–9.

McGuire, G. 2004. "A Future Trade Policy for Indonesia: Which Road to Take?" UNSFIR Working Paper Series No. 04/02, UNSFIR, Jakarta.

Milanovic, B. 2002. "Can We Discern the Effect of Globalization on Income Distribution? Evidence from Household Budget Surveys." World Bank Policy Research Paper 2876. Washington, DC: E-Library World Bank Group.

Nugraha, K., and P. Lewis. 2013. "Towards a Better Measure of Income Inequality in Indonesia." *Bulletin of Indonesian Economic Studies* 49, 1: 103–12.

OECD (Organisation for Economic Co-operation and Development). 2010. *Measuring Globalisation: OECD Economic Globalisation Indicators 2010.* Paris: OECD.

Prebisch, R. 1949. "Growth, Disequilibrium and Disparities: Interpretation of the Process of Economic Development." *En: Economic Survey of Latin America* 164, 12: 3–85.

–. 1962. "The Economic Development of Latin America and Its Principal Problems." *Economic Bulletin for Latin America* 7, 1: 1–22.

Ram, R. 1984. "Population Increase, Economic Growth, Educational Inequality, and Income Distribution: Some Recent Evidence." *Journal of Development Economics* 14, 3: 419–28.

Rubinson, R. 1976. "The World-Economy and the Distribution of Income within States: A Cross-National Study." *American Sociological Review* 41, 4: 638–59.

Salvatore, D. 2007. *International Economics.* Hoboken, NJ: John Wiley and Sons.

Sato, S., and M. Fukushige. 2009. "Globalization and Economic Inequality in the Short and Long Run: The Case of South Korea 1975–1995." *Journal of Asian Economics* 20, 1: 62–68.

Singer, H.W. 1949. "Economic Progress in Underdeveloped Countries." *Social Research* 16, 1: 1–11.

Soubbotina, T.P., and K.A. Sheram. 2000. *Beyond Economic Growth: Meeting the Challenges of Global Development.* Washington, DC: World Bank.

Spilimbergo, A., J.L. Londoño, and M. Székely. 1999. "Income Distribution, Factor Endowments, and Trade Openness." *Journal of Development Economics* 59, 1: 77–101.

Stiglitz, J.E. 2002. *Globalization and Its Discontents.* London: Penguin Books.

Tadjoeddin, M.Z. 2013. "Miracle That Never Was: Disaggregated Level of Inequality in Indonesia." *International Journal of Development Issues* 12, 1: 22–35.

Todaro, M.P. 1999. *Economic Development.* 7th Ed. London: Pearson.

Tsai, P.-L. 1995. "Foreign Direct Investment and Income Inequality: Further Evidence." *World Development* 23, 3: 469–83.

Vadila, Y., and B.P. Resosudarmo. 2020. "Tariff Reform and Income Inequality in Indonesia." *Regional Science Policy and Practice* 12, 3: 455–75.

Yusuf, A.A., and A. Sumner. 2015. "Growth, Poverty, and Inequality under Jokowi." *Bulletin of Indonesian Economic Studies* 51, 3: 323–48.

Zhang, X., and K.H. Zhang. 2003. "How Does Globalisation Affect Regional Inequality within a Developing Country? Evidence from China." *Journal of Development Studies* 39, 4: 47–67.

5

A Child's Growth Is a Nation's Growth

Children's Well-Being and Inequality
in Indonesia

SANTI KUSUMANINGRUM, ARIANTO PATUNRU,
CLARA SIAGIAN, and CYRIL BENNOUNA

For over two decades, since the overthrow of the Soeharto regime in 1998, Indonesia has institutionalized democracy and maintained positive economic growth. It attracted international attention as it overcame political turmoil and transitioned into democracy in 1998. With a gross national income per capita of US$4,050 in 2019 (US$12,000 in terms of purchasing power parity), Indonesia is currently classified as an upper-middle-income country (World Bank 2020).

Its economy was severely damaged by the 1997–98 Asian Financial Crisis; indeed, it was the worst-affected country in the Southeast Asia region. The economy plunged into the negative, inflation soared, and unemployment crept up. Almost a decade and a series of key reforms were required before it recovered. These reform efforts, which actually began during the 1980s, led to the introduction of measures to improve trade activities, the development of the capital market and banking sector, the upgrading of customs procedures, and the relaxation of investment requirements, among others (Patunru and Rahardja 2015).

Thanks to economic reform during the recovery period, Indonesia successfully weathered the 2007–08 Global Financial Crisis. It has demonstrated relatively strong economic growth of an average 5.5 percent per year since 2000, and its poverty rate has continued to decline (World Bank 2016). As the fourth-most populous country and the sixteenth largest according to land mass, Indonesia has been dubbed "Asia's third giant" (Reid 2012).

As a member of the G20, the head of the Association of Southeast Asian Nations (ASEAN) in 2011 and of the Asia-Pacific Economic Cooperation forum in 2013, Indonesia is also gaining international prominence. Its participation in multinational economic forums has spurred its policy makers to continue reforms in order to maximize the benefits of this greater global integration. Trade openness has also helped reduce poverty in Indonesia (see Chapters 3 and 6 in this volume), whereas restricting trade may have the opposite effect (see Chapter 7).

Although studies show that trade and globalization can help reduce poverty, they rarely examine how these forces affect specific population groups, especially children. This tendency also holds for studies on the relationship between globalization and inequality (such as Chapters 2 and 4 in this volume). The present chapter attempts to fill this critical gap. We show that, despite the straightforward trend of declining aggregate poverty in Indonesia over the past two decades, the trends related to child poverty have been more complicated and therefore merit greater attention from academics and policy makers alike.

In addition to its encouraging performance on the global economic stage, Indonesia is predicted to enjoy a demographic dividend between 2020 and 2030, in which profitable opportunities should be created by an increased ratio of working-aged individuals to those who are too young or too old to work (Government of Indonesia 2015–19; Hayes and Setyonaluri 2015). Albeit debatable, this prediction drove President Joko Widodo to devise Indonesia's 2015–19 Medium Term Development Plan (RPJMN) to capitalize on the surge in the working-age population. The RPJMN is the first national planning document to explicitly recognize the potential of Indonesia's demographic dividend. Perceiving that the dividend is conditional on an increasing labour supply, workers being able to save and invest their earnings, and the quality of human capital, the RPJMN sets out a number of policies and programs across a range of sectors to meet these preconditions (Hayes and Setyonaluri 2015).

The Indonesian census of 2010 recorded that 81.3 million individuals, more than a third of the population, were under the age of eighteen and were therefore legally defined as children. According to the National Socio-Economic Household Survey (SUSENAS) 8.4 million children were living below the international poverty line (IPL) standard of US$1 purchasing power parity (PPP) per capita per day, a number that rose dramatically to 44.3 million children when the US$2 PPP/capita per day IPL was used. Conservatively, when the national poverty line estimate is used, about 13.8 million

Indonesian children were living below the poverty line as of 2009. Despite the encouraging decline in national poverty during recent years, with a slightly faster rate of decrease for children, poverty remains much more prevalent among children than among the general population (SMERU and UNICEF 2013).

Household income is a useful indicator of children's ability to develop healthily. However, crude monetary measures such as poverty lines based on household income or expenditure fail to reflect a number of critical contributing factors (SMERU and UNICEF 2013). Poverty line measures assume that all children live in a household, that households have steady and quantifiable incomes, that all households are financially competent and secure, and that all children in a family benefit equally from its income. These arbitrary measures also assume that the living standards of children whose households are slightly above the poverty line will differ categorically from those who are slightly below the line. However, many Indonesian households that have risen out of poverty are still positioned precariously above the line, and a simple shock, whether an increase in food or oil prices, a natural disaster, or a health emergency, can plunge them back below the threshold (World Bank 2012b).

Increases in household income, moreover, are no guarantee of amplified spending on well-being, just as low household income is no guarantee that a child will be neglected or abused. A study of trends in National Socio-Economic Household Survey (SUSENAS) data from 2003 to 2013, for example, found that when Indonesia's income poverty dropped most precipitously (between 2003 and 2008), episodes of illness actually increased significantly over a short period, which the researchers attributed not only to disasters but also to possible negative health-related behaviour as a result of rising income (Hanandita and Tampubolon 2015). Relative household poverty measures, such as the "poorest 40 percent," share many of these above-mentioned limitations, namely an arbitrary threshold for defining poverty and an assumption that the household is an adequate proxy for the child. These measures still take for granted that parents can and will spend their income responsibly on improving the living standards of their children, while also being insensitive to the heterogeneity of living standards among the sub-groups in the "poor" category (Minujin et al. 2006; Ostria 2013).

Finally, from a human rights perspective, poverty is more than an insufficiency of economic or monetary resources; rather, it involves a multitude of social and political deprivations. Poverty entails the inability to secure the right to health, adequate housing, food, safe water, and education. Focusing only on income thresholds also deflects attention from the capabilities that children need to enjoy an adequate standard of living and other fundamental rights (OHCHR 2010, 2014).

A growing body of evidence confirms that poverty and well-being occur on multiple dimensions in Indonesia, all of which should be considered (Hadiwidjaja, Paladines, and Wai-Poi 2014). Amartya Sen (2004, 78), for example, uses his widely adopted capability approach framework to argue that an income-centred approach cannot grasp the reality and dynamics of human capabilities, including basic ones such as "the ability to meet one's nutritional requirements, the wherewithal to be clothed and sheltered, the power to participate in the social life of the community." It has become clear that neither income thresholds nor relative income measures acknowledge the vital importance of fulfilling children's human rights, whether intrinsically or as a means of preparing them to realize their full potential.

In this chapter, we join a large and growing community of social scientists, policy makers, and program practitioners around the globe in asserting that the multidimensional deprivation of children's fundamental rights is a more meaningful and valid measure of their poverty than one-dimensional monetary measures (Alkire, Roche, and Vaz 2015; Bessell 2015; Hjelm et al. 2016; Minujin et al. 2006). This is not a new proposition in Indonesia, where the constitution not only upholds a child's right to life and protection, but also to "grow and to develop," stating that this development should be secured through the fulfillment of the child's basic needs "for the purpose of improving the quality of his/her life and for the welfare of the human race" (*Indonesian Constitution* 2000, arts. 28B and 28C).

Inequalities and Children's Well-Being in Indonesia

When children's basic nutritional, health, educational, and protection needs are unfulfilled by their caregivers and the state, they fail to meet their full potential. Among the many consequences of this situation is a diminished ability to contribute their energy, intellect, and creativity to the economy. In turn, this developmental shortfall and the inability to access services to remedy it can lock individuals and their families into cycles of low income earning across generations, thus hampering national growth (Fink et al. 2016; Heckman 2011; Woodhead, Dornan, and Murray 2013). Individuals in low- and middle-income countries often incur greater risks to their well-being than their counterparts in wealthier circumstances, such as insufficient access to nutritious food, clean water, vaccines, and skilled health providers, as well as exposure to violence, exploitation, and abuse (Walker et al. 2011).

In those countries, individuals who live in low-income households (not to mention those who do not belong to a household) face even greater risks, and among those, children often endure the greatest ramifications of exposure to those risks.

A growing body of evidence shows that in low- and middle-income countries, young children who live in poverty encounter specific risks that have a negative impact on their healthy development and therefore their opportunities for success over the long term (Chopra et al. 2012; Walker et al. 2011). For example, they typically struggle to access quality education, from preschool to university. If they do succeed in enrolling, they cannot always benefit from their schooling in the same way as their wealthier peers, whether because they are hungry, tired from working before and after class, sick, developmentally delayed, or simply because their parents are undereducated or illiterate and therefore unable to help them with homework and test preparation. These factors, together with pressures to contribute to the family income, mean that such children disproportionately drop out of school. All of this creates a vicious cycle whereby these children ultimately have less opportunity than their better-off peers for economic participation and success, locking them in the poverty trap (Fink et al. 2016; Woodhead, Dornan, and Murray 2013).

Indonesia is no exception to such patterns. Throughout the country, children encounter numerous risks to their well-being, and existing public services cannot meet the need. Children everywhere, but especially in rural areas and city slums, have poor access to nutritious food, quality health care, clean water and sanitation, legal identity services, appropriate educational opportunities at each school level, and infrastructure and services adapted to special needs (Kusumaningrum 2014; Patunru and Kusumaningrum 2012; PUSKAPA 2016).

Discussions of poverty in Indonesia are incomplete without some consideration of inequality. To be sure, Indonesia has realized positive economic growth and has succeeded in reducing poverty. Moreover, after making commendable achievements on the Millennium Development Goals (MDGs), the government has committed to even more ambitious progress under the Sustainable Development Goals (SDGs). Notably, in addition to decreasing extreme poverty, Indonesia has reduced the number of underweight children who are younger than five, has diminished child mortality, and has established universal basic education (SMERU and UNICEF 2013; UNICEF 2012a, 2012b, 2012c; World Bank 2012a, 2012b, 2013, 2016). These indicators of success, however, come with the caveat that inequality has nonetheless persisted, and many children and families still struggle to fulfill their basic needs. Despite improvements in health and education, the development of these children remains at risk (World Bank 2012a).

If we apply the US$2 per day income threshold, for example, we find that about half of Indonesians live around the poverty line (World Bank 2012a). Sixty-five percent of them reside in rural areas. Forty-two percent of rural households have children whose growth is stunted, increasing their risk of long-term cognitive deficits, emotional and behavioural problems, and poor achievement at school (World Bank 2012a). What is more, the deprivation of basic rights is not only unevenly distributed across provinces, but also within districts and even among household members. The life expectancy gap between some provinces is greater than ten years (Mahendradhata et al. 2017). Indeed, certain children face disproportionately higher levels of deprivation, not only because of their family income, but also because of differences in their (dis)abilities, the sequencing of their birth, their gender, or simply because they live in the "periphery," outside of the state's focal point (Hanandita and Tampubolon 2016; SMERU and UNICEF 2013).

During the next decade, Indonesia hopes to reap the rewards generated by its demographic bonus. However, it may not achieve this goal due to the challenges of poverty and inequality that may prevent almost half of its population – including more than a third of its children – from enjoying such progress (World Bank 2012b). Such an outcome is likely without greater efforts to translate the country's economic growth into an equitable redistribution of resources so that the poor may access the public services necessary to improve their lives (OECD/ADB 2015).

Poverty and multiple deprivations of rights in Indonesia, as in many other countries, do not exist in a vacuum. In addition to the national dynamics described above, global factors also affect children, largely by influencing the local social ecologies in which they live. Beyond the more obvious areas, such as children's increasing access to technology, and international influences, such as regional economic performance, can have a range of effects on the quality of life for children. Examples here include opening or closing work opportunities for their parents, or creating pressures on national budgeting that ultimately determines children's access to health care and education (Thompson 2012). In short, globalization offers both opportunities and drawbacks where the well-being of children is concerned (Thompson 2012).

This chapter argues that Indonesia's demographic dividend will realize its potential only when children are supported to reach their developmental potential. To achieve this, the government and its partners must allocate sufficient resources to address children's various deprivations, in part by providing equitable access to services. In this chapter, our intent is not to find evidence of associations between inequalities, children's well-being, and globalization. Assessing and explaining the role of globalization in children's well-being is a "complex intellectual task" that lies beyond the scope of this essay (Rizzini and Bush 2002). Nevertheless, we suggest that globalization and making both regional and international comparisons wherever data are available should always be considered in analyzing and advocating for domestic policy changes, including ones related to addressing inequality and improving the lives of children.

The inequality experienced by children has no single cause, but this chapter focuses on shortcomings in their access to basic public services and how individual characteristics and contextual factors contribute to the systematic underservicing of some groups. We draw on previous studies and reports produced by UN agencies, international NGOs, and research institutions regarding the impact of inequality on Indonesian children, particularly in connection with health, nutrition, education, and birth registration. Of course, these four subjects cover a wide range of sectors and disciplines, but it is instructive to consider them together, as doing so provides a more holistic understanding of how children experience poverty and may thereby inform more integrative services to meet their needs. Deprivations in any of these four basic areas can have downstream effects in each of the others. For example, malnourishment in early childhood can delay or reduce cognitive growth. Compounding this, many children who cannot access nutritious food also struggle to access education, which stimulates cognitive growth. What is more, birth registration, along with the registration of other vital events, has increasingly been used to facilitate individual and family access to health, education, and social protection services. Thus, children whose caregivers cannot secure official recognition of their legal identity will commonly lose several opportunities across the life course. Even if they do manage to enroll in school and succeed there, they will be unable to secure certain rights as adults, from applying for civil service jobs, to acquiring a passport to enjoy safe migration, to accessing banking and financial services, and, in some cases, even registering to vote. If improvements do not occur in these areas, Indonesia will continue to develop unevenly, at the risk of spoiling the tremendous national growth opportunity presented by the emerging demographic bonus (Hayes and Setyonaluri 2015).

FIGURE 5.1
Under-5 mortality rate in Southeast Asia, 1990–2016

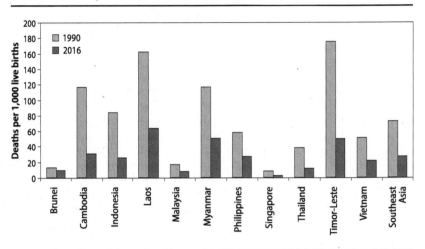

Note: These are point estimates with 90 percent confidence intervals.
Source: Based on data in UN IGME (2017).

Inequality in Child Health, Nutrition, Education, and Birth Registration

Health

Indonesia's performance in the health arena has produced some encouraging news. In 1960, the life expectancy of Indonesians was forty-nine years, which improved significantly to sixty-nine years in 2014 (World Bank 2016). The under-five mortality rate (per 1,000 births) dropped from 54 in 2000 to 26 in 2016 (UN IGME 2017). In fact, Indonesia outpaced most of its neighbours between 1990 and 2015, ultimately matching Southeast Asia's regional average (Figures 5.1 and 5.2). The infant mortality rate (per 1,000 births) declined from 38 in 2000 to 22 in 2016 (UN IGME 2017; World Bank 2012a, 2016). However, Indonesia's 2016 rate remained above the average for all lower-middle-income countries in the East Asia and Pacific region, which was 14 per 1,000 live births (UN IGME 2017). Indonesia also falls behind the region's developing country average in terms of births attended by skilled medical staff, rates of immunization, and rates of access to improved sanitation facilities (World Bank 2012a). Moreover, 37 percent of Indonesian children under the age of five are stunted, and 12 percent are wasted (World Bank 2012a).

FIGURE 5.2

Annual under-5 mortality reduction rate in Southeast Asia, 1990–2016

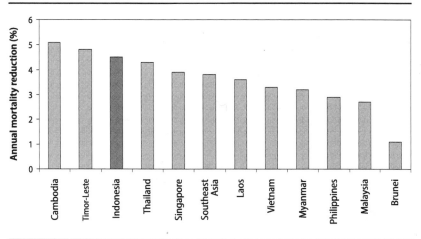

Source: Based on data in UN IGME (2017).

Several researchers have identified significant regional and income-related disparities in health outcomes across Indonesia (World Bank 2012a). Location is a critical determinant of whether a child can access health and nutrition services. Whereas the average distance to a health facility is only five kilometres nationally, the average in Papua and Maluku is more than thirty kilometres, according to 2013 estimates (Mahendradhata et al. 2017). Paired with the poor transportation infrastructure in these provinces, which create longer time burdens for patients, such distances have been found to predict lower immunization coverage and lower usage of postnatal care (Schröders et al. 2015). Vaccine cold chains rarely extend to midwives outside of facilities, and studies have revealed that community health centres themselves often do not have essential vaccines in stock (Barber, Gertler, and Harimurti 2007). Despite the national government's efforts, supplemented by international partners such as Gavi, the Vaccine Alliance, immunization coverage has not increased significantly over the past several years. Rather, decentralization of the health sector has slowed efforts to improve vaccination coverage in some areas, lowering the national average and widening the disparity of coverage between differing populations (Mahendradhata et al. 2017). Supply-side readiness is a key challenge, especially in the eastern part of the country. Managing, regulating, and integrating a growing private sector under the universal health insurance scheme (Jaminan Kesehatan Nasional, or JKN) is another key issue (World Bank 2016).

Adding to the challenge of accessing health facilities, especially in rural areas, is Indonesia's disproportionately small health workforce. For example, as of 2011, the country had among the lowest physician-to-population ratios in the Southeast Asia region, with twenty-nine of thirty-three provinces falling below the WHO-recommended ratio of 1:1,000 (Anderson et al. 2014). Although the supply of physicians has expanded, largely due to investments from private medical schools, this rate of increase has barely kept up with population growth. What is more, according to a World Bank analysis from 2010, only 20 percent of physicians were based in rural areas, where about half of the population lived (Rokx et al. 2010). The heavy concentration of private hospitals and medical universities in cities probably contributes to this urban bias. Nurses and midwives, often the only medical professionals who are regularly available to rural populations, are also in critically short supply, leaving many people to depend on volunteers in village health posts (*posyandu*) and traditional healers (*dukun*). These shortcomings have obstructed progress on several basic child health outcomes in many parts of the country. Whereas Indonesia has been relatively successful in diminishing the infant mortality rate and the under-five mortality rate, the drop in neonatal mortality rates has stagnated in recent years, and significant regional disparities in mortality reduction remain (SMERU and UNICEF 2013).

Furthermore, these child survival indicators are unequally distributed across the country. According to the 2012 Indonesian Demographic and Health Survey (IDHS), for children at every age, urban mortality was about two-thirds that of rural mortality (BPS 2013). During that year, 80 percent of births in urban areas occurred in a health facility, 90 percent of them handled by a skilled provider. By contrast, just 47 percent of rural babies were born in a facility, and 75 percent of these deliveries were overseen by a skilled health attendant. Of course, the rural-urban disparity in child survival outcomes is not entirely attributable to health system access and quality issues, but also to other deprivations that are most severe in the countryside. For example, insufficient access to improved water and sanitation infrastructure in rural areas has repeatedly been shown to predict negative child survival outcomes (Schröders et al. 2015).

Nor is geography the only determinant of child survival. Birth order is a significant predictor of a child surviving its first year of life. Infant and child mortality rates for the lowest wealth quintile across the country were more than double those in the highest quintile, as of 2013 (Mahendradhata et al. 2017). The 2012 IDHS, moreover, reported that the mortality rate for first-born infants was 35 deaths per 1,000 live births, compared to 71 deaths per 1,000 live births for infants who were seventh-born or later (BPS 2013). Although socio-economic factors are certainly at play here, the higher mortality rate for later-born infants is also connected with their mother's health. In particular, short intervals between births heighten the risk of death for both mother and baby. The mother's age is another strong predictor of child survival, with the youngest and oldest mothers being most likely to lose the baby (and to die themselves during delivery). Maternal education is also associated with child survival. The IDHS, for example, found that mothers who had no education were more than four times as likely to lose an infant than those who had more than a high school education (BPS 2013). A final predictor of child survival is the mother's nutrition. For instance, mothers who take iron and folic acid supplements during pregnancy have significantly reduced risks of neonatal, infant, and under-five mortality (Dibley et al. 2012).

Nutrition

Efforts to improve child nutrition outcomes in Indonesia have been similarly mixed. Historically, the country has had an intractably high prevalence of stunted growth, with 37 percent of children under five being stunted as of 2013 – the second-highest prevalence among nine ASEAN member states, behind Laos alone (ASEAN, UNICEF, and WHO 2016). Also in that year, Indonesia had the highest prevalence of wasting (12 percent) and obesity (12 percent) among children under five in the Southeast Asia region. An additional 20 percent of under-five children were underweight, a situation that has not greatly improved during the past several years (Mahendradhata et al. 2017). Again, these country-level prevalence estimates provide no sense of the subnational distribution of malnutrition within Indonesia, masking large discrepancies between populations across the country.

Stunting, for instance, is the tangible proof of unequal deprivation. The proportion of stunted children in the poorest Indonesian quintile is nearly twice that of the richest quintile (UNICEF 2012c). Unsurprisingly, studies show that individuals with low purchasing power typically eat fewer and less nutritious meals than those whose purchasing power is higher (Schröders et al. 2015). In fact, Indonesia still has a critical gap in iodized salt consumption, with only 58 percent of households consuming an adequate amount as of 2013, despite evidence that the IQ scores of iodine-deficient children are lower than those whose diet includes appropriate amounts of iodized salt (PUSKAPA 2016). According to the 2012 IDHS, children and mothers in higher wealth quintiles also had greater consumption of iron and vitamin A than their counterparts in lower wealth quintiles (BPS 2013). Children who do not consume adequate amounts of micro- and macronutrients are at greater risk of being underweight and stunted, having slow cognitive development, and being susceptible to both infectious disease morbidity and premature death.

Not all consumption is dependent on household income, and a range of other household, community, cultural, economic, and environmental factors influence child nutrition and healthy growth. For example, the prevalence of stunting is 1.7 times higher among children whose household head lacks formal education than among those whose household head has a tertiary education (UNICEF 2012c). Additionally, stunted children are more prevalent in rural areas (40 percent) than in urban centres (33 percent). Of course, food availability and consumption are not homogeneous throughout urban areas: many slums have poor access to fresh food supply chains, insufficient clean water, and low purchasing power, all of which compromise children's access to suitable food. Studies also reveal that exclusive breast-feeding for infants under six months old is less common in the city than in the countryside, though it is relatively low nationwide, at about 40 percent (Schröders et al. 2015). Other studies have found evidence of increasing obesity, especially in urban settings, with a rising number of households facing the "double burden" of under- and over-nutrition (Doak et al. 2005; Hanandita and Tampubolon 2015; SMERU and UNICEF 2013). Beyond the crude urban-rural binary, studies indicate that nutrition rates and dietary diversity vary widely throughout Indonesia, in accordance with local agricultural and culinary traditions, and beliefs about what infants should be fed (Schröders et al. 2015).

Education

In education, primary school enrolment and literacy have improved sizably since the 1980s (Patunru and Kusumaningrum 2012). Gross enrolment rates for primary education are over 100 percent for all income quintiles (World Bank 2013).[1] Indonesia's success in reaching universal primary education, for all boys and girls, is praiseworthy (SMERU and UNICEF 2013; UNICEF

2012a; World Bank 2012a, 2013). Nonetheless, inequalities persist in the education system, where poverty and differences in the quality of schools due to geographic and urban-rural disparities reportedly contribute to the failure of poorer children to progress across educational levels (World Bank 2012a). The 2010 census found a large number of out-of-school children and revealed that they were unevenly distributed across the country between urban and rural areas (UNICEF 2012a). Even though almost all children enjoy access to primary education, and the enrolment rate in early childhood education and development (ECED) is increasing, children from poor families and rural areas remain far less likely to access ECED than their wealthier and urban counterparts (World Bank 2012a).

Children from poor households and rural areas also face greater challenges with remaining in school beyond the primary level (World Bank 2012a). Differences in gross enrolment rates start to show at the junior secondary level. In terms of geographic divides, for example, 55 percent of rural children were enrolled in junior secondary school, compared to 80 percent in urban areas (World Bank 2012a). At the senior secondary level, 80 percent of children from the richest income quintile were enrolled, compared to 30 percent of those from the poorest households (World Bank 2013). The same source also pointed out disparities in access to education across provinces. For example, in Papua approximately 43 percent of children who were of age to attend junior secondary school were doing so, compared to 75 percent in West Sumatra. High school dropouts also tended to live in the more remote areas (World Bank 2013).

Despite this situation, equality is improving in Indonesia's educational system. Between 2006 and 2010, the share of children enrolled in schools increased for those from poorer households. In addition, these children were staying longer in school, which meant that more of them were continuing their education beyond the primary level (World Bank 2013).

Access to education is about more than enrolment. It entails the enjoyment of quality schooling, where all students have an equal opportunity to succeed, regardless of their gender, ethnicity, physical ability, or household income and location. Unfortunately, inequalities in resources influence learning outcomes. For example, disadvantaged groups in Indonesia have poorer cognitive function than their more advantaged peers. According to one study, inequalities in per capita expenditure, use of improved sanitation, and maternal high school attendance contributed to disparities in child cognitive function (Maika et al. 2013).

Indonesia participates in several international student assessments, including the Program for International Student Assessment (PISA). Established by the Organisation for Economic Co-operation and Development (OECD), PISA is conducted every three years (since 2000) to assess fifteen-year-old students on reading, mathematics, and scientific literacy (World Bank 2013). In most countries, PISA results consistently show that poverty is linked to substandard performance in school. Across OECD countries, students from poorer backgrounds are on average twice as likely as students from richer backgrounds to perform badly in reading (OECD 2013).

For Indonesia, PISA data, when disaggregated by wealth, reveal that even when children from poorer families do manage to stay in school, their performance is inferior to that of children from richer families (World Bank 2012a). The 2012 PISA showed that Indonesia's score was among the lowest of the sixty-five participating countries, ranking sixty-fourth in math and science and sixty-first in reading. This indicated that Indonesia was producing poor educational outcomes, even in comparison to other Southeast Asian countries. It was among the countries with the largest percentage of low performers in at least one subject (OECD 2016b). Indonesia's 2015 PISA results, however, were not all bad news: the incidence of grade repetition decreased by at least 10 percentage points, alongside Costa Rica, France, Latvia, Macao (China), Malta, Mexico, and Tunisia (OECD 2016a).

The 2015 data showed some other improvements, albeit limited. Of the seventy-two countries tested, Indonesia ranked sixty-fifth in math, sixty-fourth in science, and sixty-sixth in reading. Scores also varied by province, indicating that inequalities persist in education across the country (OECD 2016a; PUSKAPA 2016). Despite its progress, a recent OECD analysis categorized Indonesia's educational system as among those with "deteriorated equity," where socio-economic status still significantly predicted student performance between 2006 and 2015 (OECD 2017).

Birth Registration

Birth registration is widely recognized as an indicator of child protection. Furthermore, the lack of a birth certificate and other forms of legitimate identification has increasingly been perceived as an element of deprivation because such documents open the door to services and livelihoods (Lamont, Beljean, and Clair 2014; Szreter 2007). Consequently, the ownership of birth certificates and other types of identification has been included in many multidimensional poverty measurements, such as Multidimensional Overlapping Deprivation Analysis (MODA), Multi Cluster Indicators

Survey (MCIS), and Multidimensional Poverty Index (MPI). The lack of identification may also influence an individual's sense of personhood as a legitimate and recognized citizen (Brubaker and Cooper 2000). A study on individual deprivation measures in six countries noted that in Angola, the majority of respondents saw the lack of identification as a deprivation in and of itself, a notion that was especially pronounced among female participants (Wisor et al. 2015).

The association between the lack of documentation and the denial of basic services is strongly evident globally as well (AbouZahr et al. 2015; Dunning, Gelb, and Raghavan 2014; Oomman et al. 2013; Phillips et al. 2015). In many settings, having a birth certificate and other forms of civil registration is linked with a child's ability to stay in school (Corbacho, Brito, and Osorio Rivas 2012; Musarandega 2009), the provision of legal and social protection (Apland et al. 2014), and protection during emergency situations (Ward, Ridsdel, and Panta 2014).

In Indonesia, birth certificates and other types of documentation are increasingly required for school enrolment and graduation (Duff, Kusumaningrum, and Stark 2016; Jackson et al. 2014; Kusumaningrum et al. 2016; Sumner and Kusumaningrum 2014), and birth certificates are used as a primary reference of proof of age in the juvenile justice system. Civil registration also provides firm footing for children when they transition into adulthood. Possessing a birth certificate facilitates transnational and international migration as well as finding employment in formal sectors (Apland et al. 2014), accessing banking and increased financial inclusion, and securing land and property rights (Musarandega 2009). This trend is also observed in Indonesia, especially with the growing modernization of the government's management and information systems. The lack of proper identification among adults who work in the informal economy greatly hinders them from registering with the public social security system and causes difficulties for their next of kin in claiming benefits and compensations (ILO 2009; Setyonaluri and Radjiman 2016). A World Bank report also discusses a government regulation called "Know Your Customer," whose purpose is to increase prudence among Indonesian financial institutions by requiring that they meticulously verify their customers' identification. The report points out that the regulation will add more barriers for people in accessing various financial services (World Bank 2010).

In recent years, the government has consolidated its efforts to improve the provision of basic services and to aid identity verification in various social assistance schemes by streamlining databases and management information systems using legal identity documents and unique individual population registry numbers (Nomor Induk Kependudukan, or NIK) (Schmitt, Muyanto, and Van Langenhove 2014). As a result, individuals must now present their NIK and official identification documents to claim national health insurance (JKN) and social security entitlements (Kusumaningrum et al. 2016). Although the current social assistance management system for programs targeting children does not require ownership of identification as a basis for eligibility, it does demand that parents present proof of identity when they make claims for benefits (Singh 2013; SMERU and UNICEF 2013).[2] In addition, the system does not allow migrating families to automatically carry over their benefits when they move between districts. They must first secure the proper identification to confirm their new place of residence. This requirement makes it difficult for families who migrate seasonally or relocate to informal settlements to continue claiming their benefits during their move or after their return (Singh 2013). All these policy changes suggest that children who are currently unregistered, especially those from poor families, might be prevented from accessing the necessary entitlements to overcome their various deprivations, a trend that is likely to persist.

Millions of Indonesian adults and children do not have the necessary legal identity documents, a situation that disproportionately affects those living in poverty. Regional data indicate that from 2010 to 2015, only 69 percent of Indonesian children possessed a birth certificate. In fact, the country had the second-lowest registration in Southeast Asia (UNICEF 2016), far

FIGURE 5.3
Percentage of registered children in selected Southeast Asian countries, 2010–15

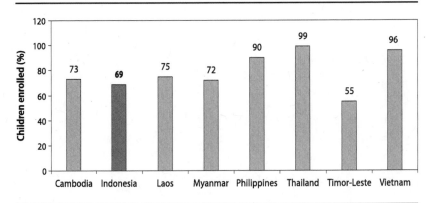

Source: Authors' illustration based on data in UNICEF (2016).

lower than neighbouring countries with a similar level of GDP per capita, such as Vietnam and the Philippines (96 and 90 percent, respectively), and well below its poorer neighbours such as Cambodia, Myanmar, and Laos (see Figures 5.3 and 5.4). The 2015 SUSENAS estimates that only 63 percent of Indonesian children were able to produce a copy of their birth certificate for an interviewer. This suggests that more than 30 million Indonesian children do not have one. Children in low-income families are less likely to be registered than their more affluent peers. According to the 2015 SUSENAS data, birth certificate ownership among children from the poorest 20 percent of Indonesians was around 63 percent, whereas it was 95 percent among children from the richest 20 percent.[3] Compared to other countries in the region, Indonesia has the highest richest-to-poorest ratio of children's birth certificate ownership (UNICEF 2016).

Geographical location plays a major role in access to civil registration. Children who live in rural and remote areas are half as likely to have their births registered as those who live close to a city (Sumner and Kusumaningrum 2014). Distance and the prohibitive costs associated with acquiring identity documents are some of the main barriers for rural families in registering their children (Sumner and Kusumaningrum 2014). Families and individuals must travel to the district capital to process their registration, as

FIGURE 5.4
Percentage of registered children among the poorest and richest
20 percent in selected Southeast Asian countries, 2010–15

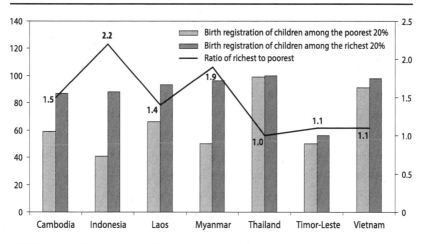

Source: Authors' illustration based on data in UNICEF (2016).

civil registrar offices are mostly located there. The long-distance travel and the back-and-forth processes increase transportation costs and entail a loss of wages during transit time (Bennouna et al. 2016). Analysis of SUSENAS 2015 shows that 37 percent of respondents had not registered the birth of a child because of the associated costs, while 7 percent had been impeded by the distance of registration offices. Some families seek assistance from middlemen, who are often village staff, to process their application, usually with some monetary compensation (Kusumaningrum et al. 2016). Unsurprisingly, regional disparities also play a role in birth registration rates. Estimates from SUSENAS 2015 show that only 38 percent of children in Papua were registered, compared to almost 91 percent in Central Java. In addition, homeless families or those who live in slums also have difficulty in acquiring legal identity documents, as they cannot present proof of residency. Rahardjo (2006) notes that poor families are often trapped in a Catch-22: accessing housing programs provided by the local government hinges on their ability to produce the requisite identification, which they cannot secure without first providing a proof of residency.

The marital and personal registration status of parents is another important factor in determining whether children will be registered. As all types of legal documentation are tightly interwoven in Indonesia, parents' lack of proper identification directly affects their children's legal identity document ownership. A child is 4.5 times more likely to be registered when one of his or her parents has a birth certificate (Sumner and Kusumaningrum 2014), suggesting that ownership of legal identity documents is intergenerational. A 2015 study conducted in three remote Indonesian areas found that almost one in five adults surveyed could not produce either a national ID or family card with his or her name on it (Kusumaningrum et al. 2016). Until recently, the children of parents who had no proof of legal marriage could not be registered under their father's name, denying their legal rights. This has created a barrier, especially given the estimates that more than half of couples who identify themselves as married are not registered as such and do not have a marriage certificate (SMERU and PEKKA 2014). Almost 75 percent of children from these couples do not possess birth certificates. An analysis of the Unified Database (BDT), which contains data on the poorest 40 percent of Indonesians in 2015, further shows that 76 percent of couples in the BDT do not have legal proof of marriage (Sumner 2016). In addition, children whose parents subscribe to customary beliefs are also disadvantaged, as customary marriages cannot be registered. Due to a stipulation in the Marriage Law (Law No. 1 of 1974), the state is prohibited from registering a civil marriage or one that was performed outside of an officially recognized religion.

Disability in the family is also associated with birth certificate ownership. Children whose parents have a physical or sensory disability are five times less likely to be registered than those whose parents have no disability (Sumner and Kusumaningrum 2014).

Policy Responses

In 1990, Indonesia ratified the UN Convention on the Rights of the Child (Indonesian Presidential Decision 1990; United Nations 1989) and subsequently issued a number of laws and regulations concerning children's well-being. The most fundamental of these was the 2000 amendment to the constitution, which stipulated: "Every child has a right to live, grow and develop, and to be protected from violence and discrimination" (*Indonesian Constitution* 2000, chapter 10A, s. 28b (2)). This change marked the beginning of a further shift on child-related issues in Indonesia's regulatory agenda.

In addition to the Law on the National Health System (Law No. 36 of 2009), the Law on the National Education System (Law No. 20 of 2003), and the Law on Population Administration (Law No. 23 of 2006 and amended as Law No. 24 of 2013), along with their implementing regulations, various child-related regulations were produced in Indonesia's legislative framework, guided by the basic rights outlined in the Convention on the Rights of the Child regarding survival and development, education, participation, and protection.[4] Most of these regulations have been translated into programs and policies that have directed the country's investments, including in matters related to the topics examined here: health, education, and birth registration.

Investing in Health

Health care has not historically been a high budgetary priority in Indonesia, though expenditures have increased significantly over the past decade in accordance with efforts to strengthen the health system (National Research Council, 2013). With the passing of the National Health System Law No. 36 of 2009, 5 percent of the state budget was allocated to health (exclusive of salaries) (World Bank 2013), and local governments had to assign at least 10 percent of their budget to health (exclusive of salaries). With the 2014 implementation of the national health insurance policy, expenditures reportedly continued to increase, and 2016 was the first year in which state spending on health effectively reached 5 percent of the annual budget. Under the current administration, it rose by 21.4 percent in 2015 and increased again by 42.8 percent in 2016 (Negara 2016).

Still, Indonesia's investment in national health care remains among the lowest in the world, even when measured against lower-middle-income countries and across the East Asia Pacific region (World Bank 2016). As of 2014, Indonesia had the tenth-lowest health expenditure of the fourteen countries in the World Health Organization's South-East Asia and Western Pacific Regions, spending only 2.8 percent of GDP, compared to 7.1 percent in Vietnam (highest ranking) and 4.2 percent in Malaysia (eighth-highest ranking) (Mahendradhata et al. 2017; WHO 2017). The public sector accounted for 39.2 percent of this funding, with much of the rest coming from private out-of-pocket spending. Health services are supplied by both the public and private sectors, with the public sector commonly taking a dominant role in providing these services in rural areas and for secondary levels of care (World Bank 2016).

It remains to be seen how Indonesia's efforts to strengthen its health system and its increased expenditure will affect investments in public health, particularly in child-centred programs. The continuing decentralization of health planning and management authority will probably complicate attempts to diminish disparities in child health outcomes, as some areas choose to prioritize children's health whereas others do not. Furthermore, health expenditures are mainly aimed at curative and rehabilitative care, with a very small portion (less than 1 percent) earmarked for risk reduction and the promotion of healthy behaviour (World Bank 2016).

Investing in Education

A 2013 World Bank report identifies Indonesia as advanced in the allocation of its education budget. Due to a constitutional amendment of 2002, the government is mandated to spend 20 percent of its total budget on education, a "20 percent rule" that was fully realized in 2009. As a result of this, Indonesia became one of the top spenders on education in the Southeast Asia region, in terms of the share of total government spending. Only Thailand apportions a greater share (World Bank 2013). However, when Indonesia's spending on education is calculated as a share of its GDP (currently at 3.7 percent), the country still falls behind Thailand, Vietnam, and Malaysia, though it considerably outperforms Laos, Cambodia, the Philippines, and Singapore (World Bank 2013).

Even though the government has significantly increased its education budget, this minimum earmarking policy can be problematic. First, it weakens the government's ability to distribute resources efficiently and optimally across sectors based on the actual needs of the population and ministries. For example, the government cannot shift resources into underfunded sectors, including social assistance programs, which will be discussed below. Second, spending pressure for such a large allocation might not create the right incentives for the education sector to plan for and implement long-term programs. Third, the earmarking policy involves administrative hurdles that are human-resource intensive and inflexible, and that further encumber spending efforts (World Bank 2013).

In terms of distribution of education spending, Indonesia is at the low end for both primary and secondary education, falling below Mexico, Malaysia, Vietnam, and Thailand. The distribution is worse in secondary education, where the differences are greatest. Spending on early childhood education and development (ECED) is minuscule compared to that for other levels of education. Even though the national and subnational commitment toward ECED is growing, its funding represents less than 1 percent of the education budget (World Bank 2013).

Education policies can address inequality when they promote equal access to educational resources and target schools with a high concentration of low-performing students and those from poorer families. Such intervention will help to remove the obstacles to the development of talent that stem from economic and social circumstances (OECD 2017). Research on early childhood development suggests that investing in ECED can be very effective for addressing income inequalities and for changing the developmental path of children from poor backgrounds. ECED services have improved educational outcomes for children, particularly those who live in poverty (World Bank 2012a). Investments in facilitating access to ECED are critical for reducing poverty rates and lessening regional income disparities, as preschool and kindergarten help to create early pathways for improved development and educational attainment (Anderson et al. 2003; National Scientific Council on the Developing Child, 2007). Indonesia needs to expand access to and increase the quality of ECED and senior secondary education. Spending needs to focus on ECED, which would change the developmental trajectory of children from poor backgrounds, and on secondary education, which would increase the availability of skilled labour (OECD/ADB 2015; World Bank 2013).

Investing in Birth Registration

Unlike for health and education, information about the government's investment in birth registration is not commonly explored and published. Birth registration also differs from health and education in that it is not a dedicated sector of the government. Instead, it is a function of the Ministry of Home Affairs (MOHA), where it is part of the ministry's Population Administration and Civil Registration directorate. Consequently, its budget is a segment of a much larger sector. This situation is typical of almost all child-protection-related issues. More often than not, their budgets are subsumed under a much broader area, such as the women's empowerment sectors (Carvalho and Koteng 2014).

The Government of Indonesia missed its 2011 goal of achieving universal birth registration (Government of Indonesia 2008). Subsequently, it aimed to increase registration by 20 percentage points by the end of 2019 (Government of Indonesia 2015–19). In other words, its intent is to issue birth certificates for more than 30 million unregistered children while simultaneously dealing with approximately 4.5 million newborns every year (Sumner and Kusumaningrum 2014).

To achieve this goal, the government included birth registration in the Medium Term Development Plan (RPJMN), which stated that from 2015 to 2019, the government would allocate 22.2 billion rupiah or approximately US$1.6 million to "increase the coverage of birth certificates." By a crude estimate, this represented a disbursement of US$0.053 or merely IDR 700 for each child who did not have a birth certificate. In addition to that, the government assigned IDR 28.7 billion or approximately US$2.15 million to "civil registration policy sensitization," IDR 67.4 billion or approximately US$5.0 million to "register all individuals," and IDR 41.2 billion or approximately US$3.1 million to "population registration policy sensitization" (Government of Indonesia 2015–19). These figures were indicative budgets subject to the actual allocation made by the government in the annual work and expenditure plan.

Aside from financial investment, over the course of five years, the government introduced several technical changes aimed at simplifying the civil registration process. Administrative costs of processing applications were removed, although late fees still applied in many areas, in accordance with local government policies. Late registration for children who had passed their first birthday no longer needed court approval, and the budget was increased to finance court fee waivers and circuit courts for late registration of marriages, especially in the Religious Court (Buffardi and Yon 2016). In

2016, a MOHA regulation discontinued the requirement that parents who wished to register a child must produce legal proof of their marriage before both their names could appear on the birth certificate, though this exemption is still limited to couples whose family cards claim them to be married. All these adjustments, however, were technical in nature. They have yet to address the structural and discriminatory barriers within civil registration, such as the marriage prerequisite for complete birth certificates just discussed, the fragmented marriage registration system in which Muslim couples are served by the Ministry of Religious Affairs, with offices available in subdistricts, whereas non-Muslims register directly with MOHA offices that tend to reside in the district capitals, and the requirement that families furnish proof of residency.

General Policies on Poverty Reduction and Social Protection

To reduce poverty across Indonesia, the RPJMN (Government of Indonesia 2015–19) set out to expand the population's access to five essential services – legal identity, health, education, social care, and basic infrastructure. The same document also cites access to sustainable livelihoods and strengthening of an integrated social protection system as the other two key pillars of poverty reduction. Specifically for children, the government operationalized the RPJMN into a National Plan of Action for Child Protection that focused on developing essential services, creating family-based social protection, and addressing child vulnerability (Government of Indonesia 2016). The plan adopted a life cycle approach, in which it identified the risks and protective factors of three developmental periods: the first thousand days after birth, the first decade after birth, and adolescence.

Indonesia also began to implement several social assistance programs on various timelines, using several intervention models and targeting differing categories of beneficiaries (Yulaswati 2016). The programs are aimed at families and individuals, and some have specific eligibility criteria, mainly for health and education (see Table 5.1).

At the time of writing, Indonesia's national health insurance program was gradually transitioning into the universal health coverage scheme JKN. As seen on Table 5.1, JKN is the largest single-payer universal health insurance in the world, which in 2016 covered around 171 million people or around 65 percent of the population (BPJS Kesehatan 2016). Within this scheme, the government pays the premiums for the poorest 40 percent of the population under the Program Indonesia Sehat (PIS). Almost half of JKN expenditure comes from the national government through PIS (World Bank 2016).

TABLE 5.1
Social assistance programs (as of June 13, 2016)

Program	Coverage	Benefit
Target group: Households at the poorest 35% (and above 25%)		
Program Indonesia Sehat (PIS)/Indonesian Health Program	21.8 million households/ 88.2 million individuals	IDR 19,225/mo/person
Target group: Households at the poorest 25% (and above 11.25%)		
Program Simpanan Keluarga Sejahtera (PSKS)/ Indonesian Family Saving Program	15.5 million households/ 65.6 million individuals	IDR 200,000/mo for 4 months
Program Indonesia Sehat (PIS)/Indonesian Health Program	15.5 million households/ 65.6 million individuals	IDR 19,225/mo/person
Program Indonesia Pintar (PIP)/Indonesian Education Program	15.5 million households/ 65.6 million individuals	Primary school: IDR 450,000/year/child Junior secondary school: IDR 750,000/year/child Senior secondary school: IDR 1,000,000/year/child
Program Beras Sejahtera (Rastra)/Indonesian Food Subsidy Program	15.5 million households/ 65.6 million individuals	IDR 1,600/kg of rice (15 kg/household)
Target group: Households at the poorest 11.25%		
Program Keluarga Harapan (PKH)/Indonesian Conditional Cash Transfers Program	6 million households/ 28.6 million individuals	IDR 950,000 to IDR 3,700,000/3 mo/household for maximum 6 months
Program Indonesia Sehat (PIS)/Indonesian Health Program	15.5 million households/ 65.6 million individuals	IDR 19,225/mo/person
Program Indonesia Pintar (PIP)/Indonesian Education Program	15.5 million households/ 65.6 million individuals	Primary school: IDR 450,000/year/child Junior secondary school: IDR 750,000/year/child Senior secondary school: IDR 1,000,000/year/child

Source: Yulaswati (2016).

In addition to JKN, various pensions and workers' compensation schemes were also transitioning into an integrated system known as BPJS Ketenagakerjaan, or labour social security, which includes coverage for workers in the informal economy (Bappenas 2014). Similarly, a few changes were made in the rest of the programs that were temporary and designed with specific eligibility criteria, commonly categorized as social assistance programs. The rice subsidy program for the poor (called Raskin) was in the process of transitioning into a food assistance program (Rastra). The Family Hope Program (PKH), a conditional cash transfer scheme, is reaching up to 6 million of the poorest households. In addition, what had been known as "scholarships for the poor," where beneficiaries were identified by schools, became PIP – household-based assistance for school-aged children. The government has also worked to improve program coverage and cohesion by using the poverty Unified Database (BDT) to target beneficiaries, allowing for households to benefit from a number of programs (Bappenas 2014).

Child well-being cuts across the social security and social assistance programs mentioned above, especially ones that support health and education. PKH, the cash transfer scheme, arguably supports child well-being since it was designed for families with expecting mothers and children below a certain age, conditional on their participation in locally available health and education facilities. In 2014, PKH started to introduce Family Development Sessions for its beneficiaries, which encompass financial literacy, basic health and care, and child protection – all intended to strengthen the family's capacity to break away from poverty and sustain its well-being. For example, evidence shows that PKH has benefitted children's educational and health outcomes (Program Keluarga Harapan 2011). Sadly, no program offers birth registration as part of its benefit package, even though the role of birth certificates in predicting children's chances of accessing education and to some extent health care is well understood. This is a missed opportunity since evaluation of various child-related cash transfer programs, both conditional and unconditional, showed that the programs have indirect and implementation effects on birth registration coverage (World Bank 2018). Specific programs designed to address issues of child well-being often function in silos. Interventions tend to be reactive and tertiary, lacking investment in prevention. In addition, a huge gap remains between the number of children in need and those being served (Kusumaningrum 2014; SMERU and UNICEF 2013). Reaching more of these children through effective programs would require greater budgetary investment.

Conclusion

Partially as a result of globalization and trade, Indonesia has achieved steady democratic and economic growth over the past several decades. However, this trend has not benefited every segment of the population, and children still endure unacceptable levels of poverty. All too often, policy makers and researchers overlook their experiences and needs, which can have disastrous consequences for Indonesia's long-term growth, not to mention its human rights commitments.

Although health and education expenditure has risen in Indonesia, the country must invest more strategically to catch up with other lower-middle-income nations in the Southeast Asia region and to ensure that progress is shared evenly among all citizens. Dispersing the education budget in a more flexible manner, especially on ECED and secondary education, is one way forward. Efforts to improve education should be geared toward bettering school quality, not only quantity. In regard to birth registration, a substantial financial investment is imperative, especially in remote areas, but the government can make a considerable impact by delegating the registration function to lower levels of government and through mobilizing frontline workers from the health and education sectors to aid the process. Pairing child and family welfare assistance with birth registration assistance can significantly increase birth certificate ownership, while ensuring that the poorest children can access much-needed assistance programs.

Over the next decade, Indonesia is predicted to enjoy a demographic dividend, but this economic bonus will be realized only if it is accompanied by increasing human capital. Thus, it is critical that national and local governments formulate policies that invest in the healthy and equal development of all children. Multidimensional poverty, however, remains Indonesia's big problem, and it is harming children in ways that may affect national growth for generations to come. Although the poverty rate has been reduced, inequality persists, excluding millions of children from Indonesia's economic gains and thus eroding its human development and national growth potential. Commendable as they are, the policies that attempt to address children's poverty and inequality are not always translated into effective programs and practice. Revenues are limited, and resources are not always allocated and spent appropriately to substantially improve the well-being of children.

Notes

1 Gross enrolment rates can exceed 100 percent when, because of late or early enrolment, or grade repetition, students are placed in a grade below that corresponding to their official age group.
2 An example of relevant programs is Program Keluarga Harapan (PKH), a household conditional cash transfer program targeting poor households with pregnant mothers and school-aged children.
3 These figures include respondents who answered, "yes but cannot show" regarding birth certificate ownership for children aged zero to seventeen in the household.
4 These include, for example, the Law on Human Rights (Law No. 39 of 1999), the Law on Child Protection (Law No. 23 of 2002) later amended as Law No. 35 of 2014, the Law on Elimination of Domestic Violence (Law No. 23 of 2004), the Law on Citizenship (Law No. 12 of 2006), the Law on Protection of Witnesses and Victims (Law No. 13 of 2006), the Law on Anti-Trafficking (Law No. 21 of 2007), and the Law on Social Welfare (Law No. 11 of 2009), the National Program for Indonesian Children. Also relevant is a series of national action plans on the elimination of the worst forms of child labour, of the sexual exploitation of children, and of trafficking in women and children; the 1997 Presidential Instruction on the implementation of children's well-being; and the inclusion of a paragraph on children's welfare in Indonesia's Guidelines of State Policy 1993. Moreover, there are the Ministerial Decree No. 2 of 2010 on the National Action Plan on the Prevention and Response to Violence against Children, followed by the National Strategy on the Elimination of Violence against Children 2016–20, the Presidential Instruction No. 5 of 2014 on the National Movement against Sexual Violence against Children, and the National Plan of Action on Child Protection as an operationalization of Presidential Regulation No. 2 of 2015 on the National Medium Term Development Plan 2015–19.

References

AbouZahr, C., D. de Savigny, L. Mikkelsen, P.W. Setel, R. Lozano, and A.D. Lopez. 2015. "Towards Universal Civil Registration and Vital Statistics Systems: The Time Is Now." *The Lancet* 386, 10001: 1407–18. DOI:10.1016/s0140–6736 (15)60170–2.

Alkire, S., J.M. Roche, and A. Vaz. 2015. "Changes over Time in Multidimensional Poverty: Methodology and Results for 34 Countries." OPHI Working Paper 76. Oxford: Queen Elizabeth House, University of Oxford.

Anderson, I., A. Meliala, P. Marzoeki, and E. Pambudi. 2014. *The Production, Distribution, and Performance of Physicians, Nurses, and Midwives in Indonesia: An Update.* Washington, DC: World Bank.

Anderson, L.M., C. Shinn, M.T. Fullilove, S.C. Scrimshaw, J.E. Fielding, J. Normand, V.G. Carande-Kulis, and Task Force on Community Preventive Services. 2003. "The Effectiveness of Early Childhood Development Programs: A Systematic Review." *American Journal of Preventive Medicine* 24, 3: 32–46.

Apland, K., B.K. Blitz, D. Calabia, M. Fielder, C. Hamilton, N. Indika, R. Lakshman, M. Lynch, and E. Yarrow. 2014. "Birth Registration and Children's Rights: A Complex Story." http://eprints.mdx.ac.uk/17346/.

ASEAN, UNICEF, and WHO. 2016. *Regional Report on Nutrition Security in ASEAN.* Vol. 2. Bangkok: UNICEF.

Badan Pusat Statistik (BPS) (Statistics Indonesia). 2013. *Indonesia Demographic and Health Survey 2012.* Jakarta: Statistics Indonesia, National Population and Family Planning Board, Kementerian Kesehatan, and ICF International.

Bappenas. 2014. "Perlindungan Sosial di Indonesia: Tantangan dan arah ke depan." Retrieved from https://www.bappenas.go.id/files/5114/2889/4558/Perlindungan_Sosial_di_Indonesia-Tantangan_dan_Arah_ke_Depan.pdf. Jakarta: Indonesian Ministry of National Development Planning, Direktorat Perlindungan dan Kesejahteraan Masyarakat.

Barber, S.L., P.J. Gertler, and P. Harimurti. 2007. "Differences in Access to High-Quality Outpatient Care in Indonesia." *Health Affairs* 26, 3: w352–w66.

Bennouna, C., B. Feldman, R. Usman, R. Adiputra, S. Kusumaningrum, and L. Stark. 2016. "Using the Three Delays Model to Examine Civil Registration Barriers in Indonesia." *PLOS ONE* 11, 12: e0168405.

Bessell, S. 2015. "The Individual Deprivation Measure: Measuring Poverty as If Gender and Inequality Matter." *Gender and Development* 23, 2: 223–40.

BPJS Kesehatan. 2016. "Ringkasan Eksekutif Laporan Pengelolaan Program dan Laporan Keuangan Jaminan Sosial Kesehatan 2016." Badan Penyelenggara Jaminan Sosial Kesehatan. Jakarta. https://bpjs-kesehatan.go.id/bpjs/dmdocuments/b39df9ae7a30a5c7d4bd0f54d763b447.pdf.

Brubaker, R., and F. Cooper. 2000. "Beyond 'Identity.'" *Theory and Society* 29, 1: 1–47.

Buffardi, A.L., and K.M. Yon. 2016. "Realising the Right to Legal Identity." Overseas Development Institute. https://www.odi.org/sites/odi.org.uk/files/resource-documents/10716.pdf.

Carvalho, M.A., and Z. Koteng. 2014. "Systematic Assessment of the Child Friendly City/District (CFC/D) Initiative in Indonesia." https://www.academia.edu/24158781/Systematic_assessment_of_the_Child_Friendly_City_District_CFC_D_initiative_in_Indonesia_Final_Report.

Chopra, M., A. Sharkey, N. Dalmiya, D. Anthony, and N. Binkin. 2012. "Strategies to Improve Health Coverage and Narrow the Equity Gap in Child Survival, Health, and Nutrition." *The Lancet* 380, 9850: 1331–40. DOI:10.1016/s0140-6736(12)61423-8.

Corbacho, A., S. Brito, and R. Osorio Rivas. 2012. "Birth Registration and the Impact on Educational Attainment." Inter-American Development Bank. http://publications.iadb.org/handle/11319/4060.

Dibley, M.J., C.R. Titaley, C. d'Este, and K. Agho. 2012. "Iron and Folic Acid Supplements in Pregnancy Improve Child Survival in Indonesia." *American Journal of Clinical Nutrition* 95, 1: 220–30.

Doak, C.M., L.S. Adair, M. Bentley, C. Monteiro, and B.M. Popkin. 2005. "The Dual Burden Household and the Nutrition Transition Paradox." *International Journal of Obesity* 29, 1: 129–36.

Duff, P., S. Kusumaningrum, and L. Stark. 2016. "Barriers to Birth Registration in Indonesia." *The Lancet Global Health* 4, 4: e234–e35. DOI:10.1016/S2214-109X (15)00321-6.

Dunning, C., A. Gelb, and S. Raghavan. 2014. "Birth Registration, Legal Identity, and the Post-2015 Agenda." Center for Global Development. http://www.cgdev.org/ publication/birth-registration-legal-identity-and-post-2015-agenda.

Fink, G., E. Peet, G. Danaei, K. Andrews, D.C. McCoy, C.R. Sudfeld, M.C. Smith Fawzi, M. Ezzati, and W.W. Fawzi. 2016. "Schooling and Wage Income Losses Due to Early-Childhood Growth Faltering in Developing Countries: National, Regional, and Global Estimates." *American Journal of Clinical Nutrition* 104, 1: 104–12.

Government of Indonesia. 2008. *Rencana Strategis 2011: Semua Anak Indonesia Tercatat Kelahirannya* [Strategic Plan 2011: All Indonesian children registered]. Government of Indonesia.

–. 2015–19. *Rencana Pembangunan Jangka Menengah Nasional.* Adopted through Government Regulation (Peraturan Pemerintah) No. 2 of 2015.

–. 2016. *Rencana Aksi Nasional Perlindungan Anak.* Adopted by the Indonesian Coordinating Minister for Human Development and Culture, January 27.

Hadiwidjaja, G., C. Paladines, and M. Wai-Poi. 2014. "The Many Dimensions of Child Poverty in Indonesia: Patterns, Differences and Associations." SMERU Working Paper. http://www.smeru.or.id/cpsp/Paper,%20Abstact,%20CV/0101_ Grace-paper.pdf.

Hanandita, W., and G. Tampubolon. 2015. "The Double Burden of Malnutrition in Indonesia: Social Determinants and Geographical Variations." *SSM-Population Health* 1: 16–25.

–. 2016. "Multidimensional Poverty in Indonesia: Trend over the Last Decade (2003–2013)." *Social Indicators Research* 128, 2: 559–87. DOI:10.1007/s11205-015-1044-0.

Hayes, A., and D. Setyonaluri. 2015. "Taking Advantage of the Demographic Dividend in Indonesia: A Brief Introduction to Theory and Practice." Jakarta: United Nations Population Funds. https://indonesia.unfpa.org/sites/default/files/ pub-pdf/Buku_Policy_Brief_on_Taking_Advantage_on_Demographic_Dividend_ 02c_%282%29_0.pdf.

Heckman, J.J. 2011. "The Economics of Inequality." *Education Digest* 77, 4: 4–11.

Hjelm, L., L. Ferrone, S. Handa, and Y. Chzhen. 2016. *Comparing Approaches to the Measurement of Multidimensional Child Poverty.* Innocenti Working Paper 2016–29. Florence: UNICEF Office of Research.

ILO. 2009. *Extending Social Security Coverage to Informal Economy Workers: Way Forward.* Jakarta: ILO.

Indonesian Constitution. 2000. Undang-undang Dasar Republik Indonesia, 2nd Amendment, August 18.

Indonesian Presidential Decision. 1990. Keputusan Presiden, No. 36 of 1990, August 25.

Jackson, M., P. Duff, S. Kusumaningrum, and L. Stark. 2014. "Thriving beyond Survival: Understanding Utilization of Perinatal Health Services as Predictors of

Birth Registration: A Cross-Sectional Study." *BMC International Health and Human Rights* 14, 1: 306. DOI:10.1186/s12914–014–0038–3.

Kusumaningrum, S. 2014. "Family-Focused Social Protection in Indonesia: A Journey to Address Children's Vulnerability." In *Family Futures*, ed. J. Griffiths, n.p. Leicester, UK: Tudor Rose.

Kusumaningrum, S., C. Bennouna, C. Siagian, and N.L.P.M. Agastya. 2016. *Back to What Counts: Birth and Death in Indonesia*. Jakarta: Center on Child Protection Universitas Indonesia in collaboration with the Ministry of National Development Planning and Kolaborasi Masyarakat dan Pelayanan untuk Kesejahteraan.

Lamont, M., S. Beljean, and M. Clair. 2014. "What Is Missing? Cultural Processes and Causal Pathways to Inequality." *Socio-Economic Review* 12, 3: 573–608. https://doi.org/10.1093/ser/mwu011.

Mahendradhata, Y., L. Trisnantoro, S. Listyadewi, P. Soewondo, T. Marthias, P. Harimutri, and J. Prawira. 2017. *The Republic of Indonesia Health System Review: Health Systems in Transition, 7*, 1. Asia Pacific Observatory on Health Systems and Policies. https://apps.who.int/iris/handle/10665/254716.

Maika, A., M.N. Mittinty, S. Brinkman, and S. Harper. 2013. "Changes in Socioeconomic Inequality in Indonesian Children's Cognitive Function from 2000 to 2007: A Decomposition Analysis." *PLOS ONE* 8, 10: e78809. DOI:10.1371/journal.pone.0078809.

Minujin, A., E. Delamonica, A. Davidziuk, and E.D. Gonzalez. 2006. "The Definition of Child Poverty: A Discussion of Concepts and Measurements." *Environment and Urbanization* 18, 2: 481–500.

Musarandega, R. 2009. "Integrated Human Rights and Poverty Eradication Strategy: The Case of Civil Registration Rights in Zimbabwe." *International Social Science Journal* 60, 197–98: 389–402.

National Research Council. 2013. *Reducing Maternal and Neonatal Mortality in Indonesia: Saving Lives, Saving the Future*. Washington, DC: National Academies Press. https://www.nap.edu/catalog/18437/reducing-maternal-and-neonatal-mortality-in-indonesia-saving-lives-saving.

National Scientific Council on the Developing Child. 2007. Science of Early Childhood Development. https://46y5eh11fhgw3ve3ytpwxt9r-wpengine.netdna-ssl.com/wp-content/uploads/2015/05/Science_Early_Childhood_Development.pdf.

Negara, S.D. 2016. "Indonesia's 2016 Budget: Optimism amidst Global Uncertainties." *Perspective* 3. ISEAS: Yusof Ishak Institute. http://www.iseas.edu.sg/images/pdf/ISEAS_Perspective_2016_3.pdf.

OECD. 2013. *Are Countries Moving towards More Equitable Education Systems?* Paris: OECD.

–. 2016a. *PISA 2015 Results in Focus*. Paris: OECD.

–. 2016b. *Who Are the Low-Performing Students?* Paris: OECD.

–. 2017. *Where Did Equity in Education Improve over the Past Decade?* Paris: OECD.

OECD/ADB. 2015. *Education in Indonesia: Rising to the Challenge*. Paris: OECD.

OHCHR. 2010. Human Rights and Extreme Poverty. UN General Assembly, Sixty-fifth Session Item 69 (b). https://undocs.org/A/65/259.

–. 2014. Extreme Poverty and Human Rights. UN General Assembly. Resolution adopted by the General Assembly on 18 December 2014 [on the report of the Third Committee (A/69/488/Add.2 and Corr.1)]. https://undocs.org/pdf?symbol =en/A/RES/69/183.

Oomman, N., G. Mehl, M. Berg, and R. Silverman. 2013. "Modernising Vital Registration Systems: Why Now?" *The Lancet* 381, 9875: 1336–37. DOI:http://dx. doi.org/10.1016/S0140-6736(13)60847-8.

Ostria, M. 2013. "Comparative Child Poverty Measures." Backgrounder No. 169. National Center for Policy Analysis. https://www.readkong.com/page/comparative -child-poverty-measures-4318104?p=1.

Patunru, A.A., and S. Kusumaningrum. 2012. "Reducing Inequality: Learning Lessons for the Post-2015 Agenda (Comprehensive Case Studies of Indonesia)." http://www.cpcnetwork.org/wp-content/uploads/2015/02/Inequality-and -Children-in-Indonesia_final.pdf.

Patunru, A.A., and S. Rahardja. 2015. *Trade Protectionism in Indonesia: Bad Times and Bad Policy.* Sydney: Lowy Institute for International Policy. https://www. lowyinstitute.org/publications/trade-protectionism-indonesia-bad-times-and -bad-policy.

Phillips, D.E., C. AbouZahr, A.D. Lopez, L. Mikkelsen, D. de Savigny, R. Lozano, J. Wilmoth, P.W. Setel. 2015. "Are Well Functioning Civil Registration and Vital Statistics Systems Associated with Better Health Outcomes?" *The Lancet* 386, 10001: 1386–94. DOI:10.1016/s0140-6736(15)60172-6.

Program Keluarga Harapan. 2011. "Main Findings from the Impact Evaluation of Indonesia's Pilot Household Conditional Cash Transfer Program." Jakarta, World Bank Office.

PUSKAPA. 2016. *Pathways Out of Adversities: An Exploratory Study.* Jakarta: Indonesian Ministry of Education and Culture, PUSKAPA, and SurveyMETER.

Rahardjo, T. 2006. "Forced Eviction, Homelessness and the Right to Housing in Indonesia." Paper presented in conference entitled *Homelessness: A Global Perspective*, New Delhi, January 9–13, 2006. https://tjahjonorahardjo.blogspot. com/2011/10/forced-eviction-homelessness-and-right.html.

Reid, A., ed. 2012. *Indonesia Rising: The Repositioning of Asia's Third Giant.* Singapore: Institute for Southeast Asian Studies.

Rizzini, I., and M. Bush. 2002. "Globalization and Children." *Childhood* 9, 4: 371–74. DOI:10.1177/0907568202009004001.

Rokx, C., J. Giles, E. Satriawan, P. Marzoeki, P. Harimurti, and E. Yavuz. 2010. *New Insights into the Provision of Health Services in Indonesia: A Health Workforce Study.* Washington, DC: World Bank.

Schmitt, V., R. Muyanto, and T. Van Langenhove. 2014. *Rancangan Sistem Rujukan Terpadu Untuk Perluasan Program Perlindungan Sosial di Indonesia Latar belakang dan dasar hukum, rancangan sistem rujukan terpadu, dan peta jalan penerapannya.* Jakarta: International Labor Organization.

Schröders, J., S. Wall, H. Kusnanto, and N. Ng. 2015. "Millennium Development Goal Four and Child Health Inequities in Indonesia: A Systematic Review of the Literature." *PLOS ONE* 10, 5: e0123629.Sen, A. 2004. "Capabilities, Lists, and Public Reason: Continuing the Conversation." *Feminist Economics* 10, 3: 77–80. DOI:10.1080/1354570042000315163.

Sen, Amartya. 2004. "Capabilities, Lists, and Public Reason." *Feminist Economist* 10, 3: 77–80. doi:10.1080/1354570042000315163.

Setyonaluri, D., and D. Radjiman. 2016. "Social Protection for Informal Workers in Indonesia: A Case Study of Micro, Small, and Medium-Sized Enterprises." In *Social Protection for Informal Workers in Asia*, ed. S.R. Handayani, 308–37. Manila: Asia Development Bank. https://www.adb.org/sites/default/files/publication/203891/sp-informalworkers-asia.pdf.

Singh, S. 2013. "Social Protection and Its Effectiveness in Tackling Child Labour: The Case of Internal Child Migrants in Indonesia." http://www.smeru.or.id/cpsp/Paper,%20Abstact,%20CV/0203_Simrin-paper.pdf.

SMERU and PEKKA. 2014. *Menguak Keberadaan Dan Kehidupan Perempuan Kepala Keluarga: Laporan Hasil Sistem Pemantauan Kesejahteraan Berbasis Komunitas.* Jakarta: SMERU, PEKKA.

SMERU and UNICEF. 2013. "Child Poverty and Disparities in Indonesia: Challenges for Inclusive Growth." http://www.smeru.or.id/en/content/child-poverty-and-disparities-indonesia-challenges-inclusive-growth.

Sumner, C. 2016. *Pencatatan Kelahiran bagi Seluruh Warga Indonesia: Arah dan Strategi Kerjasama.* Jakarta: Plan International.

Sumner, C., and S. Kusumaningrum. 2014. *Indonesia's Missing Millions: A Baseline Study on Legal Identity.* Jakarta: Australia Indonesia Partnership for Justice.

Szreter, S. 2007. "The Right of Registration: Development, Identity Registration, and Social Security – A Historical Perspective." *World Development* 35, 1: 67–86.

Thompson, Ross A. 2012. "Changing Societies, Changing Childhood: Studying the Impact of Globalization on Child Development." *Child Development Perspectives* 6, 2: 187–92. doi:10.1111/j.1750-8606.2012.00234.x.

UN IGME (United Nations Inter-Agency Group for Child Mortality Estimation). 2017. *Levels and Trends in Child Mortality: Report 2017.* New York: UNICEF.

UNICEF. 2012a. "Education and Early Childhood Development (ECD)" *UNICEF Indonesia Issue Briefs*, October."

–. 2012b. "Maternal and Child Health." *UNICEF Indonesia Issue Briefs*, October."

–. 2012c. "Maternal and Child Nutrition." *UNICEF Indonesia Issue Briefs*, October. "

–. 2016. *The State of the World's Children: A Fair Chance for Every Child.* New York: UNICEF.

United Nations. 1989. *Convention on the Rights of the Child.* General Assembly Resolution 44/25 of 20 November 1989, entry into force 2 September 1990.

Walker, S.P., T.D. Wachs, S. Grantham-McGregor, M.M. Black, C.A. Nelson, S.L. Huffman, H. Baker-Henningham et al. 2011. "Inequality in Early Childhood: Risk and Protective Factors for Early Child Development." *The Lancet* 378, 9799: 1325–38. DOI:10.1016/S0140-6736(11)60555-2.

Ward, P., J. Ridsdel, and N. Panta. 2014. "Birth Registration in Emergencies: A Review of Best Practices in Humanitarian Action." Woking, UK, Plan International. http://www.planusa.org/docs/reports/2014-Birth-Registration-in-Emergencies.pdf.

WHO. 2017. "Global Health Expenditure Database." Geneva, World Health Organization. http://apps.who.int/nha/database.

Wisor, S., S. Bessell, F. Castillo, J. Crawford, K. Donaghue, J. Hunt, A. Jaggar, A. Liu, and T. Pogge. 2015. *Individual Deprivation Measures: A Gender-Sensitive Approach to Poverty Measurement.* Canberra: Australian National University.

Woodhead, M., P. Dornan, and H. Murray. 2013. *What Inequality Means for Children: Evidence from Young Lives.* Oxford: Young Lives.

World Bank. 2010. *Improving Access to Financial Services in Indonesia.* Jakarta: World Bank Office.

—. 2012a. *Early Childhood Education and Development in Indonesia: Strong Foundations, Later Success - A Preview.* Jakarta: World Bank.

—. 2012b. *Protecting the Poor and Vulnerable Households in Indonesia.* Jakarta: World Bank.

—. 2013. *Spending More or Spending Better: Improving Education Financing in Indonesia.* Washington, DC: World Bank Group.

—. 2016. *Indonesia Health Financing System Assessment: Spend More, Right, and Better.* Washington, DC: World Bank Group.

—. 2018. *Incentives for Improving Birth Registration Coverage: A Review of the Literature.* Washington, DC: World Bank Group.

Yulaswati, V. 2016. "Penanggulangan Kemiskinan dan Kesejahteraan Sosial (Presented in Bappenas FGD, June 13, 2016)." Paper presented to the Indonesian Ministry of National Development Planning, Jakarta, June 13.

6

Reducing Rural Poverty through Trade?

Evidence from Indonesia

RICHARD BARICHELLO and FAISAL HARAHAP

Among the many debates associated with globalization is one that focuses on the effects of increased international trade. This is not the only element of globalization, but it is an important one and oftentimes controversial. Even today, popular support for increased trade is diminishing as a reflection of the dispute over its benefits, its costs, and their distribution. In the Asia Pacific Legal Culture and Globalization series, the effects of increased globalization and trade on a set of variables that pertain to human rights are examined empirically. This volume explores the impact of increased trade on the two human rights dimensions of poverty and income inequality. Both concern the trade effects on the distribution of income, with the lower end (the left-hand side) of the income distribution being the central issue for poverty, and with the whole distribution and its spread being the key for income inequality.

This chapter focuses on poverty, specifically on *rural* poverty. In every country, including Indonesia, incomes are typically lowest in rural areas, and the greatest share of residents who live below the poverty line also dwell there. Consequently, any examination of a country's poverty must include its rural poverty.

Further, the poorest people in all countries have nothing but their labour by which to earn income. By definition, they have few assets, whether they be land, physical capital, or the human capital represented by higher-valued skills. So, if we are to examine this subset of the population and are concerned about reducing its poverty, we must focus on the labour market, particularly agricultural or rural labour markets. What will reduce poverty is raising agricultural wage rates, largely those of unskilled labour.

There are a variety of policy tools that could possibly change these wage rates. We can organize them into two groups: the first could attempt to increase the demand for agricultural labour, and the second could encourage agricultural labour to work in other sectors and raise agricultural wages through a reduced supply of agricultural labour.

For the first group, one set of tools involves government policies to increase the supply of rice, such as by raising its price or lowering rice input costs. To this should be added a further set of policy tools, of trade protection such as raising tariffs or imposing import quotas. The second group of tools includes labour market policy options, using the mechanism of migration from rural to more rapidly growing urban areas and jobs in the nonagricultural sector, where wage rates are higher.

Both groups are used or observed widely in Indonesia. Like most food crops in the country, rice is protected with trade restrictions and is on an import basis in most years (Indonesia is typically a net importer of rice). These protectionist policies are accompanied by strong public rhetoric about their importance for reducing rural poverty, which on the surface may seem plausible.[1] But migration, mostly from the countryside to urban areas, is also substantial. It is widely known as an important element of human capital (like education and health investments) and therefore a source of increased income.

This chapter examines the relative merits of these two policy groups. Given the government's substantial attention to using trade policy tools – restricting trade in this case – our test conforms closely to the theme of this volume, of what can be expected from these trade policies in terms of alleviating rural poverty. In other words, will they diminish poverty or worsen it?

Indonesia is a particularly good choice in addressing this question. First, though it is now classed as a middle-income country, it has grown substantially from the early 1970s and early 1980s, when the World Bank still categorized it as a low-income country. At that time, a large proportion of its population lived below standard poverty lines. After some thirty years of income growth, poverty is still a critical policy issue but is substantially reduced, as discussed in Chapter 1. Therefore, Indonesia is a good case to examine, analyzing the pattern of agricultural wage rates, to explore some sources of this poverty reduction. Second, the government policy framework has given major attention to trade restrictions to reduce poverty, and the effectiveness of this can be measured. We do not use data on trade restrictions directly, but we use rice prices instead because they do move with the kind of trade restrictions that are being employed. Third, internal migration flows are very high in Indonesia, mostly from rural to urban areas except during recessions. So again, Indonesia represents a very useful test case for examining what contribution these high levels of migration make to poverty reduction, via agricultural wage rate movements.

Issues Related to Focusing on Wage Rates

Our research concentrated on the poorest subset of the rural poor. Wage rates define income levels because, for the poorest group in society, its own labour is its only asset. Once farmers acquire some assets, they typically receive income from them, which elevates them to a higher income bracket. A village head from a coffee-growing village in South Sumatra once responded with much puzzlement to our query about his poor coffee farmers (who would necessarily own physical capital in the form of coffee trees). He said, "I have poor farmers, and I have coffee farmers in my village, but I have no poor coffee farmers."

Of course, simply owning assets does not mean that a farmer is rich, and we do not ignore those who remain relatively poor. The asset-income link is a continuum. Our results apply well to farmers who own a small amount of land. As they acquire increasing amounts of it, their incomes will also rise due to the often implicit or "shadow" returns from that land or from its actual rental income. In such cases, our income- or poverty-related results will not apply as significantly. The reason is that the effects of certain variables such as rice prices will typically raise land rental and purchase values.

To describe this process in more detail, the rise in rice prices will induce farmers to expand rice production. To reach this goal, they will require more of the necessary inputs. As a result, the demand for such inputs will rise, which typically increases the price of all inputs to varying degrees. We know from long historical experience and for sound theoretical reasons that the rental value of land (and other inputs with "inelastic" supplies) will normally rise, whereas the effect on labour wage rates will tend to be smaller. So, government policies that raise the prices of agricultural commodities usually benefit those farmers (or anyone else) who own land, whereas the benefits to wage labour will be uncertain and perhaps very modest. Thus, our focus on wage rates means that our results will apply most to the poorest farmers and will apply with decreasing accuracy as farm asset and income levels rise.

Another related question is whether rural workers have the option of moving to employment in better-paid non-agricultural positions. This strategy is feasible (and observed) if such jobs are reasonably accessible, if the workers have the necessary skills, and if the cost of moving to the jobs does not outweigh the advantages. But for many farm workers, these conditions may not all exist, and thus their reliance on the agricultural wage persists, as does its associated poverty.

What we are looking at in this research is the agricultural wage itself, to examine what determines it. Given its importance to millions of poor Indonesians, we wish to know what can raise it, and thereby reduce their poverty. We do not examine directly whether they can escape poverty by migrating to urban jobs or whether policy can add jobs in the non-agricultural sector as an anti-poverty strategy. Our results may *suggest* these policies. But we focus on people who do not have the option to move to non-farm jobs or who stay in agriculture for various reasons, such as age, low education levels, or poor health.

Some commentators have argued that because farmers should optimally be shifting their labour to the non-farm sector, those who remain in agriculture are tradition-bound or irrational. The present discussion does not consider this suggestion or even why or how poor farmers make their decisions. Our interest is solely in empirically examining the factors that explain the movements in farm wages.

An associated question is whether outside forces have any impact on agricultural wages. This question was posed as long ago as the 1950s, notably by Nobel Prize winner Arthur Lewis (1954), who hypothesized that agricultural wage rates in poor countries are tied to subsistence levels and are impervious to outside (market) forces due to the very large and endogenous supplies of labour in rural communities. Related arguments claim that agricultural wage rates are not subject to normal supply and demand forces, as in neoclassical economic theory, but rather are institutionally determined by forces outside agriculture, at least until the country reaches a higher income status when outside economic forces will have some effect. Our work provides an empirical test of this hypothesis, without taking a position on this debate. If these Lewis-type explanations are borne out by our data, we will find that our predicted model does not work well.

A modern interpretation of what we are testing here is whether farm and non-farm labour markets are closely linked or "integrated." If the wage rates in the two markets move closely together (correlated to some acceptable degree), unlike the Lewis hypothesis, there is only one mechanism by which this can happen systematically. Labour must be moving from one market to another. In other words, there must be migration. If labour does not move, any correlation in the wage rates of the two markets would arise only by coincidence. We have no systematic time-series data to show domestic migration flows, aside from a number of cases of anecdotal evidence. This is another advantage of using labour prices across these two markets: they can show us that migration is occurring to a significant extent if the prices are sufficiently highly correlated.

The Migration Process

Labour mobility in the Southeast Asian agricultural sector has long been an object of study. Two examples among many include Hayami and Kikuchi (1982), who examined the Philippine rice economy of the late 1970s, and Naylor (1991), whose work focused on the mid-1980s rice economy of Java, West Sumatra, and South Sulawesi. These scholars noted that farming families were heavily involved in off-farm work. This includes farm workers holding jobs in the local village, rural village workers migrating to jobs in regional towns, and onward migration from those towns to large cities. The pattern included systematic semi-permanent relocation and thus entailed more than just seasonal migration.

The Indonesian government has placed no restrictions on migration, at least not since the country became independent (post-1946). This policy of not restricting domestic migration differs from what is found in China and Vietnam, where rural-to-urban migration was made illegal for lengthy periods, followed by times in which strong incentives were imposed to discourage it. During the past thirty years, Indonesia has seen large rural-to-urban migration flows, which diminish only in times of recession or at the micro level, when individuals are unsuccessful in their bid to relocate. In 1998–99, the period of the Asian Financial Crisis in Indonesia, many urban construction workers returned to the countryside, even if this reversal was somewhat short-lived.

For agricultural workers, migrating to urban areas is a risky venture. Urban areas are home to attractive jobs whose wage rates are higher than those in rural areas, even considering the higher cost of urban living. But some of these jobs are in the "protected sector" (famously described and modelled by Harris and Todaro 1970). Paying relatively well and few in number, they are often in the manufacturing sector of large cities. Obtaining such jobs can be difficult, which is one aspect of risk for migrants. What are more abundant and nearby to farm workers are jobs in the service sector. These are also distributed more widely, including in many small towns. Anyone who loses patience with the wait time for either the high-wage manufacturing jobs or the mid-wage service-sector jobs may choose to return to the countryside (what we describe above as failed individual migration).

Rigg, Promphaking, and Le Mare (2014) build on this by arguing that much rural-to-urban migration is not permanent and thereby shed doubt on the social value of this labour movement in alleviating poverty. Although they cite evidence of a reverse migration in Thailand from the city back to the country, these data must be seen in the context of an aggregate net outflow of labour from the agricultural sector that is clear in any country with moderate or better economic growth rates and strikingly clear across Southeast Asia and among younger cohorts. What is important for our work is whether the shift to urban jobs and the response to urban job signals, as given by urban wage rates, are strong enough to dominate the influence of agricultural labour market wage signals.

Farm Production and Migration Decisions

The situation facing poor farmers when they make their farming and migration decisions can be summarized as follows. When considering their farming options, they observe their output prices and input costs, from which they choose to plant certain crops. If, for example, the price of rice rises, they will choose to grow more rice and will thus need to use more of all inputs, including land and labour. In their attempts to rent more land or hire more labour, it is possible they will push up the prices of both. How much these prices rise depends on the overall scarcity of land (its supply elasticity, to be precise). If land is relatively scarce and used primarily for agriculture, so that its allocation to rice will come at the expense of other profitable uses, its price (or shadow price, if it has a limited rental or purchase market) would have to rise. If labour is scarce and agriculture is its primary source of employment, its (shadow) price would likewise increase.

But another possibility is that labour is used widely in many sectors, so more labour could be attracted into rice growing with only a small wage increase. If agricultural workers were regularly migrating to better-paying non-farm employment, only some reduction in their *flow* to such jobs could provide the extra labour for expanded rice production. In these latter cases, the wage rate in rice would not be greatly affected. Therefore, an increase in rice prices would have little impact on rural poverty because agricultural wage rates would not have changed. Actually, it would *exacerbate* poverty because all poor rice consumers would now pay more for the foodstuff and would become worse off. This situation is entirely plausible because the poorest rice farmers are often, sometimes typically, net rice consumers (they produce less rice than they consume in a year so must buy the difference) (McCulloch 2008). In the initial scenario, where the wage rate *rises* following an increase in the rice price, whether this will reduce or increase poverty is uncertain because it will depend on how many farmers are net rice consumers (who lose) and how many are net rice producers (who gain).

All the scenarios presented above are certainly possible, and it will depend on a set of economic parameters (that are location-specific and might change over time) as to whether wage rates would rise or remain the same after rice prices increased. Given that rice prices in Southeast Asia often vary due to trade policy, a policy that restricts trade to raise rice prices, as in Indonesia, could make poverty worse or could have mixed results.

One aspect of this situation is *not* uncertain. All empirical evidence gathered over time from around the world demonstrates that an increase in the price of rice is highly likely to raise the price of land. Therefore, any policy that protects farmers by increasing trade barriers will have one clear result: land will become more expensive. Anyone who owns it will benefit. So, persons who are wealthier due to owning land, whether or not they are farmers, will be helped by trade barriers. Furthermore, by helping these relatively well-off farmers, such a protectionist trade policy will increase income (or wealth) inequality. This eventuality is likely, but because we lack data on Indonesian land prices, we are unable to test it.

Among farmers who are contemplating a move to a non-agricultural job, the income situation for the poorest among them is clear. Given that non-agricultural wages are normally higher in a growing economy, *if* farmers are free to migrate, have the skills to obtain the desired employment, and can relocate with relatively few costs (such as with good transport infrastructure), their income would rise due to migration. However, even this case depends on several "ifs." Importantly, if the migration process involves sufficiently large numbers of people, the wages of those who remain in agricultural work will also improve. Once the supply of labour in farming communities dwindles, the wages for such work will rise, as has strikingly occurred since the mid-1980s in China. Migration can become a rising tide that lifts all boats.

The conclusion is that any number of possible results could occur when we ask if changes in openness to trade (i.e., reducing trade barriers) in the agriculture sector will raise or lower rural poverty. And we cannot even say for certain whether an open internal migration policy would significantly lessen rural poverty. To resolve these questions requires empirical estimation that is both country- and time-specific. We now turn to that task.

Our Model

To test the hypotheses outlined above, what we wish to do empirically is test for the determinants of rural wage rates. We begin with a neoclassical model of the farm labour market, using the familiar elements of demand and supply. But for reasons of data availability over a lengthy period and formal time-series econometric requirements, we could not estimate structural equations. So, we took a simplified approach of using a reduced form representation of this market that included only demand variables. This approach is relatively standard in price transmission models that measure the integration of two markets, which is basically what we want to do.

Our model, with the farm wage rate as the dependent variable, started with the non-farm wage rate as the first explanatory variable. However, keeping it that simple would be tantamount to admitting that only the non-farm-sector demand for farm labour is relevant. It is the case that many variables raising the demand for non-farm labour will work through the non-farm wage rate, so using this price makes it unnecessary to add those other demand-inducing variables separately.

But we also want our model to allow for the possibility that agricultural-sector variables may affect the demand for farm labour. So, we added what is arguably the most important variable in the Indonesian agricultural sector, the price of rice. Rice is the largest agricultural commodity in Indonesia, and it is particularly dominant on the island of Java.

Our choice of a third explanatory variable was determined by the data that we had for the non-farm wage rate. That variable is the manufacturing wage rate. But if one examines the non-farm employment to which agricultural labour migrates, it is much more commonly in the service sector. So, we chose a variable that would act as a proxy for service-sector demand, namely the non-farm GDP growth rate. We use such a proxy due to the difficulty of getting appropriate service-sector wage rates.

This gives us a model in which we try to explain the farm wage rate using three variables, the manufacturing-sector wage rate, the growth rate of non-farm GDP, and the price of rice. Our desire for additional variables was constrained by our inability to obtain data that spanned the 1980s to the early 2000s and the difficulties involved in using formal time-series econometrics procedures. In effect, we traded the possibility of left-out variable bias for the advantage of a longer time series to get cleaner estimates. Given these caveats, our model will answer three important questions: Do agricultural factors affect farm wage rates? Do urban, manufacturing, or service-sector variables affect farm wage rates? And how do their effects differ in size?

Data

Our data are for the three original provinces of Java: West, Central, and East Java. We have quarterly data for 1983 to 2009, 108 observations in total, which nicely cover a wide range of underlying economic conditions. This includes the earlier years when incomes were significantly lower, and labour market integration was also arguably lower. Data from the outer islands were not available for such a lengthy period, limiting us to data from Java. Some might argue that Javanese data are the most likely to show the integration of agricultural and industrial labour markets. However, that hypothesis is not so obvious. Workers from the outer islands may have stronger incentives to migrate to large urban areas due to the larger gap between local non-Java rural wage rates and Javanese urban wage rates than that between rural and urban wage rates in Java, leading to comparable market integration.

We obtained our data from Indonesia's Badan Pusat Statistik (BPS) (Statistics Indonesia), its central statistics bureau. The agricultural wage rate is an average across the three tasks of land preparation, planting, and harvesting, measured at the province level, denoted by RUW. The urban wage is obtained from country-level manufacturing wage rates (URW), a measure that reflects wages in what Harris and Todaro (1970) refer to as the formal sector. Although service sector wage rates may have been more desirable than manufacturing wage rates, they were not available over this period. However, as a proxy for the service sector wage rate, we used non-agricultural GDP to capture all elements of urban-sector labour demand, especially service-sector demand, that were not captured by the manufacturing wage rate. These data were available on a quarterly basis (2007 = base year). The two wage rates were transformed into real terms by deflating them with the relevant consumer price index (CPI), agricultural wages by the rural CPI and the urban wage rate by the urban CPI (also with 2007 = base year). The agricultural price (AGP) is measured by the rice price index as a proxy variable. The data for that index are obtained from the monthly farmers' terms of trade statistics published by BPS at the provincial level. These are farm-gate prices, collected by BPS every month and averaged across the three months of each quarter, with a base year of 2007. All data were transformed into logarithms, allowing coefficients to be interpreted as elasticities.

Wage Rates and the Operation of Labour Markets

Before turning to our regression results, we must take the important step of examining the data to understand how the manufacturing and agricultural labour markets operate, just as one would advisedly do in scrutinizing any commodity market.

Here it is necessary to determine the extent to which these labour markets operate freely. Do certain government regulations restrict their operation or prevent them from operating at reasonably competitive levels? Over the period of study and particularly for the lower end of the wage distribution, the most important labour market regulation is arguably the minimum wage. It was introduced during the 1970s, but it was small and was not seriously enforced until the 1990s (Chun and Khor 2010). Even by 1997, the fine for non-compliance was the equivalent of only fifty dollars, regardless of how many people a firm employed. But during the 1990s, the minimum wage became important: it was raised three-fold nominally from 1993 to 2000 and by 50 percent in real terms from 1993 to 2007. But even so, it was enforced only for large firms and only seriously there in the later 2000s. In rural areas, it has never been a meaningful issue. For our work, it would possibly and at best marginally be important only for the manufacturing wage rate in the very last years of our data. It would have had no direct impact on the agricultural wage rate.

Second, can we "ground-truth" our wage rate data to detect any patterns that help confirm their accuracy and even offer insights for our entire data period? The manufacturing wage rate is charted in Figure 6.1. It shows an average annual compound growth at 2.1 percent, from 19,000 rupiah in 1983 to 38,000 rupiah in the mid-2000s, using 2007 rupiah as the base year. The rate clearly declined for five quarters during the 1997–98 Asian Financial Crisis (AFC) but then moved up strongly. On the whole, it tracks the overall growth of the Indonesian economy well, with no major surprises.

The agricultural wage rate is shown in Figure 6.2, covering the same period, also in real terms, but deflated here by the rural CPI. It grows over the whole period at an average annual compound rate of 2.84 percent per year,

FIGURE 6.1
Manufacturing wage rate, in rupiah, 1983–2009

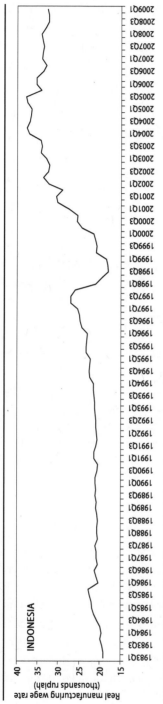

Source: BPS, 2010.

FIGURE 6.2
Agricultural wage rate, in rupiah, 1983–2009

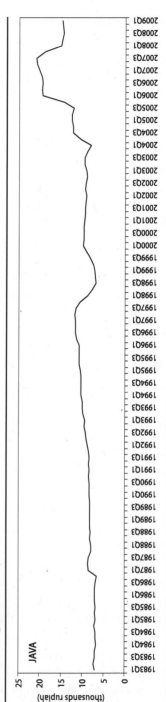

Source: BPS, 2010.

faster than the manufacturing wage so therefore showing convergence. Like the manufacturing wage rate, it increases smoothly and steadily until the 1998 AFC and then drops sharply for the five quarters of the crisis. However, after the AFC, it stays flat in real terms for four years, unlike the manufacturing wage, then rises quite dramatically from the end of 2005, from 12,000 to 19,000 rupiah in only three quarters.

An examination of our data reveals that the manufacturing and agricultural wage rates behaved roughly as expected. The former was quite predictable throughout the entire period, given the economy's performance. The latter followed suit, paralleling the manufacturing wage until the advent of the AFC. But after 1999, the two markets began to display puzzling differences in timing, as the agricultural wage remained flat for four years, whereas the manufacturing wage rose.

One explanation for this might be that the service sector wage, as a reflection of the open informal sector, tracks the overall economy most accurately and that the agricultural wage moves more closely to it than to the manufacturing wage. The manufacturing wage may have rebounded soon after the crisis, as the formal sector was most affected by increased export profitability. But the rest of the economy grew more slowly, providing little expansion in service-sector jobs, little wage growth, and hence fewer options for farm labour to migrate to those jobs and push up agricultural wages due to the reduced supply of agricultural labour. On the labour supply side more directly, it is possible that agricultural workers were cautious about relocating to off-farm employment after wages and jobs crashed in 1998, waiting to see if such jobs were really being created and available to them.

Econometric Estimation

Our estimating strategy follows the steps outlined in Figure 6.3. The first test, the unit root test, helps choose the right estimation technique, given the time-series nature of our data. This test checks whether the variables in a series are stationary or non-stationary. A stationary series allows us to use a simple ordinary least squares (OLS) model for our estimation, but for a non-stationary series we need more sophisticated models.

Formally, a stationary process is one whose joint probability distribution does not change when shifted in time. This particular feature can strongly influence a *series* behaviour or properties. When a trend is stationary, we can remove the underlying trend, which is *only* a function of time, and can capture the true underlying trend, which is not influenced by the change in time, season, etc. If a variable is not stationary, the standard assumptions for

FIGURE 6.3
Statistical methodology

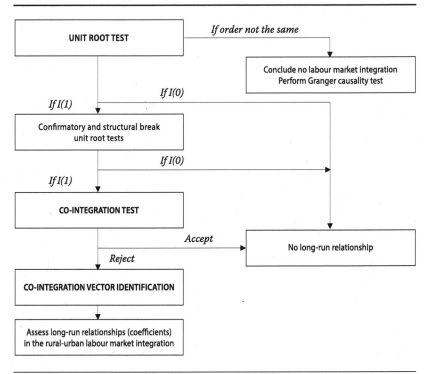

asymptotic analysis will not be valid. In other words, if we don't have a stationary series, we cannot validly examine hypothesis tests for the coefficients of our regression variables in an OLS model and would instead need a more complex model.

In our first step, we utilized three unit root methods to test each of the log-formed time-series variables (rural wage rates, real urban wage rates, agriculture prices, and urban unemployment). Our three unit root test methods are ADF (Augmented Dickey-Fuller) tests, the PP (Philippe-Peron) test, and DF-GLS (ERS) – a more advanced/sophisticated test (Harahap 2012). The null hypothesis is that the series is non-stationary or has unit roots. The results are that we fail to reject the null hypothesis for all three unit root tests, which confirms the existence of unit roots or a non-stationary series.

As a second step, to confirm the unit root results, we perform the Kwiatkowski-Phillips-Schmidt-Shin (KPSS) unit root test. Unlike the three other tests, KPSS considers a stationary series as its null hypothesis. The results from KPSS are consistent with those of the ADF, PP, and DF-GLS tests, confirming the existence of unit roots.

Third, we perform a structural break unit root test to confirm that the suspected non-stationary test results are not simply due to 'a structural break in the data. We use the Lanne Lutkepohl and Saikkonen (LLS) test, with the break date assumed to be unknown. The results of the LLS unit root test provide further evidence for the existence of unit roots when breaks are allowed. The test values for all three test statistics for each time-series variable are all quite similar across functional specifications as well as across time-series variables, and they do not provide evidence against the existence of unit roots.

Now that we have confirmed the existence of unit roots, we use a co-integration technique to determine whether or not a long-term equilibrium exists among the non-stationary variables. We perform a Johansen co-integration test on all the confirmed non-stationary time-series variables (rural wage rates, real urban wage rates, agriculture prices, and urban un-employment) altogether.

For West Java, our results show at a 5 percent level of significance that both maximum eigenvalue and trace tests indicate the presence of at least one co-integrating relation in every model specification. For Central Java, the results show at least one co-integrating relation in every specified model at a 5 percent level of significance. The results for East Java are mixed. Four of six tests show at least one co-integrating relation at a 5 percent level of statistical significance. The other two tests do not find such a relation, indi-cating that we should proceed with caution in interpreting the East Java results.

The last step is to find the magnitude and direction of the most stable long-run relationship for each of the three provinces. By "stable," we are referring to a model whose residuals are behaving normally, independent of each other and with equal variance. This step is essentially about "model fitting." The equations that were estimated for each of the three provinces are given in the Appendix, but the results are summarized in Table 6.1. The dependent variable is the agricultural wage rate, denoted as RUW in the Appendix results. All variables used in the regressions are in logarithms, allowing the coefficients in Table 6.1 to be interpreted as elasticities.

Results

All values in the Table 6.1 results are elasticities, showing the percent change in the farm wage rate (our dependent variable) for a 1 percent change in

TABLE 6.1
Long-run equilibrium regression results

Explanatory variables	West Java	Central Java	East Java
Rice price	0.14	0.17	0
Manufacturing wage rate	0.26	0.53	0.14
Urban GDP growth rate	0.14	0.19	0.19
Constant	4.50	0.88	6.83

each of the three explanatory variables. Recall that we are most interested in comparing the impact on farm wage rates of the agricultural demand for labour, using the effect of rice prices (AGP), with the effect of the urban demand for labour, considering the manufacturing wage rate and the urban GDP growth rate (as a proxy for the service-sector wage rate). First, the manufacturing wage rate is highly important in determining the farm wage rate. Averaged across the results for these three provinces, farm wages rise by 0.3 percent for a 1.0 percent increase in the manufacturing wage rate.[2] When we examine the other measure of urban or non-farm demand for labour, the urban GDP growth rate, it raises the farm wage rate by almost as much as the manufacturing wage rate, with an average elasticity of 0.17.[3] If we added these two coefficients together, the effect of urban-sector labour demand rising by 1.0 percent causes at least a 0.47 percent (possibly 0.85 percent, using the restricted equation) increase in the farm wage rate.

By contrast, a 1.0 percent increase in the rice price has a 0.1 percent effect on the farm wage rate. On the basis of these more conservative coefficients, this farm price variable has only one-fifth the effect on farm wage rates as do the non-farm wage rates. If we disaggregate this effect, the manufacturing wage rate has three times the effect on farm wages as does the rice price, and the urban GDP growth rate has two times the effect on farm wages.

Another perspective on the relative effect of these three variables is to compare their impacts over the first decade of the 2000s, from 2000 to 2009. The year 2000 marked the introduction of a rice tariff of approximately 25 percent.[4] If we use our average Java-wide rice price coefficient of 0.1, this tariff would have raised farm wages by 2.6 percent, once and for all. In other words, the tariff was introduced once and left at that level, so it will have had a one-time impact on the wage rate. Urban GDP was growing at 5 to 7 percent per year during this decade, so this factor would have raised farm wage rates, if we use our elasticity estimate of 0.17, by 1.0 to 1.5 percent per year, or 10–15 percent over the decade. Note that the continuous growth of GDP each year gives a stronger effect on this basis alone than does a one-time rice tariff increase. Manufacturing wage rates also rose steadily, and if they increased only as fast as GDP, this would have augmented farm wage rates by an additional 1.5 to 2.1 percent per year, or 15–21 percent over this decade.

To put these together, farm wage rates would have risen by 25.0 to 36.0 percent over the decade due to urban demand factors, whereas the one-time rice tariff increase boosted farm wages by only 2.6 percent. The non-farm factors raised wage rates by at least ten times more than rice prices did during that decade. Putting this in the context of trade policy, specifically more open trade, we see that shifting to more open trade in rice (lowering the tariff wall and hence lowering the rice price) will have a tiny negative effect on farm wage rates, and this will be contrasted with the benefit to all consumers, farm families included, of lower rice prices for their consumption.

Implications and Conclusions

These results have many implications, but of greatest interest for this volume is what we learn about how increases in trade will affect rural poverty. In much of its agricultural sector (notably in rice and other field crops), Indonesia has pursued a policy of erecting trade barriers to raise farm rice prices. As discussed earlier, this policy will hurt everyone who consumes rice, with an especially large impact on the urban and rural poor who do not produce it. But even the farmers who grow some rice but whose production is so small that they must purchase it at some point in the year (net rice consumers) will be hurt. Our question is will the larger farmers who are net rice producers be helped by the increase in rice prices? It is widely held that they will benefit from greater production or less trade.

We focus on the poorest segment of the rural population, those who own little or no land and who therefore must depend on their only asset, their labour. An increase in rice prices will help them only if their wage rate rises. Our results show that this effect for Java from 1983 to 2009 is very small indeed. An increase in rice prices of ten percent will raise agricultural wage rates by only 1 percent, averaged across the three provinces of Java.

In other words, if Indonesia increased trade in rice by lowering its formidable trade barriers, this step would have only a small detrimental effect on wage rates and hence on the poorest stratum of rural Indonesia (Java). This group would include poor farmers who not only own little or no land but who live in more remote locations, older farmers who feel unable to move, and those who have few other skills and thus cannot enter the non-farm labour market. These are the truly poor, and yet the protectionist rice-price-raising policy practised by Indonesia has only a small positive effect on their incomes, unless they own enough land. Against this would be arrayed the considerable benefits to all Indonesian rice consumers, which would be of significance to everyone who lives in poverty.

Would anyone be disadvantaged by a policy of decreasing trade barriers? Yes, if land rents drop, the price of land would also drop, hurting rice landowners. Such an outcome is not trivial, but the cost is borne in proportion to the amount of land a farmer owns. The poor farmers who own little land would not be greatly hurt. People who own larger amounts, a group that includes many non-farmers, are not particularly poor and will bear the brunt of this policy change of lowering rice trade barriers. In other words, our results indicate that increased trade has little negative effect on poor rice farmers, and it would be substantially offset by the gains in lower rice prices for all poor rice consumers across the country. Our results suggest that lowering trade barriers and increasing rice trade would clearly be classified as a "pro-poor" policy.

Another important result from our study, which is tangential to the impact of trade on poverty, is the effect of migration on poverty. Our work reveals that the non-farm sector has a very large effect on farm wages. Quantitatively, over a decade it has roughly ten times the effect that raising rice tariffs does. This effect arises both from migrants moving to off-farm jobs, forcing farm wages upward to be competitive, and from the reduced supply of labour to agriculture when migration occurs, also pushing up farm wage rates. Therefore, for a policy that seeks to alleviate poverty, at least under the labour market conditions of Java, enabling continued migration and keeping strong economic growth in the non-farm sector would be very effective.

Summary

Our study gives a clearer view than much of the past literature on Indonesian rural-urban labour market linkages and their role in determining rural wage rates. Wage rate patterns in both sectors appear largely predictable and show considerable co-movement, especially prior to 1998. Our findings confirm that, in the long run, agricultural wage rates are mostly determined by non-farm factors and only modestly affected by farm prices.

This means that the government policy of raising rice prices with tariffs and import quotas has a very limited long-term impact on rural wages and the poorest farmers in Java. Specifically, the 25 percent import tariff from the year 2000 raised rural wage rates by a mere 3 percent in West Java, 4 percent in Central Java, and 0 percent in East Java, for an overall average increase for Java of about 2 percent, and this was a one-time increase. By contrast, the urban manufacturing wage plus urban GDP growth raised wages each year over the subsequent decade by ten times as much.

The 1983–2009 data for Java also have clear implications for poverty alleviation. First, employing wage rate data is very useful for examining poverty among the poorest rural residents, those with little or no land, specifically by determining the factors that are effective in raising those wage rates and measuring how much they influence it. Second, increased migration is a much more powerful tool to raise farm wage rates and thereby reduce rural poverty. A host of policies can help achieve this result.

But, on balance, lowering trade barriers to reduce domestic food prices will also lessen poverty directly. What we show is that diminishing trade barriers has a very small negative effect on the wage rates of the farmers who produce the food. The case of the agricultural sector cannot be used to argue against trade liberalization and deregulation, at least not for Indonesia over this period if we are worried about the more serious dimensions of rural poverty. There is no poverty-trade trade-off in evidence here; the two are largely complementary. One must be cautious, however, in extrapolating from these results to other cases. They are country-specific and possibly time-specific as well, depending on labour market conditions.

Appendix 1:

For West Java:

$$RUW = 0.26 \, URW + 0.14 \, AGP + 0.14 \, UGDP + 4.54 \tag{1}$$
Chi-square statistic = 2.30; p-value = 0.052

For Central Java:

$$RUW = 0.53 \, URW + 0.17 \, AGP + 0.19 \, UGDP + 0.88 \tag{2}$$
Chi-square statistic = 1.87; p-value = 0.060

For East Java:

$$RUW = 0.14 \, URW - 0.70 \, AGP + 0.19 \, UGDP + 0.02t + 6.83 \tag{3}$$
Chi-square statistic = 7.77; p-value = 0.05

Further zero restriction of AGP coefficient gives higher significance (Chi-square statistic = 9.03, p-value = 0.06) and revised coefficients of 0.59 URW and 0.86 UGDP.

Explanatory Note: Coefficient on AGP for East Java in Table 6.1

In discussing these results, we should note the 0 value for the rice price elasticity for East Java. As can be seen in the Appendix equation for East Java, the original coefficient was negative (−0.7). But we must also recall that we found mixed statistical results about the existence of a co-integrating relationship (by one test no such relationship was statistically significant). A positive coefficient was expected, a zero coefficient is possible, but a negative coefficient is very difficult to explain. Given these statistical cautions about this long-run relationship, we suspect the coefficient is not significant at all. Hence, we report a 0 value in Table 6.1 for East Java. When we re-estimated this equation, restricting its coefficient to zero, the model shows higher elasticities for the manufacturing wage (0.59 instead of 0.14) and the urban GDP growth rate (0.86 instead of 0.19). Supporting our suspicion of the insignificant effect of the rice price, the revised (restricted) equation has a higher level of statistical significance than the original (unrestricted) equation.

Notes

Acknowledgments: We wish to acknowledge the helpful comments from workshop participants at the University of California-Davis, Iowa State University, the Thailand Development Research Institute, the China Center for Agricultural Policy, the Asian Development Bank Institute, Institut Pertanian Bogor, and Padjajaran University. We also thank two referees for their valuable suggestions. This research was funded in part by SSHRC.

1 The fallacy in this rhetoric about higher rice prices reducing poverty is documented in McCulloch (2008).

2 This would be even higher, 0.46, if we used the results of the more significant "restricted" equation for East Java (see the Appendix).

3 This too would rise, by a factor of 2, to 0.39 if we used the results of the restricted equation for East Java.

4 Translating a specific tariff into an *ad valorem* tariff.

References

Badan Pusat Statistik (BPS) (Statistics Indonesia). 2010. "Indonesian Bureau of Statistics Online Data Base." Jakarta. Accessed January 7, 2010. http://www.bps.go.id.

Chun, Natalie, and Niny Khor. 2010. "Minimum Wages and Changing Wage Inequality in Indonesia." ADB Economics Working Paper Series No. 196. Asian Development Bank. https://www.adb.org/sites/default/files/publication/28407/economics-wp196.pdf.

Harahap, Faisal. 2012. "Estimating Long-Run Elasticities of Rural Wage Determinants in Indonesia: The Johansen Cointegration Method." Master's thesis,

University of British Columbia. https://open.library.ubc.ca/cIRcle/collections/ubctheses/24/items/1.0072966.

Harris, John, and Michael Todaro. 1970. "Migration, Unemployment and Development: A Two-Sector Analysis." *American Economic Review* 60, 1: 126–42.

Hayami, Yujiro, and Masao Kikuchi. 1982. *Asian Village Economy at the Crossroads.* Baltimore: Johns Hopkins University Press.

Lewis, Arthur. 1954. "Economic Development with Unlimited Supplies of Labour." *Manchester School* 22: 139–91.

McCulloch, N. 2008. "Rice Prices and Poverty in Indonesia." *Bulletin of Indonesian Economic Studies* 44, 1: 45–64.

Naylor, Rosamond. 1991. "The Rural Labor Market in Indonesia," Chapter 5 in Pearson, Scott, Walter Falcon, Paul Heytens, Eric Monke, and Rosamond Naylor, *Rice Policy in Indonesia.* Ithaca, NY: Cornell University Press.

Rigg, Jonathan, Buapun Promphaking, and Ann Le Mare. 2014. "Personalizing the Middle-Income Trap: An Inter-Generational Migrant View from Rural Thailand." *World Development* 59, 7: 184–98.

7

Is Greater Openness to Trade Good?

What Are the Effects on Poverty
and Inequality?

ARIANTO PATUNRU

In the midst of growing integration, be it at the global or the regional level, Indonesia has been a latecomer. Whereas Southeast Asian countries have started to engage in the increasing trade in parts and components, Indonesia's trade in finished manufacturing products is still larger than that of parts and components (Fung, Iizaka, and Siu 2010). The trade integration characterized by product fragmentation is expected to grow, rather than contract, despite the current slowdown following the Global Financial Crisis of 2007–08. Therefore, Indonesia should position itself to take full advantage of this trend.

Indonesia rebounded well after the 2007–08 financial crisis – along with China and India, it experienced impressive positive growth in 2009. Unfortunately, its resilience fuelled a widespread belief that pulling back from trade in particular, or even globalization in general, would be the wisest course. As the argument goes, Indonesia survived the storm because of its relatively low exposure to trade. Its export to GDP ratio is less than 30 percent, compared to that of Thailand, for example, which stands at around 70 percent, or Singapore, with almost 200 percent. However, as Patunru and Zetha (2010) and Basri and Rahardja (2010) suggest, Indonesia was saved by a combination of good policies and good luck. In particular, the low export share of its GDP exists more by default than by design. Studies of its economic inefficiency show that its low competitiveness in the global market is in part caused by high logistical costs, especially from its poor transport infrastructure (Patunru and Tarsidin 2012). In short, Indonesia's poor performance in the world market is a consequence of constraints in the supply side. Basri and Patunru (2008) similarly argue that the most binding constraints in its supply side include logistics and infrastructure issues.

Other studies and reports highlight another important factor in Indonesia's suboptimal economic development – poor connectivity across regions *within* the country. The poor transportation infrastructure has contributed to significant price disparities from one province to another, even for basic goods. In remote villages in Papua, for example, a sack of cement can cost three times the Indonesian average. Considerable differences occur in the prices of basic staples, such as sugar and cooking oil (Basri 2010). Bad connectivity also contributes to the high cost of providing goods for trade purposes. As the story goes, importing a mandarin orange from China to Jakarta is cheaper than shipping it from Pontianak in Kalimantan (Borneo), a distance of about seven hundred kilometres. Similarly, anyone who wishes to transport goods from Central Kalimantan to its next-door neighbour South Kalimantan would find that sending them directly overland is more difficult than flying them across the Java Sea to the Jakarta airport and back.

Yet another impediment to Indonesia's participation in the global market is government policy. As a relatively young country, Indonesia has experienced swings in policy with regard to trade and investment. Its first president, Sukarno, adopted a command socialism that was inward looking and opposed to foreign investment (although ironically foreign debt was high under his tenure). When his presidency ended in 1966, the per capita income was less than that in 1938, total foreign debt was almost twice the GDP, and the country saw hyperinflation of more than 500 percent.

The new order under the next president, Soeharto, took almost the opposite approach. The economy was much more open and friendly to foreign investment. A stable economic and political environment transformed the country into one of the fastest-growing economies in Southeast Asia. Unfortunately, after more than two decades in power, Soeharto became too complacent. His policies became imprudent and protectionist in favour of his family and cronies. Corruption and rent-seeking activities were rampant. When the Asian Financial Crisis struck in 1997, the fundamentals were already weak. As a result, though Thailand was at the epicentre of the crisis, Indonesia was the hardest-hit country in the region. Its economy plunged, inflation skyrocketed, and unemployment inched up. To save the economy from falling further, Indonesia turned to the International Monetary Fund

(IMF) for assistance. The IMF aid came with a long list of conditions that required Indonesia to undergo structural reform. The IMF program contributed to pushing Indonesia to implement successful unilateral trade liberalization – some regarded this as the boldest trade reform in its history (Basri and Patunru 2012). It included a complete deregulation of agricultural trade and the removal of most non-tariff barriers.

However, in retrospect, many observers demonstrated that several IMF prescriptions – monetary, banking, and exchange rate policies – were misplaced and did more damage to the economy (Grenville 2004; Ito 2012).

The interest in free trade after the IMF reforms turned out to be short-lived. In 2001, protectionism returned, focusing initially on food crops and then on trade regulations and licensing requirements for textiles, steel, sugar, and cloves (Basri and Patunru 2012). This protectionist trend continues, and to some extent is even exacerbated, under the current president, Joko Widodo (Patunru and Rahardja 2015). The major difference between the current protectionism and that of the previous era is that most protectionism now takes the form of non-tariff barriers, such as import bans, export quotas, labelling, licensing, and domestic content requirements.

Whereas trade protectionism has experienced its ups and downs, one sector is consistently characterized by policy makers' preference for full protection: rice. Even under his relatively liberal regime, Soeharto nurtured an ambition to reach self-sufficiency in rice. Today, other commodities such as maize, sugar, soybeans, and beef are the focus of similar ambitions (Nehru 2013).[1] Proponents of this view argue that protecting domestic production means protecting the farmers and hence the poor. In this chapter, I aim to debunk this fallacy. Using rice as a case study, I show that the domestic price of rice has increased far above the international price, that most of the poorest farmers are net consumers, not net producers, of rice, and that contrary to the self-sufficiency argument, trade restriction is bad for the poor. Much of this chapter is based on the core empirical facts of rice production and consumption, followed by a simple simulation of a price change to observe its possible effects on producers and consumers. Interested readers can also consult Chapter 6 in this volume, which provides a formal model and econometric tests to arrive at a similar conclusion.

The Dynamics of Indonesia's Rice Prices

Indonesia is the largest consumer of rice in Southeast Asia. It is the fourth-largest importer of rice in the world, after China, Iran, and Saudi Arabia, with total imports of more than 1 million tonnes in 2018 (Burton 2019).

Despite this, the government constantly attempts to restrict imports. As a consequence, the domestic price has risen significantly. As rice has a considerable weight in the inflation basket, its price increase helps drag the headline inflation up.

Figure 7.1 shows the real price of rice in Indonesia during the fifty years from 1969 to 2020. It remained relatively stable from the mid-1970s to the late 1990s, as the government provided heavy subsidies for inputs (seed, fertilizer, and pesticides, as well as credit) and invested in irrigation and rice research, owing to a major windfall associated with two oil price shocks in the 1970s (Fane and Warr 2008; McCulloch and Timmer 2008). The government also gave Bulog (the state logistics agency, established in 1967) a mandate to stabilize prices, as well as an import monopoly. Such support imposed a heavy burden on the state budget, especially when the oil boom ended in the 1980s. Since then, rice output has grown more slowly, and the price rose steadily in the lead-up to the Asian Financial Crisis, peaking in September 1998.

As part of its loan conditions with the IMF, Indonesia agreed to liberalize the rice market in the aftermath of the Asian Financial Crisis. Bulog's import monopoly was discontinued, and private traders could now import rice. As a result, the price dropped from 8,000 rupiah in September 1998 to 5,000 rupiah per kilogram in April 2004 (at constant 2012 prices).[2] As McCulloch and Timmer (2008) note, from 1999 to 2004 when trade was more open, prices were more stable than when Bulog exercised its monopoly.

But stabilization by market was temporary. In 2004, the government imposed an import ban. As a consequence, prices started to increase rapidly. From May 2004 to May 2006, the price of rice more than doubled, from 5,000 rupiah to more than 10,000 rupiah per kilogram. This is obviously far higher than what the government saw as the "normal" price of rice – about 4,200 rupiah.[3] A drought in mid-2006 also hit paddy production and pushed up prices. As food has a large weight in the inflation basket – as rice does in the food category – the inflation rate soared (Figure 7.2).[4]

Given the situation, the government had no choice but to lift the import ban in September 2006. Within weeks, prices went down, and the inflation rate dropped back to single digits during the next month. However, rather than automatically linking the prices to market dynamics, the government reinstated Bulog's import monopoly. Subsequently, a similar situation often recurred. Figure 7.3 shows the 2014–19 period, with rice imports still constrained, resulting in high inflation for food items that in turn drags up headline inflation.

FIGURE 7.1

Rice price adjusted for inflation, 1969–2020 (rupiah per kilogram)

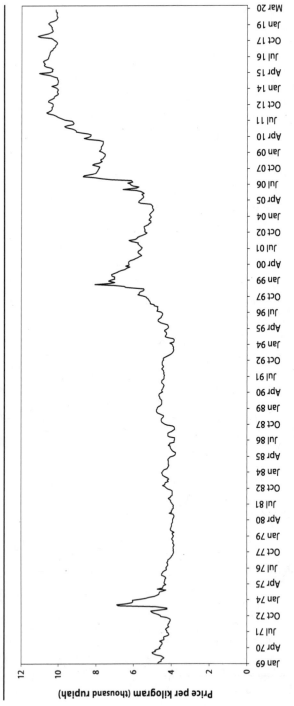

Notes: The prices from January 1969 to January 2006 are the retail prices of the Medium rice variety, collected from Neil McCulloch (pers. comm., 15 June 2006), World Bank (2006), and Bulog database (Bulog 2006). The prices from February 2006 to October 2006 were estimated based on the price of the IR-64 rice variety in Jakarta's Cipinang wholesale market, adjusted with the average price difference between the two series from 1995 to 2006 (i.e., retail margin over wholesale prices). The prices from November 2006 until March 2020 are the retail prices of Medium rice, collected from Badan Pusat Statistik (BPS) (Statistics Indonesia) (BPS 2020a). The nominal prices were deflated by the consumer price index (CPI), indexed at 2012 = 100, calculated from the BPS database.

FIGURE 7.2
Inflation and food prices, 2004–08 (%, year-on-year)

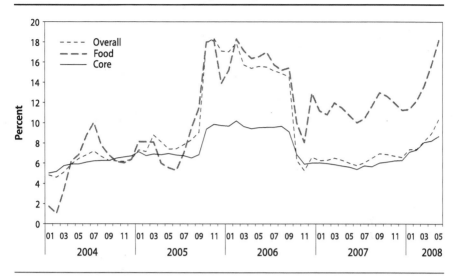

Notes: The year-on-year inflation series are calculated from BPS's consumer price indices. The base year for these indices is 2002.

FIGURE 7.3
Inflation and food prices, 2014–19 (%, year-on-year)

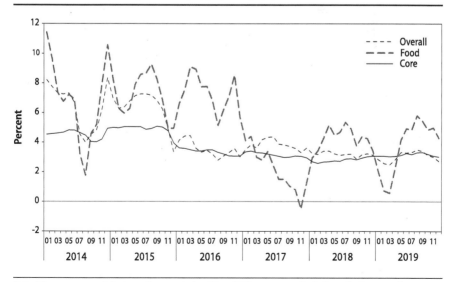

Notes: The year-on-year inflation series are calculated from BPS's consumer price indices. The base year for these indices is 2012.

Domestic and World Prices

Figure 7.4 compares the price of rice in Indonesia with the world price from 1995 to March 2020. The latter is represented by the border price of the Thai 25 percent broken variety, as Thailand is a world-leading exporter of rice, and Thai 25 percent broken rice is very similar to Indonesia's IR-64 and Medium rice varieties. The figure shows that until 2004, the Indonesian price closely paralleled the world price.[5] It started to deviate from the world price in 2005. As discussed above, this coincided with the government-imposed ban on importing rice.

In 2007–08, the world experienced a rice price crisis, due to a combination of trade restrictions by major rice suppliers, panic buying by key importers, the weak dollar, and record high oil prices (Childs and Kiawu 2009). As a result, the world price tripled from November 2007 to April 2008, leaving the Indonesian domestic price behind. As McCulloch and

FIGURE 7.4
Domestic and world rice prices, 1995–2020 (rupiah per kilogram)

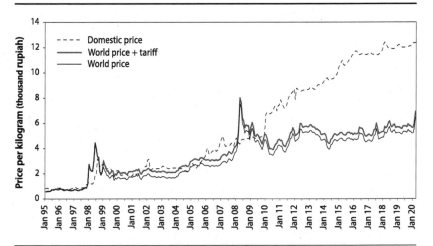

Note: The domestic price series is represented by the wholesale price of IR-64 rice, as quoted in Cipinang, the biggest wholesale market in Jakarta, collected from Neil McCulloch (pers. comm., 15 June 2006) for January 1995 until May 2009 and from BPS afterward (BPS 2020a). Prices from June 2009 until December 2009 were estimated using the cost of Medium rice, adjusted with the average margin between the retail and wholesale prices from November 2006 until May 2009. The world price series is represented by the wholesale price of Thai 25 percent broken rice, collected from the Bank of Thailand database (via CEIC Database) and converted to rupiah, with an additional shipping and handling cost of twenty dollars a ton and an import profit of five US dollars a tonne. The "world price + tariff" series is the same as the world price but with the addition of a 20 percent tariff in 1999 and specific tariffs of 430 rupiah per kilogram from January 2000 until December 2006, 550 rupiah per kilogram from January 2007 until November 2007, and 450 rupiah per kilogram from December 2007 onward.

Timmer (2008) point out, the higher world price would improve the profitability of Indonesia's rice products and hence create a window of opportunity for the government to reconsider its trade policy.

This moment, in which the domestic price was below the world price, lasted from March 2008 to March 2009. But policy reform did not take place. Instead, a combination of import monopoly and tariff remained. A tariff of 430 rupiah per kilogram had been imposed since December 2006, after which it was adjusted to 550 rupiah per kilogram in January 2007 and to 450 rupiah per kilogram in December 2007. In addition, imports had to be approved by Parliament – a fact that lengthened the process of stabilizing prices.[6]

With reform momentum lost, when the world price went back down, the Indonesian price was still on the rise, and in fact skyrocketed from December 2009 to March 2010. It has been increasing since then, making the divergence even greater. By the end of 2012, for example, the gap had reached 65 percent. The World Bank (2015) estimates that in 2013 a 12 percent rise in the price of rice increased the poverty rate by 1.3 percentage points. This is roughly equivalent to 3 million people.[7] If, as a major consumer of rice, Indonesia has an impact on the world price, then the true market price would lie somewhere between the bold and dashed lines on Figure 7.4. Assuming this coincides with a price gap of 25 percent, the high domestic price of rice kept 6 million Indonesian people in poverty in 2012.

If tariffs are the only restriction, the imported rice will sell domestically for the world price plus the tariff. Figure 7.4 implies that tariffs are not the only factor in the divergence between domestic and world prices. Clearly, non-tariff barriers play a role as well, especially the import ban. Since February 2014, the domestic price has been more than double that of the world price, but only about 10 percent of this increase is due to tariffs. It is true that some of the price differences might result from geographical barriers such as poor logistics; however, these may account for "only" about 10 percent.[8] Therefore, it is fair to say that such a large price difference in rice is due to trade restrictions, particularly the import ban.

Indonesia's Rice Imports

According to Dawe (2008), the geography of Indonesia hinders the production of sufficient rice to feed the population (it lacks both extensive flat lands and dominant river deltas that provide abundant water). In this, it resembles the other consistent net importers (Philippines, Malaysia, Japan, Sri Lanka) and differs from the consistent net exporters (Thailand,

FIGURE 7.5
Rice net imports-to-production ratio (%, 5-year moving average)

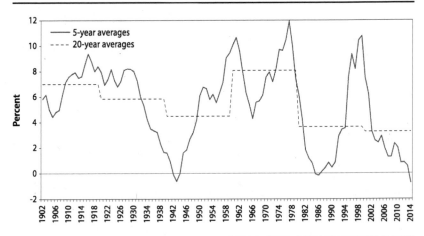

Notes: Data from 1900 to 2000 are from Dawe (2008) and Rosner and McCulloch (2008). Data from 2000 to 2010 are from BPS (BPS 2020a). Some export data were missing (2010–14), so I used information from media source to calculate the net import-to-production ratio (Daniel 2015). I used a paddy-to-rice conversion factor (paddy-rice milling ratio) of 0.63 (Rosner and McCulloch 2008).

Myanmar, Indochina). Unsurprisingly, therefore, Indonesia has been importing rice for a very long time.

Figure 7.5 shows Indonesia's net imports (that is, imports minus exports) of rice relative to domestic production since 1902. The five-year and twenty-year moving averages are included. One underappreciated fact is that Indonesia has been importing rice for more than a hundred years. There were only a few times when exports outweighed imports, resulting in negative net imports. These include brief periods in the early 1940s, the mid-1980s, and in 2014.[9] Otherwise, imports could be substantial. In the late 1970s, for example, the net import-to-production ratio reached 12 percent. That is, around 12 percent of the domestic need for rice was supplied by imports. Interestingly, after an increase in 1999 following the removal of the import ban, the import-to-production ratio declined steeply. This implies that even when imports are not banned, the amount of imported rice does not necessarily increase. Arguably, the stable production during the early 2000s made imports less attractive, despite the liberal period in 1999–2003.

The foregoing analysis, however, has assumed that production data *are* reliable. This is a contentious topic. Rosner and McCulloch (2008) argue that data for rice production (and consumption) are not dependable. They show that production is generally overestimated (whereas consumption is underestimated). They conclude, therefore, that prices are the only accurate indicator of the balance between supply and demand for rice. If it is true that the production data are underestimated, the net import-to-production ratios in Figure 7.5 should be higher. The bias might even be larger in recent times, considering the 2016 spat between Indonesian government officials over the inaccuracy of rice production data.[10]

Table 7.1 illustrates this problem with quantity data. If one relies on the published BPS statistics regarding consumption and production of rice, Indonesia would appear to be abundantly endowed with rice production, far exceeding its total consumption.[11] In fact, if the data were correct, the total demand would be less than half of total domestic production. Yet, the final column in Table 7.1 reveals that the country still imported rice. Even if one adjusts the production figures downward by 17 percent (Rosner and McCulloch 2008), the excess supply figures remain very large.[12] In 2018, BPS finally adjusted its sampling method. Ruslan (2019) shows that the pre-2018 method could lead to 40 percent overestimation of rice production, relative to the new method.

Rice, Poverty, and Inequality

Although food and rice have consistently declined in the total household expenditures of Indonesians between 2002 and 2012, the shares are still significant, especially in lower-income groups (Table 7.2). Four-fifths of the population still devote more than half of their total expenditure to food. Rice takes 17.5 percent of the total expenditure of the poorest 20 percent, compared to less than 4.0 percent of the top 20 percent. The ratio of 5 (i.e., 25.56/5.5 and 17.5/3.8) did not change in the ten years between 2002 and 2012. This indicates that higher rice prices have the greatest impact on lower-income groups.

At the same time, rice also creates employment opportunities, especially for the poor. As Table 7.3 shows, the poorest 20 percent of the population earned more than 50 percent of their income from the agriculture sector in 2012, an increase from 36 percent in 2002. On the other hand, the richest 20 percent of Indonesians obtained only 10 percent of their income from agriculture in 2012; it was 4 percent in 2002. This indicates that agriculture played an increasingly important role as an income source between 2002 and 2012. The subset of food crops provided just over 20 percent of the income for the poorest households and less than 2 percent for the richest ones. In other words, almost 80 percent of the income of the poorest households did not come from this subset. Since the National Socio-Economic

TABLE 7.1
Consumption, production, and import of rice in Indonesia

	Consumption (kilogram per capita per week)	Population (millions)	Annual demand (000 tons)	Domestic supply of rice (000 tons)	Excess supply (000 tons)	Imports (000 tons)
2007	1.74	226	21,197	36,009	14,812	1,407
2008	1.80	232	22,512	38,005	15,494	290
2009	1.76	235	22,334	40,571	18,237	250
2010	1.73	239	22,283	41,876	19,593	688
2011	1.72	242	22,476	41,427	18,951	2,751
2012	1.68	245	22,265	43,505	21,240	1,810
2013	1.64	249	22,035	44,906	22,871	473
2014	1.63	252	22,196	44,633	22,437	844

Notes: Per capita consumption, population, production, and import data are from BPS. Annual consumption assumes fifty-four weeks. Rice supply is calculated from BPS production estimates, with a paddy-rice conversion rate of 0.63 (BPS 2018). "Excess supply" is domestic supply minus annual demand.

TABLE 7.2
Food and rice in total expenditure (%)

Expenditure		Food		Rice	
Quintile		2002	2012	2002	2012
Lowest	1	71.9	67.1	25.6	17.5
	2	69.6	62.9	20.2	12.9
	3	67.2	58.3	16.3	10.3
	4	63.0	53.8	12.0	7.9
Highest	5	47.3	38.4	5.5	3.8

Sources: McCulloch (2008); 2012 SUSENAS survey (BPS 2019).

TABLE 7.3
Sectoral contribution in total income (%)

Expenditure		Agriculture		Food crops	
Quintile		2002	2012	2002	2012
Lowest	1	36.0	52.2	19.8	21.8
	2	28.7	41.9	15.5	14.1
	3	21.8	34.8	11.6	10.5
	4	13.6	26.5	6.8	6.6
Highest	5	4.3	10.7	1.8	1.8

Note: Agriculture includes food crops, horticulture, plantations, fisheries, animal husbandry, forestry, and other types of agriculture.
Sources: McCulloch (2008); 2012 SUSENAS survey (BPS 2019).

Household Survey (SUSENAS) does not specifically address rice under sources of income and instead lumps it into the category of food crops, it is fair to say that rice actually plays quite a small role as an income source.

This is also consistent at the aggregate level in the agricultural sector. As Table 7.4 shows, agriculture accounted for less than 40 percent of adult employment. Furthermore, from 2005 to 2012 employment shifted from agriculture to other sectors, such as social services and transport. However, more than 70 percent of the rural poor still depended on agriculture (down from 75 percent in 2005), as did less than one-third of the urban poor.

Although three-quarters of the rural poor work in the agricultural sector, Table 7.5 shows that only 35 percent of poor households depended on rice farming in 2004, a number that dropped to 20 percent in 2012. As expected, most of these poor households are in rural areas. In 2004, 42 percent of the

TABLE 7.4

Adult employment by sector, location, and poverty status

	Urban		Rural		Total		
	Poor	Non-poor	Poor	Non-poor	Poor	Non-poor	All
2005							
Agriculture	35.5	10.7	75.0	57.7	63.4	36.0	40.0
Trading	22.2	31.4	6.9	15.7	11.4	22.9	21.2
Industry	17.6	18.4	8.4	9.6	11.1	13.7	13.3
Social services	9.5	20.6	2.9	6.8	4.8	13.2	11.9
Transport	7.4	8.4	2.0	4.4	3.6	6.3	5.9
Building	6.4	5.9	3.1	3.9	4.1	4.9	4.7
Mining and quarrying	0.7	1.0	1.3	1.5	1.1	1.3	1.3
Finance, insurance, building rent	0.5	3.1	0.1	0.3	0.3	1.6	1.4
Electricity	0.2	0.5	0.1	0.1	0.1	0.3	0.2
	100.0	100.0	100.0	100.0	100.0	100.0	100.0
2012							
Agriculture	26.7	10.6	72.1	53.8	56.8	32.6	34.7
Trading	18.6	26.0	5.5	13.9	9.9	19.8	19.0
Industry	17.0	16.9	8.6	9.2	11.4	13.0	12.8
Social services	15.7	25.5	4.5	10.7	8.3	18.0	17.2
Transport	7.8	10.4	1.9	4.0	3.9	7.1	6.9
Building	12.3	6.8	5.9	6.0	8.1	6.4	6.5
Mining and quarrying	1.3	1.1	1.2	1.8	1.3	1.5	1.5
Finance, insurance, building rent	0.3	2.1	0.1	0.4	0.2	1.2	1.1
Electricity	0.3	0.6	0.1	0.1	0.1	0.3	0.3
	100.0	100.0	100.0	100.0	100.0	100.0	100.0

Sources: McCulloch (2008); 2012 SUSENAS survey (BPS 2019).

rural poor worked in the agricultural sector, and this too diminished to 27 percent in 2012. In contrast, only 18 percent of the rural poor were employed in non-farming sectors in 2004, whereas more than 40 percent were in 2012. As for the non-poor, just over 20 percent were rice farmers in 2004 and less than 10 percent were in 2012. All these data suggest that the importance of rice farming as an income source has declined.

Yet, whether or not an increase in rice prices benefits those who work in the agricultural sector (or more specifically, rice farming) depends on

TABLE 7.5
Urban and rural households by farming status

	Farmers		Non-farmers
	Rice (%)	Others (%)	(%)
2004			
Urban	7.6	8.1	84.3
Poor	19.0	18.3	62.7
Non-poor	6.3	7.0	86.7
Rural	37.8	32.0	30.2
Poor	41.7	40.2	18.1
Non-poor	37.0	30.4	32.6
Total	24.8	21.7	53.6
Poor	34.5	33.3	32.2
Non-poor	23.2	19.9	57.0
2012			
Urban	3.3	4.4	92.3
Poor	9.2	10.3	80.5
Non-poor	2.9	4.1	93.0
Rural	16.6	27.3	56.0
Poor	26.7	33.0	40.3
Non-poor	15.6	26.7	57.7
Total	10.1	16.1	73.8
Poor	20.4	24.7	54.9
Non-poor	9.2	15.4	75.4

Sources: McCulloch (2004); 2012 SUSENAS survey (BPS 2019).

whether they are *net* consumers or *net* producers of rice. Any household can farm rice, but at the same time, it also consumes rice. If it consumes more of the crop than it produces, it is a net consumer. For this type of household, we would therefore expect that an increase in the price of rice would actually exert downward pressure on the family's welfare. Table 7.6 addresses this issue.

In Table 7.6, households are categorized as net producers or net consumers of rice. The first column shows the total number of households that grow rice. This can be broken down into those for whom production exceeds consumption (net producer, column 2) and those for whom it does not (rice-growing net consumer, column 3). Of course, another type of net consumer is households that consume rice but do not grow it (non-rice-

TABLE 7.6
Net producers and net consumers of rice (% of HH)

	Net producers	Net consumers		
	Rice growing	Rice growing	Non-rice growing	Total
2004 (total households: 54.3 million)				
Urban	5.5	2.0	92.5	94.5
Rural	28.3	9.3	62.4	71.7
Total	18.5	6.2	75.3	81.5
2012 (total households: 63.3 million)				
Urban	4.6	0.3	95.1	95.4
Rural	19.0	1.2	79.8	81.0
Total	11.8	0.9	87.3	88.2

Note: "Rice" is proxied by "food crops" in the SUSENAS survey. "Non-rice" agriculture includes horticulture, plantations, fisheries, animal husbandry, and other types of agriculture.
Sources: McCulloch (2008); 2012 SUSENAS survey (BPS 2019).

growing net consumer, column 4). The fifth column shows the total number of net-consumer households (that is, column 3 plus column 4).

The table indicates that in 2004, 81 percent of Indonesian households were net consumers of rice, and 19 percent were net producers. In 2012, the number of net consumers increased to 88 percent of the population.[13] Even in rural areas, just under 20 percent of total households were actually net producers of rice. Again, this confirms the conjecture that in general, increases in the price of rice would benefit only a small portion of the population.

By taking a slightly different approach, we can analyze income inequality in major rice-producing regions. Following Naylor (1991), I show income distribution in rural and urban areas for the consumers group (Table 7.7) and in rural areas for the producers group (Table 7.8). I divided the population into three income groups based on the 25 percent and 75 percent quintile of per capita expenditure (see the note under each table for the cut-off points). In this treatment, "consumers" refers to all residents in the region who consume rice, whereas "producers" is the subset of the population that owns or leases land to grow rice.[14] I show figures for major rice-producing provinces in Sumatra (North Sumatra, West Sumatra, Lampung, and South Sumatra), Java (West Java, Central Java, and East Java), and Sulawesi (South Sulawesi). Together, these regions were responsible for almost 75 percent of national rice production in 2012 (BPS 2020b).

TABLE 7.7
Income distribution: Consumers

	Income – rural areas			Income – urban areas		
	Low	Middle	High	Low	Middle	High
North Sumatra	17.5	60.5	22.0	9.7	55.0	35.3
South Sumatra	27.5	61.3	88.8	9.3	48.4	42.3
Lampung	36.3	53.4	10.3	8.4	53.3	38.3
West Sumatra	15.7	58.3	26.0	5.0	45.4	49.6
East Java	51.0	44.5	4.5	25.1	52.8	22.1
West Java	39.5	53.8	6.7	18.9	46.6	34.5
Central Java	47.6	45.2	7.1	27.0	51.6	21.4
South Sulawesi	37.2	48.3	14.5	15.3	50.1	34.6
Indonesia	35.5	52.3	12.2	15.9	47.1	37.0

Note: Expenditure/capita/month: low: Rp 1,206,268; medium: Rp 1,206,268–2,982,711; high > Rp 2,982,711.
Source: 2012 SUSENAS survey (BPS 2019).

Table 7.7 shows that almost 80 percent of rural consumers are in the low- and middle-income classes, with some provinces having about 50 percent of consumers in the low-income class (East Java and Central Java). Urban areas have a lower incidence of relative poverty than rural areas. For the latter, only two provinces (North and West Sumatra) have less than one-fourth of their total consumers fall into the low-income category.

The income distribution for producers is shown in Table 7.8.[15] The relative poverty incidence among rural producers is lower than that among rural consumers. In all the rice-growing provinces, less than 40 percent of producers are in the low-income group. However, almost three-quarters of them are in the middle- and high-income groups. This implies that policies to increase rice prices will benefit these wealthier groups more than the low-income group.[16]

To illustrate this point, I assume a scenario in which the price of rice increases by 5 percent, from 10,000 rupiah to 10,500 rupiah per kilogram. According to BPS, the average per capita rice consumption in 2012 was 1.675 kilograms per week (BPS 2020c). This translates to around 19.6 million tons of rice for one year. I distribute this amount proportionally to the provinces and income groups listed in the tables above and compute the new consumption in each province and each income group as if prices had risen by 5 percent. Assuming income elasticity of 0.7, 0.4, and 0.2 for low,

TABLE 7.8
Income distribution: Producers

	Income – rural areas		
	Low	Middle	High
North Sumatra	8.79	68.76	22.45
South Sumatra	25.11	58.81	16.08
Lampung	23.71	67.09	9.20
West Sumatra	11.78	54.24	33.98
East Java	33.25	58.91	7.84
West Java	35.70	55.70	8.60
Central Java	39.57	49.80	10.63
South Sulawesi	28.87	56.33	14.80
Indonesia	27.24	58.08	14.68

Note: Expenditure/capita/month: low: Rp 1,206,268; medium: Rp 1,206,268–
2,982,711; high > Rp 2,982,711.
Source: 2012 SUSENAS survey (BPS 2019).

middle, and high income, respectively, and compensated demand elasticity of −0.14 (Naylor 1991), I am able to calculate the change in consumer surplus. The results are shown in Table 7.9.[17] The changes in consumer surplus are all negative, indicating a loss to consumers. In general, rural consumers suffer more than their counterparts in the city. Across income groups, the distribution varies, but for Indonesia as a whole, low-income consumers in rural areas suffer the most (note that not all provinces are listed in the table).

Similarly, we can calculate the change in producers' surplus. I assume the price of paddy (rice with the husk removed) is 60 percent that of rice (Natawidjaja and Rum 2013) and that the elasticity of supply with respect to the price of rice is 0.2 (Naylor 1991; Warr 2005). The total production of paddy in 2012 was 69 million tons. After distributing this amount to the respective provinces and income groups, I calculate the new production levels if the price of paddy increased by 5 percent from 6,000 rupiah to 6,300 rupiah per kilogram. Finally, I compute the change in producers' surplus. Table 7.10 shows the results.[18] In contrast to the case of consumers, the changes in producers' surplus are all positive, indicating welfare gains. Note, however, that many of the producers' gains in the listed provinces are higher than those of average Indonesian producers as a whole. As mentioned above, these provinces are the main paddy growers, accounting for 75 percent of Indonesian production. The lower average numbers for Indonesia suggest that in other provinces the producers' gain might be small, if not negative.

To get a more comprehensive picture, we can combine the information from Tables 7.9 and 7.10, giving us the net transfers of income among

TABLE 7.9

Price increase effect: Change in consumers' surplus (million rupiah)

	Income – rural areas			Income – urban areas		
	Low	Middle	High	Low	Middle	High
North Sumatra	−47,104	−163,588	−59,619	−25,349	−144,178	−92,676
South Sumatra	−51,556	−115,272	−167,322	−11,069	−57,737	−50,537
Lampung	−72,271	−106,677	−20,618	−9,336	−59,411	−42,752
West Sumatra	−23,126	−86,179	−38,507	−2,551	−23,232	−25,414
East Java	−262,415	−229,677	−23,266	−247,554	−522,200	−218,859
West Java	−379,637	−519,198	−64,783	−153,097	−378,642	−280,806
Central Java	−324,421	−309,077	−48,628	−167,282	−320,519	−133,143
South Sulawesi	−76,660	−99,908	−30,050	−18,326	−60,119	−41,582
Indonesia	−1,732,461	−2,560,992	−598,548	−770,856	−2,289,370	−1,801,166

Note: Expenditure/capita/month: low: Rp 1,206,268; medium: Rp 1,206,268–2,982,711; high > Rp 2,982,711.
Source: 2012 SUSENAS survey (BPS 2019).

TABLE 7.10

Price increase effect: Change in producers' surplus (million rupiah)

	Income – rural areas		
	Low	Middle	High
North Sumatra	98,495	770,263	251,469
South Sumatra	281,335	658,765	180,127
Lampung	265,612	751,596	103,019
West Sumatra	131,924	607,639	380,665
East Java	372,496	659,934	87,798
West Java	399,963	623,956	96,308
Central Java	443,287	557,902	119,039
South Sulawesi	323,442	631,007	165,779
Indonesia	305,194	650,607	164,426

Note: Expenditure/capita/month: low: Rp 1,206,268; medium: Rp 1,206,268–2,982,711; high > Rp 2,982,711.
Source: 2012 SUSENAS survey (BPS 2019).

TABLE 7.11
Price increase effect: Net transfer of income (million rupiah)

	Income – rural areas			Income – urban areas		
	Low	Middle	High	Low	Middle	High
North Sumatra	51,391	606,675	191,851	−25,349	−144,178	−92,676
South Sumatra	229,779	543,493	12,804	−11,069	−57,737	−50,537
Lampung	193,341	644,920	82,402	−9,336	−59,411	−42,752
West Sumatra	108,798	521,460	342,158	−2,551	−23,232	−25,414
East Java	110,081	430,257	64,532	−247,554	−522,200	−218,859
West Java	20,326	104,758	31,526	−153,097	−378,642	−280,806
Central Java	118,866	248,825	70,411	−167,282	−320,519	−133,143
South Sulawesi	246,782	531,099	135,728	−18,326	−60,119	−41,582
Indonesia	−1,427,267	−1,910,384	−434,121	−770,856	−2,289,370	−1,801,166

Note: Expenditure/capita/month: low: Rp 1,206,268; medium: Rp 1,206,268–2,982,711; high > Rp 2,982,711.
Source: 2012 SUSENAS survey (BPS 2019).

consumers and producers, as depicted in Table 7.11. The table shows that a 5 percent increase in the price of rice would transfer income from urban areas to rural areas in rice-growing provinces. But the large negative effect for Indonesia as a whole implies transfer from small rice producers to the major producers, as well. Finally, there is also a significant transfer of income from low-income groups to high-income groups. To conclude, a price increase will hurt all consumers and will benefit producers only in the major rice-growing regions. The largest losses will be borne by low-income consumers, especially in rural areas.

We can express the consumer loss in terms of per capita loss as a percentage of annual per capita expenditures, as shown in Table 7.12. The table reveals that the impact of a price increase on consumer welfare is regressive. That is, the losses are greatest in the lower-income groups, ranging from 0.9 to 1.4 percent of per capita expenditure per year in rural areas, and from 0.8 to 1.1 percent in urban areas. By contrast, in the high-income groups the losses never reach 4.0 percent of total expenditure. Note that though these absolute magnitudes appear small, a 65 percent price increase (as experienced at the end of 2012) will imply a loss of 15 to 18 percent of total expenditure – which is not negligible, especially for the poor.

Nevertheless, as Warr (2005) points out, the (net) producer/(net) consumer framework is a partial equilibrium analysis. It assumes that a price increase would affect net consumers of rice solely by adding to the cost of

TABLE 7.12

Per capita consumer losses as % of annual per capita expenditures

	Income – rural areas			Income – urban areas		
	Low	Middle	High	Low	Middle	High
North Sumatra	1.01	0.72	0.39	1.01	0.68	0.32
South Sumatra	1.14	0.75	0.29	1.06	0.74	0.26
Lampung	1.14	0.77	0.32	1.02	0.68	0.28
West Sumatra	0.94	0.72	0.35	0.79	0.60	0.28
East Java	1.14	0.84	0.30	1.00	0.67	0.26
West Java	1.12	0.73	0.34	1.13	0.67	0.23
Central Java	1.20	0.89	0.29	1.09	0.70	0.27
South Sulawesi	1.40	0.81	0.34	0.99	0.73	0.26
Indonesia	1.16	0.76	0.34	1.05	0.65	0.24

Note: Expenditure/capita/month: low: Rp 1,206,268; medium: Rp 1,206,268–2,982,711; high > Rp 2,982,711.
Source: 2012 SUSENAS survey (BPS 2019).

putting food on the table. But it is possible that when the price rises, rice farmers see a chance to augment their profits and decide to expand. As a result, the demand for labour intensifies. This labour is likely to include the landless people who are the net consumers of rice. So, a possible income effect might counterbalance the price effect for this group, which the partial equilibrium approach misses.

Such a caveat motivated Warr (2005) to run general equilibrium simulations, taking into account the effect of rice import restrictions on both household expenditures and household incomes. Again, his study confirms that higher rice prices are bad for the poor. In particular, his results show that the rice import ban of 2004 raised the domestic rice price equivalent to a 125 percent tariff. Furthermore, such a price increase leads to a worsening in the incidence of poverty; and among farmers, only the richest benefit.

Why Protectionism Persists

If opposition to globalization does not always work in favour of the poor – in fact, as in the case of rice, trade restrictions actually harm them – why does protectionism persist? This section discusses four factors affecting the supply of and demand for protection.

First, exchange rate movements. When the rupiah depreciates, Indonesia's exports become less expensive and its imports more expensive. This works as an indirect protection for tradable domestic products. In contrast, when the real exchange rate appreciates, imports become more economically attractive, and sectors such as agriculture often ask for other forms of protection to compensate for their diminished ability to compete. In the mid-1980s, trade liberalization was bold and comprehensive. In part, this was made possible as the rupiah was depreciating against the dollar, suppressing the demand for protection (Basri and Hill 2004). Later, as the real effective exchange rate appreciated in 2005–06, the protection for rice (as measured by nominal rate of protection) increased (Patunru and Basri 2011).

Second, the problem of collective action. Using the Olsonian framework (Olson 1965), we can argue that those who are most damaged by protectionism often lack the ability to fight against it because their large numbers render the cost of organizing and coordinating their efforts prohibitively high. On the other hand, if a smaller group demands protection, it can afford the coordination costs and can hence lobby policy makers more effectively. This framework is useful in explaining the case of rice protection in Indonesia. Whereas the facts show that trade restriction hurts the poor and consumers at large, a small elite of richer farmers and traders has the ear of policy makers. In the rice industry, the call for protection often comes from farmers associations such as HKTI (Indonesian Farmers Association) and FSPI (Indonesian Farmers Union Federation). Arguably, the key members of these groups are not the poorest peasants but richer farmers and traders.[19]

Third, competitiveness. Domestic industries ask for protection mostly because they cannot keep up with foreign competitors. For Indonesia, this is most evident in the manufacturing sector. As in many other countries, the sector came under threat when China joined the WTO in 2001 (Patunru and Rahardja 2015). Immediately, industries such as shoemaking, garment production, and other light manufacturing that tend to be labour intensive had to struggle against the more competitive labour costs in China. In the case of rice growing, Indonesia as a net importer can compete with net exporters such as Thailand and Vietnam only at significantly high costs directed to irrigation, fertilizers, and pesticides.[20]

Fourth, the so-called IMF stigma. During the time of the Asian Financial Crisis, the IMF had come to Indonesia's aid. Nonetheless, it had earned a bad name among many Indonesians because its assistance came with a very long list of conditions, forcing the country to liberalize trade as part of a reform package. In addition, the media, which tend to be nationalist leaning, portrayed the process and the resulting agreement as a "new colonization," provoking the anger of many Indonesians.[21] Later studies did find that some of the IMF recommendations were misplaced. Again, the media were quick to use these studies as extra ammunition against the international financial institutions. This stigma still persists today and has even expanded beyond anti-IMF sentiments to a dislike of foreign investment in general. Populist commentators portray increased investment and financing by international institutions as signs that Indonesia is bowing down to foreigners and not heeding the wishes of its own people.

Finally, some additional factors might explain the animosity against trade in the case of rice. First is Indonesia's ambition for self-sufficiency. The belief that the country can and should achieve this goal is nowhere stronger than in the rice sector itself. Whereas per capita consumption of rice has steadily decreased, the general public still perceives rice as the most important staple food in Indonesia. Accordingly, the argument goes, it is only right to protect rice production. The strongest variant of this view even romanticizes rice and rice paddies. Two top Indonesian agricultural economists support protecting the rice sector because, after all, "for a very long time painters have portrayed golden paddy trees or rice harvesting in the fields against a background of mountains, clear water irrigation, or green dikes" (Amang and Sawit 2001, 76).

The second factor is a potentially thin world market. The proponents of protectionism argue that as Indonesia is one of the largest consumers of rice, it is vulnerable to the ups and downs of the world market (see Amang and Sawit 2001). The fact that the world market for rice was thin – it traded a limited amount of rice – was used to demonstrate this vulnerability. In particular, protectionists contend that if Indonesia were not self-sufficient, it would be prone to food insecurity as the world supply might not be enough. Although the world market is no longer thin (Dawe 2008), this view persists.

Conclusion and Implications

Ultimately, restricting Indonesia's access to globalization may hinder the eradication of its poverty. Obstructing the trade in rice has contributed to a significant increase in the domestic price, far above the international price. Given this, net rice consumers, including poor people, lose. Nonetheless, protectionism persists, despite the fact that it benefits only a small group of wealthy people to the detriment of a larger group that includes the poorest segments of society.

The present study shows the need for raising public awareness of the distributional consequences of protection. Disseminating data, evidence, and facts in ways that are easy to understand will play a key role here. Furthermore, there is a need to reduce the exposure of the poor to the negative impact of rice protection. This can be done by providing more leeway and power to consumer groups to channel the aspirations of net rice consumers.

As for policy, it is important to note that removing non-tariff barriers (such as the import ban) might be politically difficult. However, gradual reform is possible. This could take the form of a price intervention band, a pre-determined set of upper and lower international price levels beyond which the government can intervene to dampen price shock for producers and consumers.

Notes

Acknowledgments: I thank Neil McCulloch for historical data on rice and Wisnu Adiwijoyo for excellent research assistance. I am grateful for feedback from a workshop at the University of Indonesia. This research was funded by SSHRC.

1 President Joko Widodo also urged the Indonesian people to work hard to stop food imports. *Jakarta Post,* October 30, 2016.
2 This is despite a 20 percent import tariff that was briefly imposed in 1999, followed by a specific import tariff of 430 rupiah per kilogram that spanned January 2000 to December 2006.
3 In 2006, for example, Vice President Jusuf Kalla announced that the "desirable stable price range" was 4,200 to 4,300 rupiah per kilogram (Basri and Patunru 2006). This corresponds to around 6,000 rupiah at 2012 rupiah purchasing power.
4 The government cut its fuel subsidy in October 2005, a move that considerably raised the price of fuel and prompted many observers to link the cut with the upsurge in inflation and hence the increase in the poverty rate (which jumped to 17.8 percent in March 2006, after a steady decline for eight years). However, as Basri and Patunru (2006) and Patunru and Basri (2011) note, the heightened fuel prices accounted for only a small amount of the spike in the poverty rate, 77 percent of which was due to the rising price of rice.
5 As shown in Figure 7.4, the world price of rice topped the domestic price in 1998, an episode that was associated with the Asian Financial Crisis. According to Fane and Warr (2008), this massive depreciation of the rupiah was largely responsible for the discrepancy.
6 The prices were stable at the time when Bulog did not have to obtain parliamentary approval to import rice (McCulloch 2008).
7 The headcount ratio in 2013 was 11.37 percent, associated with 28.5 million people.
8 A study by the University of Indonesia finds that Indonesia's total logistical costs are around 14 percent of production costs, whereas in a best-practice situation – that of Japan – they are only 5 percent. The study attributes the difference (9 percent) to the poor logistics of Indonesia (Patunru and Tarsidin 2012).

9   The mid-1980s self-sufficiency in rice earned President Suharto an enthusiastic round of applause at a 1985 Food and Agriculture Organization of the United Nations meeting in Rome.

10 According to a Reuters article of 2016, some officials accused the Ministry of Agriculture of inflating the rice harvest data to present a rosy picture and hence keep farm subsidies flowing. Had the data been accurate, Indonesia would be awash with domestic rice supplies. On the contrary, it needed to import rice from Thailand and Vietnam. For details, see Munthe and Taylor (2016).

11 Note that the SUSENAS-based consumption data used by BPS tend to be underestimated due to, among other things, the exclusion of out-of-home consumption (Rosner and McCulloch 2008; World Bank 1992).

12 The 17 percent adjustment factor was estimated by BPS. It is the average difference in production data between household survey estimates and the eyeball estimates of agricultural field agents, as reported in their monthly observations of harvested areas.

13 McCulloch (2008) uses the 2004 SUSENAS, which has a special module on rice production. This allows him to calculate the amount of rice produced by each rice-farming household and to compare it with the consumption data. The 2012 SUSENAS, which I employed in the present study, lacks detailed information on rice production, so I classify those who work in food agriculture as net producers and those who consume rice as total net consumers. My approach is similar to that taken by Naylor (1991). Non-rice-growing net consumers are those who consume rice solely by purchasing it, whereas rice-growing net consumers are those who consume rice from their own production.

14 Following Naylor (1991), I inferred the percentage of producers in each income group by the quantity of own-produced rice in each group as a proportion of total own-produced rice for all groups combined.

15 The table concentrates solely on the distribution in rural areas because the number of rice producers in urban centres is negligible.

16 This is similar to the situation in 1984, as found by Naylor (1991), although her figures show more regressive transfers.

17 I calculate the own-price elasticity of demand for rice using the Slutsky equation – that is, own-price elasticity of demand is the compensated demand elasticity minus the income elasticity of rice multiplied by the budget share spent on rice. The budget share was calculated from the 2012 SUSENAS survey.

18 I assume that paddy is grown only in the countryside; hence, Table 7.10 does not include urban areas.

19 For example, General Prabowo Subianto, who ran against Joko Widodo for the presidency, is a former head of the HKTI.

20 In 2013, the rice paddy yield in Indonesia was 5.15 tons per hectare, whereas that in Thailand was 3.15 tons per hectare. However, Indonesia used 204,000 tons of NPK fertilizer, and Thailand used 168,000 tons. In addition, more than 65 percent of Indonesia's rice-growing area is irrigated, compared to 20 percent in Thailand (Dawe 2008).

21 For example, the photograph of President Suharto signing the agreement while IMF Director Michel Camdessus hovered over him, arms folded, was widely reproduced.

In the eyes of the Indonesian media, it was an image of Western dominance and Eastern submission.

References

Amang, Beddu, and Mohamad Husein Sawit. 2001. *Kebijakan Beras dan Pangan Nasional – Pelajaran dari Orde Baru dan Orde Reformasi* [National rice and food policy – Lessons from the new order and the Reformasi order]. Bogor: IPB Press.

Basri, Muhamad Chatib. 2010. "Navigating beyond Recovery: Growth Strategy for an Archipelagic Country: The Case of Indonesia." Paper presented at the workshop "Strategies for Asia's Sustainable Growth beyond the Global Crisis: Infrastructure, the Environment, and the Finance," Jakarta, February 15.

Basri, Muhamad Chatib, and Hall Hill. 2004. "Ideas, Interests, and Oil Prices: The Political Economy of Trade Reform during Soeharto's Indonesia." *World Economy* 27, 5: 633–55.

Basri, Muhamad Chatib, and Arianto A. Patunru. 2006. "Survey of Recent Developments." *Bulletin of Indonesian Economic Studies* 42, 3: 295–319.

–. 2008. "Indonesia's Supply Constraints." Background paper commissioned by the OECD for preparation of *Indonesia Economic Assessment: OECD Economic Surveys,* July 17.

–. 2012. "How to Keep Trade Policy Open: The Case of Indonesia." *Bulletin of Indonesian Economic Studies* 48, 2: 191–208.

Basri, Muhamad Chatib, and Sjamsu Rahardja. 2010. "The Indonesian Economy amidst the Global Crisis: Good Policy and Good Luck." *ASEAN Economic Bulletin* 27, 1: 77–97.

Badan Pusat Statistik (BPS) (Statistics Indonesia). 2018. *SKGB 2018: Konversi Gabah ke Beras.* Jakarta: Badan Pusat Statistik.

–. 2019. *Survei Sosial Ekonomi Nasional (Susenas), 2012 Core.* https://doi.org/10.7910/DVN/12TVW1, Harvard Dataverse, V1.

–. 2020a. *Rata-rata Harga Beras di Tingkat Perdagangan Besar/Grosir Indonesia (Rupiah/Kg).* https://www.bps.go.id/linkTableDinamis/view/id/963.

–. 2020b. *Production of Paddy by Province (Tonne), 1993–2015.* https://www.bps.go.id/linkTableDinamis/view/id/865.

–. 2020c. *Weekly Average Consumption of Several Food Items Commodity per Capita, 2007–2019.* https://www.bps.go.id/statictable/2014/09/08/950/rata-rata-konsumsi-per-kapita-seminggu-beberapa-macam-bahan-makanan-penting-2007-2018.html.

Bulog (Badan Urusan Logistik or Indonesian Bureau of Logistics). Accessed October 1, 2015. http://www.bulog.co.id/data_statistik_beras_eceran.php.

Burton, James. "The Top 10 Largest Rice Importers in the World." *World Atlas,* August 28, 2019. https://www.worldatlas.com/articles/the-largest-rice-importers-in-the-world.html.

Childs, Nathan, and James Kiawu. 2009. "Factors behind the Rise in Global Rice Prices in 2008." Report from the Economic Research Service, United States Department of Agriculture.

Daniel, Wahyu. 2015. "Pengimpor dan Pengeskpor Beras, Ini Datanya." *DetikFinance* 24 July. https://finance.detik.com/berita-ekonomi-bisnis/d-2974119/ri-pengimpor -dan-pengekspor-beras-ini-datanya

Dawe, David. 2008. "Can Indonesia Trust the World Rice Market?" *Bulletin of Indonesian Economic Studies* 44, 1: 115–32.

Fane, George, and Peter Warr. 2008. "Agricultural Protection in Indonesia." *Bulletin of Indonesian Economic Studies* 44, 1: 133–50.

Fung, Kwok-Chiu, Hitomi Iizaka, and Alan Siu. 2010. "United States, Japanese, and Korean FDI and Intra-East Asian Trade." *Asian Economic Papers* 9: 129–54.

Grenville, Stephen. 2004. "The IMF and the Indonesian Crisis." *Bulletin of Indonesian Economic Studies* 40, 1: 77–94.

Ito, Takatoshi. 2012. "Can Asia Overcome the IMF Stigma?" *American Economic Review: Papers & Proceedings* 102, 3: 198–202.

McCulloch, Neil. 2008. "Rice Prices and Poverty in Indonesia." *Bulletin of Indonesian Economic Studies* 44, 1: 45–63.

McCulloch, Neil, and C. Peter Timmer. 2008. "Rice Policy in Indonesia: A Special Issue." *Bulletin of Indonesian Economic Studies* 44, 1: 33–44.

Munthe, Bernadette Christina, and Michael Taylor. 2016. "RPT-Cooked in Indonesia: Phoney Rice Data Threatens Food Supply." Reuters, January 24. http://www. reuters.com/article/indonesia-rice-data-idUSL3N15701Q.

Natawidjaja, Ronnie, and Irlan A. Rum. 2013. "Food Security Situation and Policy in Indonesia." Paper presented at the 2013 Food Security Regional Dialogue, Medan, Indonesia, 26–27 June. https://blogs.adelaide.edu.au/global-food/2013/07/05/ 2013-food-security-regional-dialogue-medan-meeting-food-security-goals- with-good-policy.

Naylor, Rosamond. 1991. "Equity Effects and Rice Strategies." In *Rice Policy in Indonesia,* ed. Scott Pearson, Walter Falcon, Paul Heytens, Eric Monke, and Rosamond Naylor, 138–61. Ithaca, NY: Cornell University Press.

Nehru, Vikram. 2013. "Survey of Recent Developments." *Bulletin of Indonesian Economic Studies* 49, 2: 139–66.

Olson, Mancur. 1965. *The Logic of Collective Action.* Cambridge, MA: Harvard University Press.

Patunru, Arianto A., and Muhamad Chatib Basri. 2011. "The Political Economy of Rice and Fuel Pricing in Indonesia." In *Poverty, Food, and Global Recession in Southeast Asia: Is the Crisis Over for the Poor?* ed. A. Ananta and R. Barichello, 203–28. Singapore: Institute of Southeast-Asian Studies.

Patunru, Arianto A., and Sjamsu Rahardja. 2015. *Trade Protectionism in Indonesia: Bad Times and Bad Policy.* Sydney: Lowy Institute for International Policy. https://www.lowyinstitute.org/publications/trade-protectionism-indonesia-bad -times-and-bad-policy.

Patunru, Arianto A., and Tarsidin. 2012. "Recent Indonesian Economic Development and the Urgent Need to Remove Growth Obstacles." *Asian Economic Papers* 11, 3: 57–77.

Patunru, Arianto A., and Erna Zetha. 2010. "Indonesia's Savior: Fiscal, Monetary, Trade, or Luck?" *Public Policy Review* 6, 4: 721–40.

Rosner, L. Peter, and Neil McCulloch. 2008. "A Note on Rice Production, Consumption and Import Data in Indonesia." *Bulletin of Indonesian Economic Studies* 44, 1: 81–91.

Ruslan, Kadir. 2019. "Improving Indonesia's Food Statistics through the Area Sampling Frame Method." *CIPS Discussion Paper* 7, July. Jakarta: Center for Indonesian Policy Studies. https://www.cips-indonesia.org/area-sampling-frame-method

Warr, Peter. 2005. "Food Policy and Poverty in Indonesia: A General Equilibrium Analysis." *Australian Journal of Agricultural and Resource Economics* 49: 429–51.

World Bank. 1992. *Indonesia: Agricultural Transformation – Challenges and Opportunities, Main Report.* Washington, DC: World Bank Group. https://documents.worldbank.org/en/publication/documents-reports/documentdetail/445841468260136983/main-report.

–. 2006. *Making the New Indonesia Work for the Poor.* Washington, DC: World Bank Group. https://documents.worldbank.org/en/publication/documents-reports/documentdetail/213351468049853220/making-the-new-indonesia-work-for-the-poor.

–. 2015. *Indonesia Economic Quarterly: High Expectations.* Washington, DC: World Bank Group. https://documents.worldbank.org/en/publication/documents-reports/documentdetail/450781467992486719/indonesia-economic-quarterly-high-expectations.

8

Coffee Eco-Certification

New Challenges for Farmers' Welfare

BUSTANUL ARIFIN

One result of increased trade is the development of sub-markets for coffee with specific characteristics. Examples include organic cultivation and production using ecologically sustainable methods, or what is known as eco-certification. Eco-certification schemes have emerged from growing concerns over global environmental governance and efforts to democratize markets by increasing the role of civil society in production and trade-related activities. In practice, however, they serve as new vehicles of corporate control over global food production, trade, and consumption. Eco-certification generally connects consumers and businesses in the developed countries of the global North with producers and small farmers in developing countries of the global South.

It is expected that eco-certification promotes the sustainable production of agricultural commodities and simultaneously serves business and development interests. Eco-certification is widely expected to promote the sustainable production of agricultural commodities while simultaneously serving business and development interests. This change in global commodity chains will particularly influence the export potential of a developing country's agricultural economy and hence the welfare of its farmers. For suppliers in developing countries, global standards are becoming de facto market requirements. In the face of this trend, the Southern actors in business, civil society, and government need to redefine their positions, moving away from traditional, possibly non-sustainable coffee-farming practices, to better alternatives and improved processing and post-harvest activities. The supply chain of export commodities needs to change to reflect the structure of commodity value chains.

Ninety percent of Indonesian coffee is produced by smallholders who farm one or two hectares and who have limited access to technology, market information, and financial schemes. Coffee is grown at higher elevations, requiring an agro-ecosystem of sufficient shade trees and mixed gardens, sometimes at forest margins. The ideal is agro-forestry – a system in which trees and crops are integrated – rather than the monocropping that is now seen as non-sustainable. Unsustainable farming can cause soil erosion and other forms of natural resource degradation. For smallholders, coffee farming simply does not pay enough to support a decent standard of living, even in rural areas, so these smallholder farmers are also trapped in poverty. Neither the farm-gate price nor productivity are high enough to achieve economies of scale in coffee production systems, which would improve livelihoods and regional development in general. The farm-gate price is very much dependent on the global price of coffee, as the majority of Indonesian coffee is exported to the world market, especially to Northern countries. The welfare of the farmers is also determined by the structure of global value chains and the environmental governance of markets, given the recent advent of eco-certification.

Coffee-producing regions in Indonesia have a long history of changing land use patterns, from uninterrupted forest cover, to land clearance, to intensive farming, and ultimately to community-based forestry management (van Noordwijk et al. 2002) through a complex negotiation support system. Coffee agro-forestry systems are also associated with the development of institutional arrangements in which growers are rewarded for farming in an environmentally friendly manner; the shade, timber, and multi-purpose tree species (MPTS) that are part of agro-forestry also contribute to poverty alleviation by providing farmers with additional income.

The coffee economy is also a sector with several (competing) global certifying entities, some of which have a partnership structure. Eco-certification generally requires the establishment of farmers' organizations and locally adopted codes of conduct. However, many of these standards do not guarantee that direct benefits, particularly price premiums, will reach farm labourers or local communities. The social and economic effects of eco-certification in agricultural commodity chains are still widely debated. Proponents argue that eco-certification might be a sensible solution, based on the notion of shared responsibilities to address commodity-related development challenges that contribute to pro-poor growth and encourage sustainable economies (Springer-Heinze 2007; Van Tulder and Fortanier 2009). Critics cite the unproven track record of eco-certification and claim that such global initiatives represent neoliberal discourses and new vehicles of corporate control over global food production, trade, and consumption (Raynolds, Murray, and Heller 2007; Raynolds, 2009; Fuchs, Kalfagianni, and Havinga 2011).

Differing eco-certification schemes tend to compete with each other for market share, prominence, and legitimacy, adding to the confusion (Bartley 2007). Competition among standards has occurred in the global coffee sector (Muradian and Pelupessy 2005; Raynolds, Murray, and Heller 2007;), impeding the emergence of functional links across standards. In other sectors, competition and cooperation across standards exist simultaneously (Riisgaard 2009). The mounting importance of eco-certification and the need for traceability are driving structural change in supply chains, resulting in the increased upstream penetration of exporters into coffee-producing areas.

Exporters are now developing business models whereby they train farmers in Good Agricultural Practices (GAP) and their variations depending on the objectives and characteristics of specific certification schemes. Generally, coffee exporters, including some large-scale global players, have been working more closely with local collectors and middlemen in rural areas. In addition, they have created new networks with local coffee stakeholders, farmers' groups, and/or cooperatives, and have established up-country buying stations. They have provided financial schemes and various forms of agricultural credit to sever the link between growers and local traders, who have traditionally offered loans as a means of leveraging supply. This, coupled with the cost of certification, constitutes a considerable investment, especially because the farmers are not obliged to sell their product to these exporters and are at liberty to sell it on the local roast-and-grind market if they choose.

This chapter evaluates the new globalizing elements of the coffee trade to determine their effects on market structures, farm income, and rural poverty in Indonesia. The cases of eco-certification of Robusta coffee in Lampung and Arabica coffee in Aceh and South Sulawesi are used as a model for analyzing the dynamics of the global initiatives at the field level.

Coffee Eco-Certification in Indonesia

Certification schemes in the coffee sector emerged during the early 1990s in conjunction with rising concerns about the environment and developed rapidly in this century. Sustainability perspectives and the long-term impact of coffee farming on natural ecosystems and the social-economic dimensions of livelihoods have been discussed by academics, government, the private sector, and civil society or non-governmental organizations (Glasbergen 2011, 2013; Bitzer and Glasbergen 2015; Ibnu et al. 2015). As the new development paradigms tend to seek alternatives to the distortionary effects of direct state intervention in commodity supply chains, these certification schemes are argued by some authors to democratize markets by increasing the role of civil society in regulating production and trade-related activities (Neilson, 2008; Fuchs, Kalfagianni, and Havinga, 2011). On the other hand, standards and certification institutions could serve simply as new vehicles of corporate control over global food production, trade, and consumption (Ponte, 2004; Arifin 2010).

Raynolds, Murray, and Heller (2007) also suggest that for the most part, sustainability standards in the coffee industry spring from voluntary initiatives, involving collective formulation by some stakeholders, outside the framework of government organization. These groups share common interests, such as raising consumer awareness of public health issues, fertilizer and pesticide contamination, the virtues of organic farming, and the need to protect endangered species, biodiversity, and the natural environment. The initial involvement of stakeholders was simply based on individual interests, before expanding into a more strategic agenda, including those of civil society groups, farmers' organizations, and trade unions. Given the growing demand for products that meet new standards, and the broad expansion of markets and competition, it has become increasingly necessary to ensure that sustainability standards are credible.

A number of works attempt to synthesize the major global initiatives in the coffee sector that deal with sustainability standards and environmental governance (for example, see Ponte 2004; Giovannucci and Ponte 2005; Muradian and Pelupessy 2005; Raynolds, Murray, and Heller 2007). At least four general categories of guidelines present the rules: first-party, second-party, third-party, and fourth-party "voluntary" regulatory systems. "First party" generally refers to the "Starbucks Coffee Sourcing Guidelines," which set standards for good social and environmental performance (Starbucks Coffee, 2002). Later, these guidelines evolved into Coffee and Farmer Equity (CAFÉ) Practices, which is part of the Starbucks preferred supplier program. However, third parties are responsible for monitoring compliance with the CAFÉ Practices standards and the costs of compliance itself, costs that must be paid by farmers. In return, farmers are supposed to obtain reasonable price premiums.

An example of a second-party regulatory system is the Sustainable Agriculture Information Platform, in which specific commodity guidelines govern sustainable agriculture along the food chain. Again, a third party would monitor adherence to these guidelines.

As its name suggests, third-party certification involves the private sector or NGOs in setting the guidelines and monitoring sustainability standards in the coffee industry. At least four major third-party certifications are currently operating in the coffee sector around the globe: Utz Kapeh, Organic, Fairtrade, and Rainforest Alliance. All have similar missions and objectives to improve socio-economic and environmental conditions involved in coffee production and trade. Utz Kapeh originated with Guatemalan coffee producers and the Dutch coffee company Ahold, later becoming an independent Guatemalan-Dutch NGO. Utz Kapeh developed a set of standards for third-party coffee certification, formally equivalent to the EurepGAP, a certification system for the sourcing of fruits and vegetables led by European retailers (Giovannucci and Ponte 2005).

Finally, fourth-party certification refers to the initiatives by the multistakeholder voluntary scheme and usually known as the Common Code for the Coffee Community (4C).The 4C initiative is led by the German Development Cooperation Agency and the German Coffee Association, where the steering committee consists of major stakeholders in the coffee industry. The 4C codes emphasize social and ethical principles, such as paying minimum wages, avoiding child labour, allowing trade union membership, and complying with international environmental standards on pesticide and groundwater contamination. Monitoring and auditing are conducted by third-party organizations, and the costs of this certification are to be covered by the growers. A comprehensive review of such models of eco-certification and their relationship to the development of the coffee value chain system can be found in Arifin (2010).

Empirical evidence on whether these standards have achieved their stated objectives is still inconclusive, although some suggest that coffee farmers receive both direct and indirect benefits from sustainability standards (Giovanucci and Ponte 2005). Similarly, how these standards have affected biodiversity is not yet clear, although there is speculation that they have become the necessary conditions to preserve local biodiversity in coffee-producing regions. In general, little is known about the activities of eco-certification in producing countries and what they achieve with regard to the beneficiaries whom they intend to serve (Blowfield 2007; Lund-Thomsen 2008). So far, most research has concentrated on the effects of

Fairtrade certification and organic standards. Some studies discovered a positive impact on producer organizations and the welfare of smallholder farmers (Bacon et al. 2008), but others found only small direct income and production effects (Ruben and Fort 2012; Barham et al. 2011; Beuchelt and Zeller 2011). For other certification schemes, the effects on producers do not appear clear-cut either (Ruben and Zuniga 2011; Kolk 2011; Jena, Stellmacher, and Grote 2015).

The most significant benefit of these sustainability standards is probably their potential to strengthen social capital and to improve community-cooperative governance structures in the producing regions as they generally require the establishment of farmers' organizations and locally adopted codes of conduct. Empirical evidence regarding the impact of eco-certification on the welfare of coffee farmers often seems contradictory (Beuchelt and Zeller 2011), misleading (Chiputwa, Spielman, and Qaim 2015), or inconsistent in terms of the positive effects (Ibnu et al. 2015). In Indonesia, in addition to these global eco-certification schemes, voluntary and private certification initiatives are developing, launched by local schemes (such as Inofice certification) and government schemes (such as ISCoffee).

Although Indonesia is the fourth-largest coffee exporter in the world and the second-largest exporter of Robusta, eco-certified coffee is relatively scarce in the country. Wahyudi and Jati (2012) suggest that about 25 percent of its exported Robusta is eco-certified, whereas 75 percent of its Arabica falls into this category. The Indonesian Standard Coffee certificate (ISCoffee) was initiated by the Ministry of Agriculture in 2013 and is implemented by the government (Ibnu at al. 2015). In the future, the government may require that all Indonesian coffee producers are certified according to this standard. The creation of ISCoffee was triggered not only by the existence of global certification schemes, but also by the increase in domestic coffee consumption and emerging export markets, particularly those in Africa and Asia. About 56 percent of exported Indonesian coffee targeted these new markets, and the government hoped to attach a "national identity" for sales to these markets in the form of local (or national) certification (Ibnu, Offermans, and Glarbergen 2019).

The following cases of eco-certification in three major coffee-producing provinces – Lampung, Aceh, and South Sulawesi – provide a novel description of the dynamics and development of sub-markets for Indonesia's coffee supply chain.

First, the port of Panjang in Lampung exports more coffee than any other in Indonesia, pooling beans grown across the provinces of South Sumatra,

Bengkulu, and Lampung. These provinces largely produce Robusta coffee, which is dry-processed and sold into both the domestic and world market. Because its quality is poor, it sells at a discount to world prices, so its trade operates on tight margins in a highly competitive market. Nestlé runs an instant coffee factory in Lampung, and a number of international trading companies maintain a presence near Panjang. Green bean exports from Lampung expanded from 42,000 tons in 1975 to 270,000 tons in 2010 and have been associated with a gradual loss of natural forest cover across southern Sumatra. The majority of coffee farmers in Lampung are smallholders, working two hectares or less (Arifin et al. 2008).

Buyers of smallholder coffee include exporters, roasting companies, and local factories, through the distribution systems outlined previously. Major exporters in Lampung include Aman Jaya Perdana, Indocafco, Andira Indonesia, Antara Saudara, and Indera Brothers, which absorb nearly 70 percent of total coffee production in the province. Major roasting companies include Indocafco and Nestlé, which have recently been active in promoting the sustainability standards of the global value chain. Theoretically, competition among these buyers increases price transparency and creates a market structure in which the supplier sets the price, resulting in a price premium for farmers. However, smallholders do not have the luxury of choosing the buyer with whom they do business. Instead, the market tends not to work in their favour, because buyers can unilaterally set the farm-gate price in rural areas.

Second, the Gayo highlands of Aceh produce high-quality Arabica coffee for the international specialty industry, with large buyers such as Starbucks absorbing much of it (an estimated thirty thousand tons annually). Arabica is wet-processed and frequently bought and processed by large mills located at source, with direct links into the international market. Beans are exported from Belawan in Medan at a significant premium above international market prices. Since the 1990s, various certification schemes such as Organic, Fairtrade, CAFÉ Practices, and Rainforest Alliance have made inroads into the industry, such that it is now characterized by increased product traceability, a supply chain audit culture, and the presence of various cooperatives to comply with buyer-driven demands. The Gayo highlands nestle against the Leuser Ecosystem Area, a protected zone managed by the Special Province of Aceh, with a conservation status equivalent to a national park. With solid premiums available for this coffee, and with recent high commodity prices, new coffee farms continue to be established within the Leuser Ecosystem Area.

Third, about four thousand tons of high-quality Arabica are exported from the port of Makassar, sourced from the various highland areas of South Sulawesi, the most important of which is the Tana Toraja District. This premium coffee is sold into specialty markets, with particularly strong demand from Japan and the United States. Coffee farming in Toraja is deeply embedded within traditional cultural systems and is characterized by low inputs, low productivity, and relatively stagnant production despite the strong demand. Torajan coffee is one of the highest-grown in the world, with plots as high as two thousand metres above sea level, which imparts its unique taste. There are currently no formal conservation areas in Toraja, though coffee farms are situated adjacent to, and within, land classified by the government as protected forest in the upper catchments. Although the boundaries of this forest have been regularly renegotiated in recent years to take into consideration the realities of local land use practices and to satisfy local political and economic priorities, far less land clearing occurs here than in Aceh and Lampung.

The current policy on coffee industry development is to improve quality for both export and domestic consumption and to encourage downstream industries and industry clusters. With respect to upstream farming, policies promote the application of Good Agricultural Practices (GAP), sustainable production by planting shade trees, the use of organic fertilizer and resorting to chemical alternatives only when necessary, and the employment of agro-forestry for plots inside the protection forest. Downstream from the farms, domestic processing is encouraged, as the industry is currently made up of many small players, along with four established brands taking up about 46 percent of market share. The local industry is trying to strengthen the domestic market by conducting intensive advertising campaigns and publicizing the health benefits of drinking coffee. Coffee is expected to become increasingly available due to the rapid expansion of retailers and manufacturers' attempts to improve its distribution through foodservice outlets (Kumar 2011).

Coffee Production and Poverty Incidence

Indonesia is the fourth-largest coffee producer, after Brazil, Vietnam, and Colombia, but the second-largest producer of Robusta after Vietnam. Its output in 2017 was estimated at 668,700 tons, a slight increase from the 639,400 tons of 2016 (BPS 2018). About 418,000 tons (62.5 percent) were shipped to the global market in 2017, generating export earnings of US$1.2 billion, a significant increase from those of 2016. This upward trend is due

TABLE 8.1
Coffee production, Indonesia, 2009–17 (thousands of tons)

Province	2009	2011	2013	2015	2017	% Share*
Aceh	50.20	52.30	48.28	47.40	68.50	8.07
North Sumatra	54.40	56.80	58.35	60.20	66.00	8.96
West Sumatra	33.30	30.80	32.56	34.10	21.80	4.62
South Sumatra	131.60	127.40	139.80	110.40	120.90	19.05
Bengkulu	55.40	53.80	56.45	56.60	59.60	8.53
Lampung	145.20	144.50	127.10	110.30	116.30	19.47
West Java	11.60	14.30	16.65	17.50	16.80	2.33
Central Java	16.40	10.50	20.31	22.80	18.70	2.68
East Java	54.00	37.40	56.99	66.00	65.00	8.45
Bali	14.90	10.40	17.33	17.30	17.30	2.33
East Nusa Tenggara	20.60	19.90	21.80	21.30	22.10	3.20
South Sulawesi	32.00	30.60	30.24	30.50	29.80	4.64
Others	62.90	49.90	50.04	45.00	45.90	7.67
Indonesia	682.50	638.60	675.90	639.40	668.70	100.00

Note: * Average annual share to national production.
Source: BPS (2018).

to the increase in both export volume and coffee prices in the world market, most probably because global coffee consumption has expanded. The rise in prices and export earnings provides opportunities for smallholder farmers to increase their production and productivity, with the result that their farm income could grow as well.

Indonesia devotes about 1.25 million hectares to coffee farming, spread from the western-most province of Aceh on the island of Sumatra, to Java, Sulawesi, Bali, Nusa Tenggara, and the eastern province of Papua. Lampung, South Sumatra, and East Java concentrate on growing Robusta, whereas the highlands of Aceh, North Sumatra, South Sulawesi, and Bali are suitable for Arabica. Lampung and South Sumatra account for the largest share of production (about 40 percent, combined), followed by North Sumatra, East Java, and Aceh (Table 8.1). Java produces about 13.6 percent, whereas South Sulawesi contributes approximately 4.6 percent. Only 5.5 percent comes from Bali and East Nusa Tenggara, but the specialty nature of Bali Kintamani and Flores Bajawa could provide a new opportunity in the high-quality market.

About 85 percent of Indonesian coffee is Robusta, mostly from Lampung, South Sumatra, and Bengkulu, whereas the remaining 15 percent is Arabica, grown in the highland areas of Gayo in Aceh, Sidikalang in North Sumatra, Toraja in South Sulawesi, the Kintamani Highlands of Bali, and the Bajawa region of Flores island in East Nusa Tenggara. Except for a number of large government-owned estates in East Java, coffee is nearly 90 percent grown by smallholders. On average, these farmers cultivate a plot ranging from 0.5 to 2.0 hectares in an isolated region with poor access to social services. Their low income keeps them slightly above or slightly below the poverty line. It is no coincidence that the coffee-producing regions experience a high occurrence of poverty, as rural poverty is quite considerable in Indonesia.

Actually, the incidence of poverty declined to about 26 million people in March 2018, or 9.82 percent of the total population. Sixty-one percent of poor people live in the countryside, and the remaining 39 percent reside in urban areas. Of the 15.8 million people who live in rural poverty, most are farmers, including coffee farmers, and landless labourers. The wide disparity between rural and urban areas in the incidence of poverty suggests that if agricultural development is not supported by rural development, the positive impact on the economy will be limited. Due to the tiny size of their landholdings, rice farmers and those who grow other food crops generally experience higher levels of poverty than coffee farmers and those who produce other cash crops, although the variation in any given province is attributable to many factors other than landholding size. Access to markets, financial institutions, technology, and other resources is an important determinant of rural poverty in the agricultural sector. The poverty figures for Java, the food production centre of Indonesia, are quite high: 7.5 percent in West Java, 11.0 percent in East Java, 11.3 percent in Central Java, and 12.1 percent in Yogyakarta. The vulnerability of poor people to increases in the cost of food is demonstrated by the fact that 76.7 percent of their household expenditures goes to food, while the remaining 23.3 percent is split between housing, electricity, education, and transportation. In rural areas, the price of rice has contributed to 21.0 percent of the poverty line, whereas this figure is 26.8 percent in urban centres. Because of the inelastic demand for rice, poor households generally suffer the most when its price increases, including the coffee farmers who must buy it from the market just to support their subsistence living.

All coffee-producing regions in Indonesia, except Bali, have a very high poverty incidence by province, although the rate declined significantly from 2009 to 2017 (see Table 8.2). Even though coffee farming performs an important social security function in these producing regions, the market structure and value chain system from local to global markets do not provide

TABLE 8.2
Poverty incidence in coffee-producing regions, 2007–17 (total and %)

Province	2009	2011	2013	2015	2017
Aceh	892.86	894.81	848.21	855.50	851.21
	21.80	*19.57*	*17.66*	*17.10*	*16.41*
North Sumatra	1,499.68	1,481.31	1,364.98	1,485.91	1,390.22
	11.51	*11.33*	*10.23*	*10.66*	*9.75*
West Sumatra	429.25	442.09	394.05	364.57	362.25
	9.54	*9.04*	*7.85*	*7.01*	*6.81*
South Sumatra	1,167.87	1,074.81	1,109.29	1,129.08	1,086.84
	16.28	*14.24*	*14.15*	*14.01*	*13.15*
Bengkulu	324.13	303.60	323.88	328.45	309.80
	18.59	*17.50*	*18.05*	*17.52*	*16.02*
Lampung	1,558.28	1,298.71	1,148.67	1,132.09	1,107.74
	20.22	*16.93*	*14.63*	*13.94*	*13.37*
West Java	4,983.57	4,648.63	4,339.85	4,460.68	3,971.43
	11.96	*10.65*	*9.57*	*9.55*	*8.27*
Central Java	5,725.69	5,107.36	4,718.91	4,541.41	4,324.11
	17.72	*15.76*	*14.50*	*13.45*	*12.62*
East Java	6,022.59	5,356.21	4,818.54	4,782.55	4,511.14
	16.68	*14.23*	*12.64*	*12.31*	*11.49*
Bali	788.07	690.49	669.48	696.54	687.44
	5.13	*4.20*	*4.22*	*5.00*	*4.20*
East Nusa Tenggara	1,050.95	894.77	816.65	813.09	770.95
	23.31	*21.23*	*20.14*	*22.60*	*21.62*
South Selatan	489.84	423.63	402.76	413.98	420.57
	12.31	*10.29*	*9.93*	*9.76*	*9.43*
Others	7,424.45	7,247.83	7,211.39	7,406.22	7,249.75
	23.35	*24.66*	*25.98*	*26.44*	*27.17*
Indonesia	32,529.97	30,018.93	28,310.27	28,553.18	27,177.11
	14.15	*12.49*	*11.42*	*11.18*	*10.38*

Source: BPS (2018).

enough economic returns at the farm-gate price in rural areas. The provinces of Aceh and East Nusa Tenggara are among two coffee-producing regions that have poverty rates of 16.4 percent and 21.6 percent, respectively. Two provinces in Sumatra have the highest share of coffee production yet they also have high rates of poverty. The poverty rate in Lampung in 2017 was 13.4 percent and that in South Sumatra was 13.2 percent. In short, though coffee farming has contributed significantly to export earnings for Indonesia, it has unfortunately not been able to remove coffee farmers and rural people generally from the poverty trap.

At least three main factors help explain why the coffee economy might not directly lift farmers and other rural people out of poverty. First, farmers typically do not apply Good Agricultural Practices, and most use minimum inputs, let alone chemical fertilizers and pesticides. As a result, the average yield of coffee in Indonesia is about 533 kilograms per hectare, far below the potential 3.0 tons per hectare for Robusta and 1.5 tons per hectare for Arabica. The advanced age of the trees (most are over twenty-five), as well as pests and disease, such as the coffee berry borer, also play a role in the low yield. Although most inputs are available, such as quality seedlings and fertilizers, farmers cannot afford them.

Second, traditional processing yields low-quality coffee that does not fetch a premium price, so the average farm-gate price remains low. Harvesting systems vary by region but are mostly rudimentary. Farmers pick the beans, then pulp, ferment, wash, and dry them. Most Indonesian coffee is dry-processed, to produce what is known as "naturals." Once the processing is complete, farmers sell the green beans at the farm gate, usually to traders. The traders forward them to larger traders and exporters to be shipped to the world market. Robusta is considered mainstream "fair-average quality," and overseas roasters blend it with coffee from other sources. Despite the significant increase in the world price of coffee, the considerable length of the supply chain means that farmers have a very small chance of being paid appropriately for their crop. In addition, the price-transmission elasticity of coffee and agricultural commodities in general is normally very small, far less than 0.5. This would reflect a higher change in the price of coffee in the world and retailers' markets but will constitute only a small change in the farm-gate price.

Third, as mentioned above, eco-certification has not been shown to greatly improve the welfare of farmers. It might encourage more sustainable land management practices and may have affected the price structure of coffee, although the trend remains unclear. Traders who sell organic coffee could receive a slightly higher price premium than for non-certified coffee because of the direct link with the international specialty market. However, switching to organic production may not necessarily improve the profits of farmers. Ensuring the integrity of the certified organic brand necessitates the use of thorough traceability systems, the high cost of which is borne by farmers. Even if farmers did receive a higher farm-gate price for their organic coffee, there is no guarantee that it would offset their cost of applying organic standards.

The Coffee Supply Chain

The supply chain for coffee is actually quite straightforward and not as complicated as commonly thought: passing from production centres to traders and/or roasters, the beans are then shipped throughout the world from the major ports of Surabaya and Singapore. As mentioned earlier, Robusta is grown mostly in southern Sumatra (Lampung, South Sumatra, and some in Bengkulu). Arabica, which has become increasingly popular during the last decade, is grown in Aceh, Sulawesi, Bali, and Flores. Robusta coffee from Lampung and South Sumatra is marketed to broker traders and/or exporters by local collector traders in the production centres. Large-scale traders and exporters are mostly located in the city of Bandar Lampung, the capital of Lampung Province. Nevertheless, exporters do not always sell the coffee to international markets, especially if its quality does not meet the minimum standard of export requirements. Instead, coffee from Sumberjaya and Tanggamus is sold to local processing companies that produce a typical fine ground coffee with a strong flavour under locally well-known brands such as Bola Dunia, Sinar Dunia, Sinar Baru, Siger, and Jempol. This coffee differs markedly from the instant coffee produced by modern processing companies under the Nescafé, Indocafe, and Torabika brands.

The trade flows of Indonesian coffee have been mostly concentrated in two main shipping ports, Surabaya (East Java) and Singapore. The coffee produced in Sumatra (from places like Aceh, North Sumatra, and Lampung), the island farthest to the west, mostly goes to Singapore and is then shipped to various export destinations. The production from Sulawesi, Bali, East Java, and Nusa Tenggara, that is, islands in the eastern part of Indonesia, goes to Surabaya, from where it too is transported to Singapore before being exported to other parts of the world, such as the US, Europe, and Japan. One should note that roasters in Europe usually perform a re-export activity of roast and ground coffee to other export destinations in the world, including Australia.

FIGURE 8.1
Export Destinations of Arabica (Panel a) and Robusta Coffee (Panel b)

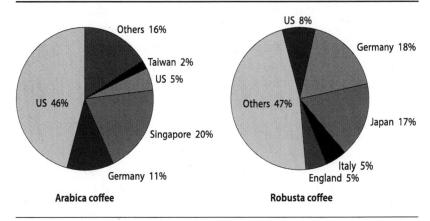

Source: International Coffee Organization, 2018.

Coffee plays a crucial role in the foreign-reserve earnings of Indonesia: in 2017, the country exported 418,000 tons at a value of about US$1.2 billion. Such exports have expanded considerably since 2001, though both volume and values have fluctuated in recent years (BPS 2018). In 2015, Indonesia exported about 502,000 tons of green coffee, generating earnings of approximately US$1.2 billion. When the world coffee price dropped in 2016, the export value of that year was just over US$1.0 billion, even though the volume was 415,000 tons, similar to that of 2017. To some extent, Indonesia also exported roasted coffee, but this declined significantly during the last decade because Indonesia diversified to export in extract forms of coffee. Recently, the demand for coffee has risen in Indonesia's domestic market, especially for higher-quality beans rather than the average and low-quality alternatives, which may affect the destination of exports. Changes in urban lifestyles, growing coffee retail centres, and modern cafes in big cities throughout the country will increase coffee consumption in the near future.

The bulk of Indonesian coffee is exported to the United States. For example, Americans consumed 74.9 thousand tons of Indonesian coffee in 2017, or about 22 percent share of total export (BPS 2018). Most of it is Arabica from the Aceh highlands and other places in northern Sumatra, as the economic relations between traders in Aceh and their American partners have improved a great deal during the last decade. European countries, such as Germany (7 percent share), Italy (7 percent), and Russia (6 percent), are the second-largest destination for Indonesian coffee. European markets are well known for preferring Robusta, and Indonesian coffee is normally the main component in blends. Japan and Malaysia are the largest Asian destinations for Indonesian coffee, having a share of 7 percent each. Other destinations include Egypt, China, Algeria, Belgium, Georgia, Morocco, Thailand, Singapore, India, and Canada.

In many coffee-producing regions of Indonesia, farmers generally have close relationships with collector traders, who often provide loans during the production process without resorting to the complicated procedures of money lending. In return, farmers must sell their crop to the collector traders, leaving smallholders with limited choices among market channels, hence creating an interlocking trading system at the village level. Interestingly, collector traders encourage farmers to harvest their coffee in bulk (*asalan*) quality, which means that traders, rather than farmers, accumulate the added value. This marked degree of dependence on collector traders puts farmers in a very weak bargaining position. As a result, the coffee market structure at the village level is biased toward collector traders whose monopsonistic behaviour distorts price transparency. The reasons why farmers tend to rely on collector traders are not restricted solely to economic choices, but also relate to the level of trust, socio-psychological factors, and other social capital of the coffee economy. These deserve a detailed investigation of the micro institutional setting and careful analysis of the roles of nonstate regulation, both of which lie beyond the scope of this chapter.

Similarly, at the level of global trade, coffee exporters are fighting to obtain a fairer price from their partners overseas. Exporters that are directly affiliated with global roasting companies usually do not have such complicated procedures in business negotiations. In the growing global value chain initiatives, buyers tend to establish subsidiary trading and roasting companies in the coffee-producing regions of developing countries. These companies generally take care of certification costs in order to capture the interests of smallholder farmers who cannot afford such extra costs. The history of coffee zone systems in Indonesia – and of other important commodities such as tea, sugar, and fertilizer – is a tale of distortions in agribusiness-related commodities. Consequently, the small farmers are also trapped in an interlocking supply chain system due to the influence of powerful global buyers up to the farm level in rural areas.

Figure 8.2 portrays the generalized coffee supply chain system in Indonesia. Small variations might occur, depending on the social capital and psychological relationship between farmers, farmers' groups, collector traders, and large-scale exporters. Due to the large number of smallholder producers,

FIGURE 8.2

Generalized supply chains distribution systems of Lampung coffee

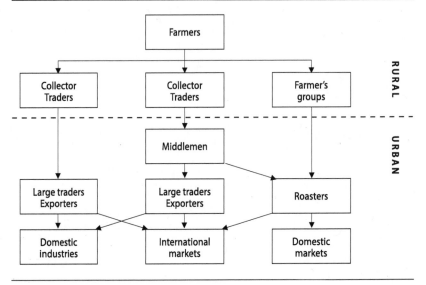

Note: see Arifin, 2010

local collectors are required to bulk up the coffee for local traders or middlemen. Local traders may dry, clean, and grade the beans before selling them to local roasters or local and international green bean processors and exporters. The processors and exporters will carry out further processing, including cleaning, drying, milling, polishing, and sorting before shipping. In some instances, they will also roast and grind beans that are too poor for export, preparing them for the domestic market.

Since 2014, some multinational corporations have assigned field managers to secure the bean sources directly at the producing regions. These individuals interact with farmers' groups, providing advice and technical assistance to increase coffee quality and developing economic and social networks of farmers and broader international markets. Such investment in social capital would provide important economic returns in the near future, developing networks for benefits to the industry.

The Government of Indonesia is also promoting higher value-added products for the export market, such as good-quality green beans and further processed products. It strongly encourages the production of specialty coffee, as the market share for this exotic item is high and is growing in consequence in the international market. Also included in this category is the well-known *luwak* coffee, named after the Asian palm civet, a small mammal. Coffee cherries are fed to the civet, fermented in its digestive tract, and collected after it excretes them. Due to growing demand from export markets and domestic retailers, some plantations are currently domesticating the animal to increase the luwak yield. Nevertheless, this coffee has been condemned by animal welfare groups. A team of scientists has recently developed enzymes whose fermentation function resembles that of the palm civet and will thus be able to produce high-quality coffee (Udi et al. 2013).

Coffee associations and stakeholders are also promoting specialty coffee for specific international buyers and some niche markets. The large price differences between Arabica and Robusta in the international market would encourage Arabica development at the farm level. A small amount of Arabica is roasted in Indonesia for the domestic specialty market, which has expanded rapidly, in parallel with the growth of the middle class, especially in urban areas. Generally, Indonesia's specialty coffee has a full body and relatively low acidity. Each region is known for its typical cupping profile, though a great deal of diversity occurs within regions. The Association of Indonesian Coffee Exporters and Industry (AEKI) has been promoting the specialty coffee from all over the country, such as Mandailing, Gayo, Lintong, Toraja/Kalosi, Bali-Kintamani, Bajawa-Flores, and Washed Java, among others. The list could become longer in the near future as the industry has the potential to develop higher coffee quality, as long as the incentive systems are as favourable as possible.

The characteristics of Indonesian specialty coffee can be summarized as follows: Mandailing and Gayo have intense flavour, with cocoa, earthy, and tobacco notes. Lintong and Toraja/Kalosi have good sweetness and body, with warm spice notes. Washed Java, both Robusta and Arabica, has good, heavy body, with a lasting finish and herbaceous notes. Lampung and Semendo have heavy body and intense flavour, with a lasting finish. Flores Bajawa, both Robusta and Arabica, has heavy body, sweetness, chocolate, and tobacco notes. Bali Kintamani is normally sweeter than other Indonesian examples, with nut and citrus notes. Finally, Papua specialty coffee, the most recent development, has heavy body, chocolate, earth, and spicy finish.

Moreover, the government and the coffee industry are developing geographical indications (GI) for Indonesian coffees, to protect the marketing rights and business practices in the international market. So far, the GI for Kintamani coffee (Bali) and Gayo (Aceh) have been priority issues as the government is serious about protecting the uniqueness of specialty coffees in the international market. However, sustainability issues are very important for the future and must be carefully examined, particularly since Arabica grows best in highland areas where protected forests and national parks are usually located. Sooner or later, more GIs will be issued as the market shifts toward coffee whose specific origins shape its flavour, rather than the cheap, bulk, and instant alternatives. Given that the private sector is aggressively accelerating its investment in product development, marketing, and communication, the coffee economy of the future will rely on more advanced principles of competitiveness, market penetration, and new market destinations.

Eco-Certification, Market Integration, and Farmers' Welfare

This section is drawn from three studies conducted during the last two decades. The first, from 2008, concentrates on incentives for smallholders (Arifin et al. 2008). The second, of 2010–11, looks at the role of global initiatives in the efficiency of Indonesia's coffee value chain (Arifin and Ogtasari 2011). And the third, of 2013–14, determines how agro-forestry and certification are of benefit to farmers (Arifin et al. 2014). The first and third studies involve fieldwork, largely conducted in Lampung, Aceh, and South Sulawesi, whereas the second study is mostly an econometric exercise using secondary data collected from various sources.

The studies suggest that the threat posed by a conversion from shaded to non-shaded growing systems galvanized the promotion of environmentally friendly production through value-chain mechanisms that provided economic incentives for farmers. The key aim of these schemes was for coffee growers to be rewarded for their roles in habitat conservation and sustainable resource management. In Indonesia, the first certified organic coffee came from the Takengon region of Central Aceh and was sold in 1992 as Gayo Mountain Organic Coffee. It was followed by other environmentally friendly certifications in Aceh, Lampung, East Java, and Sulawesi (Arifin et al. 2008).

Developing and implementing a rigorous chain of custody controls in coffee destined for the global market is an important step in excluding unsustainably grown coffee from the supply chain. However, the environmental issues involved in coffee production are complex, and problems cannot be blamed entirely on "illegal producers," who were the target of a negative World Wildlife Fund campaign concerning the diminishing numbers of tigers in Lampung's Bukit Barisan Selatan National Park, as reported in studies by WWF-Indonesia (WWF 2007). In fact, labelling such coffee as "illegal" may simply create problems for smallholders, whose farm-gate prices are considerably less than the market premium in the international market. Similarly, campaigns to shame the importers who buy beans without asking too many questions about their origin could hinder efforts to improve the asymmetrical structures of the coffee market. Buyers who represent importer trading companies in the international market might not make a point of recording and publishing the details for the origin of smallholder-grown coffee. What has been emphasized so far is more about the quality of coffee, especially the water content that can influence the flavour of Indonesian Robusta.

The certification of smallholders generally requires the formation of cooperatives to facilitate product traceability. This process is most advanced in Aceh, where up to twenty farmer cooperatives now supply certified organic coffee to the market. However, the past experience of Indonesian farmers with agricultural cooperatives has not been good, and there are indications that the most recent spate of international market-driven co-op formation is no different in this respect. Cooperatives have not generally secured the support of Indonesian farmers because they cannot provide the services supplied by traditional market mechanisms, such as hassle-free access to credit and simple marketing procedures, and because of the perceived high costs of dealing with rent-seeking cooperative structures. Our fieldwork in Aceh suggests that farmers persist in selling their beans to first-stage collectors who then supply them to "cooperatives," many of which were established by large exporters and may consist of many thousands of members (Arifin et al. 2008). The six cooperatives that we visited in Aceh employed an average of five full-time staff members. These cooperatives also offer services for their members, including credit provision, input supply or technical advice, and a price premium for organic coffee.

We found a similar case in South Sulawesi, where the process of organic certification is under way in the Toraja area. Premium-quality Arabica is grown in the Tana Toraja District, as high as two thousand metres in altitude, exported from Makassar, and sold into specialty markets, with particularly strong demand from Japan and the United States. Smallholder farmers in Toraja generally use few inputs, which could potentially put their crop in the organic category because of the low amount of chemical fertilizer and pesticides applied. Consequently, the productivity of Torajan coffee remains low, despite the growing international demand for it. However, in the near future, as in Aceh and Lampung, the protected forests of South Sulawesi might face serious encroachment from the expansion of coffee plantations (Arifin et al. 2008).

Our fieldwork showed that as a result of certification, Aceh coffee frequently fetched a slightly higher price than Toraja coffee at the point of export. However, farm-gate prices in Aceh were substantially lower than those in Toraja. We did come across one farmer in Aceh who claimed a price premium, but even he received only the same amount as the average Torajan farmer. Our stakeholder interviews indicated that the primary cause of this price difference was additional supply chain transaction costs associated with traceability requirements, the insertion of cooperatives within an existing supply chain offering few value-added services, and the price of the audit process itself. Price premiums are clearly not finding their way to farmers in Aceh and are therefore unlikely to change farmer incentive structures (Arifin et al. 2008).

We undertook an econometric study to examine the impact of eco-certification on the efficiency of coffee value chains by identifying the structure of the Indonesian coffee market (Arifin and Ogtasari, 2011). Using the price changes of Lampung-grown Robusta, we mapped the structure of the market and its degree of horizontal integration. Additional analysis was also employed regarding the direction of causality in the Lampung and Indonesian markets. Last, we used annual data series to analyze the effects of coffee prices at the global level, particularly in London and New York, on the price of Robusta in Indonesia. This corresponds to the impact of the global market on Indonesia's domestic market. A series of econometric analyses using vector autoregression and the Vector Error Correction Model were employed to examine the spatial integration of coffee markets in Indonesia and the vertical integration of global coffee markets with that of Indonesia.

Our results show that the coffee value chain in Indonesia is both spatially and vertically integrated, where the regional and national prices of coffee affect each other, implying a long-term mutually dependent relationship among Indonesian markets. About 60 percent of the variation in the Robusta price in Lampung explains the variation in the price in Indonesia, showing the market leadership of the province in Robusta. As explained previously, coffee shipped from Panjang in Lampung for the global market also includes coffee from South Sumatra and Bengkulu.

The variance of coffee prices in New York and London also had an impact on farm-gate prices in Indonesia, albeit very small. For every 1.0 percent increase in the New York and London prices, the Indonesian farm-gate price changed by 0.013 percent and 0.028 percent, respectively. The price transmission elasticity of the global price to the domestic price is 0.48, implying that the value chain system of the Indonesian market is not in an ideal or efficient condition. The study suggests policy reforms to improve coffee quality, especially that grown by smallholders. This requires better connecting farmers to the world market, dissemination of market information, the development and operation of quality assurance systems, and other related empowerment programs for stakeholders in the value chains (Arifin and Ogtasari 2011).

Finally, our 2013 field study in Lampung examined the roles of agro-forestry and certification in improving the economic and environmental benefits of coffee farmers (Arifin et al. 2014). We conducted face-to-face interviews with 408 households who used an agro-forestry system and were eco-certified by Rainforest Alliance and 4C. A cluster random sampling method was employed during data collection, focusing on two subdistricts of Pulau Panggung and Air Naningan in the Upper Sekampung Watershed, in the Tanggamus District. We also interviewed a control variable of farmers who did not pursue agro-forestry or who grew fewer than 100 shade or multi-purpose trees. The cut-off point for agro-forestry adopters versus non-adopters is actually based on the assumption that one multi-purpose tree can provide shade for four coffee trees, thus stimulating photosynthesis and nutrient absorption from the soil.

Study participants farmed 1.34 hectares per household, far below the ideal threshold to improve their livelihood and rural development in general. Those who adopted agro-forestry worked an average of about 1.42 hectares, a bit larger than that of non-adopters, which was 1.22 hectares. Agro-forestry requires extra space to accommodate the multi-purpose trees, as the protective forest canopy must maintain the supply of fresh water and other aspects of a healthy ecosystem.

In Upper Sekampung, about half of our study participants (202 households) were eco-certified, mostly via 4C (149 households, 36.5 percent) or Rainforest Alliance (53 households, 13 percent). The remaining half (206 households) were in the process of becoming certified. In terms of size, the farms of these smallholders did not vary greatly, averaging 1.35 hectares for 4C farmers, 1.20 hectares for Rainforest Alliance, and 1.35 for those who were transitioning to sustainability certification. Ninety-four percent of households owned the land, twenty-six of which rented it to farmers who lived in Sekampung or the city of Bandar Lampung.

On average, Upper Sekampung produced 386.6 kilograms of coffee per hectare, far below the national average of 533.0 kilograms, a discrepancy that is due mostly to traditional farming practices and simple processing techniques. Coffee was a profitable crop in the study sites, but ample opportunities could be explored to improve yield and quality to fulfill the increasing demand. The revenue-to-cost ratio of production was 2.72, indicating that every 1,000 rupiah expended on production costs could generate a revenue of 2,720 rupiah per hectare. Once the income gained from multi-purpose trees and other crops was included, the benefit-to-cost ratio of all farms in the study sites was 6.44, indicating that every 1,000 rupiah spent on farming activities could generate income of 6,440 rupiah per hectare.

However, Indonesia's coffee production system is not particularly efficient, as demonstrated by its very high labour costs: about 70.0 percent of total production costs of 2.3 million rupiah per hectare goes to labour, 37.22 percent of which is family labour and 32.44 percent is hired labour. By contrast, tradable inputs such as manure, other fertilizers, and pesticides account for about 21 percent of production costs. The high labour cost reflects the increasing wage rate in rural Indonesia, which could indicate that rural labour has started to move away from the agricultural sector, especially young people. The low yield of coffee production in Upper Sekampung and in Indonesia generally is mostly driven by the scanty application of modern inputs, which might diminish the quality of the crop. Interpreting the results of farm income analysis in terms of sustainable coffee production systems should be conducted with care. Coffee farming in Upper Sekampung might not be harmful to the environment, especially not in connection with soil and water contamination, as the use of chemical fertilizer is so low. However, the expansion of farming to forest margins could pose a threat, especially to protected forests and possibly to Bukit Barisan Selatan National Park, which is adjacent to coffee farms.

In this case, agro-forestry and eco-certification play important roles for sustainability in the fragile environment of the Upper Sekampung Watershed. Our income analysis showed that the benefit-to-cost ratio of the total farm for agro-forestry adopters was 6.92, significantly higher than the 5.76 ratio for farmers who did not apply agro-forestry. Every 1,000 rupiah spent in the farm could generate 6,920 rupiah for those who adopted agro-forestry and 5,760 rupiah for those who did not. Revenue from multi-purpose trees and other crops greatly contributed to the performance of the coffee-farming system in our study sites. Households that pursued agro-forestry received additional income, mostly from selling other agricultural products, such as local fruit and timber (Arifin et al. 2014).

In short, eco-certification schemes have somehow restructured coffee value chains, creating an awareness of the sustainability aspects of the production and processing of agricultural commodities and along value chains

(Neilson 2008; Arifin 2010). The demands of the private sector for better traceability, documentation, audits, and contractual relationships between the involved parties have increased considerably. Although these developments are positive, they create new costs for producers, the smaller of whom cannot afford to pay them on their own. Farmers who join a sustainability certification scheme do receive a price premium, compared to non-certified farmers (Ibnu et al. 2015), but they remain the most vulnerable and the weakest actors in the coffee value chain. They still face uncertainty about price fluctuations and market access, especially during times of global uncertainty. Market mechanisms, which have become the major driving force behind globalized private-sector certification schemes, clearly have some limitations, especially with the value chain approach and regarding quality standards and human safety.

The three case studies discussed above reveal that the new globalizing elements of environmental governance did not directly affect the livelihood of smallholder farmers in Indonesia and thus had not alleviated poverty in rural areas. This can be confirmed by comparing two ideal scenarios with the reality of coffee farming in Indonesia. First, eco-certification schemes require that farmers adapt to new social and environmental aspects of agricultural production. Their knowledge, attitudes, and technical capacities must improve, especially where Good Agricultural Practices (GAP), managerial skills, and membership in farmers' organizations are concerned. Once they attain this level, the quality and quantity of their crop will also rise, as will their access to global markets. In this scenario, the competitiveness of the farming system substantially increases, with the result that the income and welfare of farm households can improve significantly. Unfortunately, our three case studies suggest that, at best, this scenario applies only partially to Indonesia. Some farmers have obtained short-term training in agricultural practices, such as grafting techniques, pest management, and health protection from chemical pesticides. However, even this limited capacity building may not improve their welfare during the current implementation period of eco-certification.

Second, when consumers at the endpoint of the value chain willingly pay higher prices for coffee that is labelled as certified organic and ethically produced, farmers supposedly benefit. The additional price paid by consumers will trickle down to them through a market mechanism so that the coffee value chains could claim to assure an environmentally friendly and socially responsible production process. Our studies did not demonstrate that such was the case; the livelihood of smallholder farmers did not significantly improve by the small degree of market integration between global and local markets. The coffee market in Indonesia has shown more horizontal integration than vertical integration of global and local market, where Lampung coffee has served as a market leader. In this case, the value chain approach is probably too restricted to bring about sustainable change and improvements in the income of smallholders (Glasbergen 2018), which indicates that alternative strategies and additional sustainable pathways are needed.

However, there is hope for the future. Because eco-certification in Indonesia has a strong foundation in the agro-forestry system and community-based forestry management, farmers' organizations remain important mechanisms for empowerment in the agricultural sector. Coffee growers have become accustomed to the rules and regulations for natural resource conservation and to the direct economic benefits of shade trees and multipurpose trees in their farming system. Their organizations may not strictly replicate the structure of the formal cooperative but could nonetheless increase economies of scale and allow better price negotiation with large buyers, including international traders. Such improvements in social capital could be an important prerequisite among smallholder farmers, enabling them to take the opportunities to increase the quantity and quality of their product, from the application of Good Agricultural Practices, to negotiating better farm-gate prices, to employing new processing techniques to enhance the flavour of their beans.

Concluding Remarks: Improving the Certification Scheme

During the last several decades, eco-certified coffee has claimed an increasingly large share of global sales. Unfortunately, however, this trend has not had much impact on farm-gate prices for Indonesian beans, mostly because the price transmission elasticity of the global coffee price is very small. Nonetheless, eco-certification does have the potential to strengthen social capital and improve community cooperative governance in coffee-producing regions, as the partnerships generally require the establishment of farmers' organizations and the adherence to certain codes of conduct. Therefore, intermediaries such as individuals, start-up companies, civil society organizations, and others can play a crucial role in ensuring sustainability principles, thus providing links between sellers (smallholder farmers) and buyers (roasting companies, research institutes, civil society organizations, or international agencies). They could increase public awareness, serving as a clearinghouse for information, training, capacity building, negotiating, monitoring and evaluation, resolving conflicts, and absorbing transaction costs. They have also helped to generate collective action in linking smallholders with broader markets, providing support for weaker members of the community to better alleviate poverty or to ensure that the poor are not made worse off.

Improving the welfare of smallholders is a complex challenge by itself, as their economies of scale are quite limited. Policy reforms could be undertaken to upgrade the quantity and quality of Indonesian coffee, to ensure the viability of empowerment mechanisms, and to enhance social capital and other institutional arrangements, which could contribute to poverty alleviation in agriculture and rural areas. These measures include connecting coffee farmers to the world market, strengthening the competitiveness of the industry, and disseminating market information, quality assurance systems, and other related incentive systems in eco-certification.

References

Arifin, Bustanul. 2010. "Global Sustainability Regulation and Coffee Supply Chains in Lampung Province, Indonesia." *Asian Journal of Agriculture and Development* 7, 2: 67–90.

Arifin, Bustanul, Richard Geddes, Hanung Ismono, Jeffrey Neilson, and Bill Pritchard. 2008. *Farming at Indonesia's Forest Frontier: Understanding Incentives for Smallholders.* Policy Brief No. 6. Australia Indonesia Governance Research Partnership. Canberra: Crawford School of Economics and Government, Australian National University.

Arifin, Bustanul, and Harly I. Ogtasari. 2011. "The Roles of Global Coffee Initiatives for the Efficiency of Coffee Value Chain in Indonesia." Paper presented at the Seventh ASAE Conference, "Meeting the Challenges Facing Asian Agriculture and Agricultural Economics toward a Sustainable Future," Hanoi, October 13–15.

Arifin, Bustanul, Katsuya Tanaka, Ryohei Kada, and Hanung Ismono. 2014. "The Roles of Agroforestry System and Coffee Certificate in Improving Farmers' Economic and Environmental Benefits in Sumatra." Paper presented at Tropentag 2014 "Bridging the Gap between Increasing Knowledge and Decreasing Resources," Prague, September 17–19.

Bacon, Christopher M., Victor Ernesto-Méndez, María E.F. Gómez, D. Douglas Stuart, and Raúl D. Flores. 2008. "Are Sustainable Coffee Certifications Enough to Secure Farmer Livelihoods? The Millennium Development Goals and Nicaragua's Fair Trade Cooperatives." *Globalizations* 5, 2: 259–74.

Badan Pusat Statistik (BPS) (Statistics Indonesia). 2018. *Statistik Indonesia: Statistical Yearbook of Indonesia 2018.* Jakarta: BPS.

Barham, Bradford L., Mercedez Callenes, Seth Gitter, Jessa Lewis, and Jeremy Webber. 2011. "Fair Trade/Organic Coffee, Rural Livelihoods, and the 'Agrarian Question': Southern Mexican Coffee Families in Transition." *World Development* 39, 1: 134–45.

Bartley, Tim. 2007. "Institutional Emergence in an Era of Globalization: The Rise of Transnational Private Regulation of Labor and Environmental Conditions." *American Journal of Sociology* 113, 2: 297–351.

Beuchelt, Tina, and Manfred Zeller. 2011. "Profits and Poverty: Certification's Troubled Link for Nicaragua's Organic and Fairtrade Coffee Producers." *Ecological Economics* 70, 7: 1316–24.

Bitzer, Verena, and Pieter Glasbergen. 2015. "Business–NGO Partnerships in Global Value Chains: Part of the Solution or Part of the Problem of Sustainable Change?" *Current Opinion in Environmental Sustainability* 12: 35–40.

Blowfield, Michael. 2007. "Reasons to Be Cheerful? What We Know about CSR's Impact." *Third World Quarterly* 28, 4: 683–95.

Chiputwa, Brian, David J. Spielman, and Matin Qaim. 2015. "Food Standards, Certification, and Poverty among Coffee Farmers in Uganda." *World Development* 66: 400–12.

Fuchs, Doris, Agni Kalfagianni, and Tetty Havinga. 2011. "Actors in Private Food Governance: The Legitimacy of Retail Standards and Multistakeholder Initiatives with Civil Society Participation." *Agriculture and Human Values* 28: 353–67.

Giovannucci, Daniele, and Stefano Ponte. 2005. "Standards as New Form of Social Contract? Sustainability Initiatives in the Coffee Industry." *Food Policy* 30, 3: 284–301.

Glasbergen, Pieter. 2011. "Mechanisms of Private Meta-Governance: An Analysis of Global Private Governance for Sustainable Development." *International Journal of Strategic Business Alliances* 2, 3: 189–206.

–. 2013. "Legitimation of Certifying Partnerships in the Global Market Place." *Environmental Policy and Governance* 23, 6: 354–67.

–. 2018. "Smallholders Do Not Eat Certificates." *Ecological Economics* 147: 243–52.

Ibnu, Muhammad, Pieter Glasbergen, Astrid Offermans, and Bustanul Arifin. 2015. "Farmer Preferences for Coffee Certification: A Conjoint Analysis of the Indonesian Smallholders." *Journal of Agricultural Science* 7, 6: 20–35. http://dx.doi.org/10.5539/jas.v7n6p20.

Ibnu, Muhammad, Astrid Offermans, and Pieter Glarbergen. 2019. "Toward a More Sustainable Coffee Production: The Implementation Capacity of Indonesian Standard Coffee." *Pelita Perkebunan* 35, 3: 212–29.

International Coffee Organization (ICO). 2018. *Historical Data on the Global Coffee Trade.* London: International Coffee Organization (ICO). http://www.ico.org/new_historical.asp.

Jena, Pradyot Ranjan, Till Stellmacher, and Ulrike Grote. 2015. "Can Coffee Certification Schemes Increase Incomes of Smallholder Farmers? Evidence from Jinotega, Nicaragua." *Environment, Development, and Sustainability* 19: 45–66.

Kolk, Ans. 2011. "Mainstreaming Sustainable Coffee." *Sustainable Development* 21, 5: 324–37.

Kumar, Pawan. 2011. *Indonesia Food and Agribusiness Outlook: Leading the Southeast Asian Growth Story.* Utrecht: Rabobank International Food and Agribusiness Research Advisory.

Lund-Thomsen, Peter. 2008. "The Global Sourcing and Codes of Conduct Debate: Five Myths and Five Recommendations." *Development and Change* 39, 6: 1005–18. doi:10.1111/j.1467-7660.2008.00526.x.

Muradian, Roldan, and Wim Pelupessy. 2005. "Governing the Coffee Chain: The Role of Voluntary Regulatory Systems." *World Development* 33, 12: 2029–44.

Neilson, Jeffrey. 2008. "Global Private Regulation and Value-Chain Restructuring in Indonesian Smallholder Coffee Systems." *World Development* 36, 9: 1607–22.

Ponte, Stefano. 2004. *Standards and Sustainability in the Coffee Sector: A Global Value Chain Approach.* Winnipeg: International Institute for Sustainable Development.

Raynolds, Laura. 2009. "Mainstreaming Fair Trade Coffee: From Partnership to Traceability." *World Development* 37, 6: 1083–93.

Raynolds, Laura, Douglas Murray, and Andrew Heller. 2007. "Regulating Sustainability in the Coffee Sector: A Comparative Analysis of Third Party Environmental and Social Certification Initiatives." *Agriculture and Human Values* 24, 2: 147–63.

Riisgaard, L. 2009. "How the Market for Standards Shapes Competition in the Market for Goods: Sustainability Standards in the Cut Flower Industry." DIIS Working Paper 7. Copenhagen: Danish Institute for International Studies. http://hdl.handle.net/10419/44693.

Ruben, Ruerd, and Ricardo Fort. 2012. "The Impact of Fair Trade Certification for Coffee Farmers in Peru." *World Development* 40, 3: 570–82.

Ruben, Ruerd, and Guillermo Zuniga. 2011. "How Standards Compete: Comparative Impact of Coffee Certification Schemes in Northern Nicaragua." *Supply Chain Management International Journal* 16, 2: 98–109.

Springer-Heinze, Andreas. 2007. *ValueLinks Manual: The Methodology of Value Chain Promotion.* Eschborn, Germany: GTZ (Deutsche Gesselschaft fur Technische Zusammenarbeit) GmbH.

Starbucks Coffee. 2002. Corporate Social Responsibility: Annual Report. https://globalassets.starbucks.com/assets/1f4cecd10e464938a7e5cd82fcbcb5e2.pdf

Udi, Jumhawan, Sastia Prama Putri, Yusianto, Yusianto, Erly Marwani, Takeshi Bamba, and Eiichiro Fukusaki. 2013. "Selection of Discriminant Markers for Authentication of Asian Palm Civet Coffee (Kopi Luwak): A Metabolomics Approach." *Journal of Agricultural Food Chemistry* 61, 33: 7994–8001.

Van Noordwijk, Meine, S. Rahayu, Kurniatun Hairiah, Y. Wulan, A. Farida, and Bruno Verbist. 2002. "Carbon Stock Assessment for a Forest-to-Coffee Conversion Landscape in Sumber-Jaya (Lampung, Indonesia): From Allometric Equations to Land Use Change Analysis." *Science in China*, ser. C, 45: 75–86.

Van Tulder, Rob, and Fabienne Fortanier. 2009. "Business and Sustainable Development: From Passive Involvement to Active Partnerships." In *Doing Good or Doing Better: Development Policies in a Globalizing World,* ed. Monique Kremer, Peter van Lieshout, and Robert Went, 211–35. Amsterdam: Amsterdam University Press.

Wahyudi, Teguh, and Misnawi Jati. 2012. "Challenges of Sustainable Coffee Certification in Indonesia." Paper presented at "Economic, Social and Environmental

Impact of Certification on the Coffee Supply Chain," International Coffee Council 109th Session, London, September 25. http://www.ico.org/event_pdfs/seminar-certification/certification-iccri-paper.pdf.

WWF. 2007. "Gone in an Instant: How the Trade in Illegally Grown Coffee is Driving the Destruction of Rhino, Tiger and Elephant Habitat. Bukit Barisan Selatan National Park, Indonesia." https://www.wwf.or.jp/activities/lib/pdf_forest/deforestation/CoffeeReport_final.pdf.

9

Understanding Visual Disability as Development and Global Human Rights Issues

A Demographic Perspective in Indonesia

EVI NURVIDYA ARIFIN and ARIS ANANTA

The debate on the relationship between globalization and human rights is not new (Arfat 2013; Howard-Hassmann 2010; Mukherjee and Krieckhaus 2012; Tausch 2016). Globalization has been happening mainly because of the rising movement of goods, capital, services, and people, as well as the diffusion of ideas, norms, lifestyles, and technology. Various aspects of globalization have affected people's welfare, and it has been criticized as the cause of exploitation, human rights violations, and threats to human dignity.

On the other hand, globalization has improved the realization of human rights through opening market opportunities and increasing the diffusion of ideas. It can improve democracy and promote human rights. To benefit from globalization, Arfat (2013) recommends understanding the emerging social, economic, and environmental determinants of global issues. A human rights approach can then be applied to balance the forces of globalization with a just international legal framework. Howard-Hassmann (2010) proposes that social and political commitments are required to secure the positive impacts of globalization on the promotion of human rights.[1]

This chapter focuses on disability as a public health issue, where a global debate has arisen between development and human rights. Singh (2014) argues that economic globalization, through market mechanisms, has resulted in the exclusion of people with disabilities from the labour market everywhere in the world. Being gainfully employed is an important need for those with disabilities, but the labour market is not able to respond to it.

The World Health Organization (2012a) describes disability as being a result of interactions between personal factors and conditions of health and environment. It is not simply a biological construct. Neither is it merely a social construct.

Sen (2009) sees disability as part of capability deprivation. He shows that individuals with physical or mental disabilities are among the most neglected in society. They need a larger amount of resources to obtain the standard of living enjoyed by able-bodied persons. Moreover, they are often the poorest of the poor in terms of income, yet their need for income is greater than that of able-bodied individuals. Therefore, including disability in measuring poverty may significantly increase the poverty rate. The relevance of disability in overall development may have been underestimated.

Sen (2009) also argues that many disabilities can be prevented and cured. This potential is not limited to medical approaches; it also includes changing the physical and social environments, such as public infrastructure, which people live in. Preventions and cures also depend on the condition of other types of capability deprivation.

Donnelly (2013) elaborates that "rights" emerge as "suffering" comes and as "threats" to dignity arise. With this concept, visual disability is also an emerging human right issue, as society becomes increasingly modernized and digitized. The inability to see, and to read, can transform itself into a "threat" to the dignity of a human being. In a community with low education and technology, the need to see is great, but not as great as in a modern and digitized world. Visual ability is not simply an increasingly important issue in capability deprivation, but also in the wider issue of human dignity. Focusing on public health as a human rights issue, Mukherjee and Krieckhaus (2012) evaluate papers on the impact of globalization on global public health in thirty-two countries. They conclude that globalization has improved global public health. However, using the Konjunkturforschungsstelle index of globalization, Tausch (2016) refutes this finding and shows that globalization has worsened public health indicators.[2]

We contribute to the debate on development versus human rights by examining disability as both a global human rights issue and a development issue. We use both capability and human rights approaches. Vizard, Fukuda-Parr, and Elson (2011) note that the latter is concerned with values covering freedom, dignity and respect, equality and non-discrimination, and participation and autonomy, as well as mechanisms to protect and promote these values. Human rights are about accountability and obligation.

On the other hand, the capability approach deals with the substantive freedom and opportunities of individual groups. Osmani (2005) points out that this approach links the issue of poverty to that of human rights and that poverty is a shortfall in the achievement of development and human rights. As a result, and as shown by Szymanski and Bilius (2011), the rights of persons with disabilities have been getting more international attention since the 1980s.

Our main contribution is the examination of the demography of visual disability and its social-economic circumstances in Indonesia, utilizing the results of the 2010 census, the most recent at the time of writing and the first to include questions on disabilities. Before the census, data on disability were based on surveys (using samples) only. This is the first study on social and economic correlates of disability in Indonesia. The results are expected to produce a better understanding of visual disability, which in turn will help the understanding of inequity in health. As the World Health Organization and World Bank report (2011) elaborates, a demographic analysis can enhance the effectiveness of policies in removing disabling barriers and can help deliver better services to those with disabilities to participate in society. Therefore, development and human rights can go together, rather than being a trade-off.

Global Policies and Actions on Visual Disabilities

Visual disabilities are understudied, though they are frequently neither difficult nor costly to cure (Taylor et al. 2007). Moreover, most are avoidable, which can improve people's well-being by raising their capability – their freedom to be and do what they want. At the same time, providing opportunities for using visual-disability-friendly facilities may raise both the productivity and happiness of those with visual disability. Yet, untreated vision problems can lead to physical handicaps (Rudberg et al. 1993; West et al. 1997), increased incidence of falls (Jack et al. 1995; Lamoreux et al. 2008), depression (Tsai et al. 2003), social isolation, dependency, and even mortality (Gopinath et al. 2013).

According to estimates from the World Health Organization (2012b), there were 285 million people in the world with visual disabilities in 2010, of which 39 million were blind and 246 million were affected by low vision (uncorrected refractive errors). Most were fifty or older. Globally, visual disability was found to be mostly due to uncorrected refractive errors (43 percent) and cataracts (33 percent). Other causes of global visual disability are glaucoma (2 percent); age-related macular degeneration, diabetic retinopathy, trachoma, and corneal opacities (1 percent); and undetermined causes. Yet, the majority of causes (uncorrected refractive errors and cataracts) are curable at relatively affordable cost. Indeed, as Dineen et al. (2003) point out, cataracts are the main cause of blindness. Cataract surgery is relatively easy, and the rate of recovery is very high, in contrast to, for example, glaucoma. Loskutova et al. (2019) show that once people lose their visual function due to glaucoma, their treatment can only delay the progression of the disease.

Vision problems may also vary by gender and socio-economic status. Rius et al. (2012) conclude that in India, women have the highest risk of visual disability, after controlling for age and access to services. They also find that people with higher socio-economic status (those with higher income, more education, or employment in a non-manual job) have a lower risk of visual disability. Zheng (2012) concludes that visual disability among the residents of Singapore varied with ethnicity, education, income, neighbourhood, literacy, marital status, language skill, and migration status. Liljas et al. (2015) find that among older persons in a British community, sensory disabilities are associated with a decline in quality of life, social interaction, and physical functioning.

Given the rising attention to visual disability, the World Health Organization (WHO) inaugurated World Sight Day in 2000, which falls on the second Thursday of October. The global program Right to Sight was jointly initiated by the WHO and the International Agency for the Prevention of Blindness (IAPB) in 1999. It gained a strong political commitment during the fifty-sixth World Health Assembly in 2003, when resolution WHA56.26, "Elimination of Avoidable Blindness," was adopted on May 28, 2003. More than forty countries signed the resolution, including Indonesia. It urged all WHO members to set up national Vision 2020 plans no later than 2005, to establish a national coordinating committee for Vision 2020, to start implementation of the action plan by at least 2007, to include an effective information system, and to support the efficient use of resources to eliminate avoidable blindness. Attention to visual disability accelerated after the adoption of the UN Convention on the Rights of Persons with Disabilities in 2006. In 2011, the sixty-sixth World Health Assembly endorsed an action plan entitled Universal Eye Health: A Global Action Plan 2014–2019 for the prevention of avoidable visual impairment (World Health Organization 2013).

An aging population is another factor that brings sensory decline, including vision loss, to the forefront. Visual impairment is a major sensory difficulty for the elderly (West et al. 1997). As people age, eye tissue deteriorates and vision declines. Presbyopia, cataracts, age-related macular degeneration, glaucoma, and diabetic retinopathy are the most common causes of age-related visual impairment (Loh and Ogle 2004).

Therefore, visual disability has been both an emerging human rights and economic issue in aging populations, as many people cannot access proper treatment for it. Developing countries with aging populations face even more challenging situations.

In terms of policy, the World Health Organization (2012b) notes that monitoring the progress in reducing visual disability is difficult because much of the current data are not easily accessible. Therefore, the creation of effective policies to reduce the problem must be preceded by population-based studies on the subject.

This chapter uses Indonesia as a case study, as the country has been globalized and progressively digitized. As its population gets older (Arifin and Ananta 2016), the issue of sensory impairment will become increasingly relevant. Indonesia is also a developing country, with inadequate income and infrastructure for those with disabilities, including visual disabilities.

Saw et al. (2003) show that rates of low vision and blindness in some provinces on the island of Sumatra were similar to those in other rural areas in developing countries. Blindness in these areas can be avoided, as much of it is caused by cataracts and uncorrected refractive errors. Improving the overall infrastructure of eye care delivery and raising the quality of staff who treat cataracts can reduce blindness. Yet, though cataract surgery is cheap in terms of national income, it can be prohibitively expensive for the rural poor. At the same time, though myopia can be fully corrected with glasses, whose cost is relatively cheap, large numbers of Indonesians who need them do not possess a pair.

Yet, Indonesia was very quick in responding to the world program on blindness. When the WHO and the IAPB launched Vision 2020: The Right to Sight (February 17, 1999) to eliminate avoidable blindness by 2020, Megawati Sukarnoputri, the vice president of Indonesia, initiated Vision 2020 Indonesia only one year later. Vision 2020 identified five immediate priorities: cataracts, trachoma, onchocerciasis, childhood blindness (including vitamin A deficiency), as well as refractive errors and low vision. These priorities were based on the burden of blindness and the availability and affordability of programs to prevent and treat them.

Despite this, in 2016 Indonesia had the highest prevalence of blindness in Southeast Asia. One of the factors responsible was the unequal distribution of human resources, which were concentrated in large cities. In some areas, especially those that are rural and remote, there was almost no personnel to treat visual disabilities. Not surprisingly, Indonesia had the lowest cataract surgical rate in Southeast Asia, around 1,500 per one million people (International Agency for the Prevention of Blindness 2018).

To manage this issue, the Indonesian National Committee of Blindness and Ophthalmological Society of Indonesia (PERDAMI) produced a strategic plan of action on eye health. It targeted providing primary eye care services through community health centres (Puskesmas) throughout Indonesia. It aimed to have a cataract surgical rate of 3,000 per one million people and raise the ophthalmologist-to-population ratio to at least one ophthalmologist per 250,000 people (International Agency for the Prevention of Blindness 2018).

Visual Disabilities in Indonesia

Measurement

As disability is a complex multi-dimensional experience, it is not easily measured. Furthermore, Indonesian policy makers and scholars were not particularly interested in the subject until 2000. Therefore, lack of data collection and follow-up make assessment of the situation for disabled people difficult. As discussed in the World Health Organization and World Bank report (2011), the measurement of disability varies depending on the country, sources of data, question designs, sampling, concepts, and definitions.

Our concept of disability is taken from that of the World Health Organization and World Bank report (2011). Disability encompasses three categories: impairment (problems in the structure of the body, such as paralysis or blindness); activity limitation (difficulty with certain activities, such as seeing or walking); and restricted participation in society (for example, discrimination in the job market, including on the basis of age).

In this chapter, we concentrate on the second category, and we follow a set of questions developed by the United Nations Statistical Commission in 2001 (World Health Organization and World Bank 2011). Known as the Washington Group questions, they address difficulty in seeing (after wearing glasses and/or contact lenses), hearing (after wearing hearing aids), walking, remembering or concentrating, self-care (including bathing and/ or dressing), and communication in one's customary or usual language. The possible answers to the questions are "no difficulty," "some difficulty," "a lot of difficulty," and "unable."

As mentioned previously, we employ the 2010 Indonesian census for this study. It offered the first set of nationwide data on disabilities and was a full census, covering the entire population, rather than only a sample, as in previous government surveys.[3] A self-assessment on physical/mental difficulties, it targeted five kinds of difficulties: visual, hearing, walking or climbing stairs, remembering or concentrating, and self-care. Each question had three possible answers: no difficulty, some difficulty, and severe difficulty.

As noted above, our scope is limited to visual disability, which the census measured via the following question: "*Apakah (NAMA) mempunyai kesulitan Melihat, meskipun pakai kacamata?*" (Does [NAME] have any difficulty in seeing, despite using eye glasses?). Respondents could choose between three answers: *tidak* (no), *sedikit* (some), and *parah* (severe). The census classified respondents as experiencing difficulty if glasses or other treatment did not greatly improve their sight. If they could see clearly with the aid of glasses, they were classed as not suffering any difficulty. Visual difficulty was measured at a distance of thirty centimetres in well-lit conditions; if respondents could clearly discern the size, form, and colour of objects, they were categorized as having no difficulty. Severe difficulty included total blindness. It should be noted that the answers were self-reported by the respondents, and the interviewers did not independently measure their ability to see (BPS 2011).

To understand the magnitude of visual disability, we use two types of measurements – distribution and prevalence. The former shows how people with visual disabilities are distributed by age throughout the population, as well as the magnitude of their disabilities. In business sectors, distribution results may reveal potential customers for vision aids. In the realm of government policy, the size of the affected group will be important for intervention.

On the other hand, prevalence is the ratio of visually disabled people in a given age group divided by the total number of people in that age group. It captures the varying likelihood of suffering visual disability among persons in differing age groups. Readers should note that our measurement differs from the one used by the World Health Organization (2012b). It also differs from that employed in the Basic Health Surveys (Riskesdas in Bahasa, Indonesia) of 2007 and 2013, in which respondents were tested medically (Kementrian Kesehatan 2014).

Number of People with Visual Disability and their Geographical Distribution

According to the 2010 Indonesian census, 5.82 million people aged ten and above experienced some degree of visual difficulty (either "some difficulty"

TABLE 9.1
Number of population by degree of visual difficulty and age group,
Indonesia, 2010

Age	No difficulty	Some difficulty	Severe difficulty	Total
10–14	22,503,546	31,048	7,212	22,541,806
15–19	20,565,659	48,367	7,789	20,621,815
20–24	19,656,674	58,936	8,434	19,724,044
25–29	21,121,122	76,914	10,416	21,208,452
30–34	19,657,145	98,914	12,124	19,768,183
35–39	18,299,066	144,061	14,539	18,457,666
40–44	16,146,571	323,812	18,769	16,489,152
45–49	13,515,530	478,509	22,783	14,016,822
50–54	10,896,959	617,749	29,436	11,544,144
55–59	7,796,602	609,727	32,485	8,438,814
60–64	5,380,335	629,104	42,829	6,052,268
65–69	4,021,875	615,585	52,965	4,690,425
70–74	2,751,651	631,405	70,823	3,453,879
75–79	1,495,027	422,285	59,464	1,976,776
80–84	781,876	304,986	55,526	1,142,388
85–89	279,852	128,575	29,118	437,545
90–94	95,688	57,615	17,325	170,628
95+	54,167	35,354	14,841	104,362
Total	185,019,345	5,312,946	506,878	190,839,169

Source: Compiled from BPS (n.d.).

or "severe difficulty"). Of these, 5.3 million had some difficulty, almost ten times as many as those whose disability was severe (0.5 million, see Table 9.1), which is comparable to the total population of Singapore. Individuals who had visual difficulty constituted 3.05 percent of Indonesians who were ten or older. In the United States, the rate was 2.7 percent for Americans who were aged sixteen and over (National Federation of the Blind 2018).

Furthermore, Table 9.2 indicates that the percentages for Indonesians with vision problems were much larger among those who were thirty or older than for those aged ten to thirty, reflecting a natural decline in eyesight after age thirty. This phenomenon occurred in all provinces except West Papua. For West Papua, Table 9.2 gives 2.22 percent for age ten and older but 2.10 percent for age thirty and up. Table 9.2 also shows that percentages for those aged ten and over varied by province, with the highest in the six provinces of Sulawesi. This island is in eastern Indonesia, which tends to be less socio-economically advanced than western Indonesia. Its

TABLE 9.2
Visual disability by province: Indonesia, 2010 (%)

Province	Age >= 10	Age >= 30	Province	Age >= 10	Age >= 30
Aceh	3.71	7.15	West Nusa Tenggara	3.25	5.93
North Sumatra	3.01	5.59	East Nusa Tenggara	4.10	7.63
West Sumatra	4.44	7.80	West Kalimantan	3.35	6.17
Riau	3.12	5.97	Central Kalimantan	3.44	6.47
Jambi	3.47	6.37	South Kalimantan	3.29	5.85
South Sumatra	3.38	6.23	East Kalimantan	3.47	6.26
Bengkulu	3.77	6.97	North Sulawesi	4.78	7.74
Lampung	2.99	5.30	Central Sulawesi	4.58	8.34
Bangka-Belitung	2.89	5.26	South Sulawesi	4.91	8.82
Riau Islands	2.83	5.18	Southeast Sulawesi	4.26	8.36
Jakarta	3.62	6.08	Gorontalo	6.16	11.10
West Java	3.07	5.32	West Sulawesi	4.17	8.04
Central Java	2.13	3.38	Maluku	3.38	6.49
Yogyakarta	2.28	3.45	North Maluku	3.21	6.22
East Java	2.70	4.18	West Papua	2.22	2.10
Banten	2.47	4.55	Papua	1.10	4.42
Bali	2.82	4.38	*Indonesia*	3.05	5.22

Source: Compiled and calculated from BPS (n.d.).

percentage rate is at least 4.0 percent, with the highest in Gorontalo (6.16 percent) and the lowest in West Sulawesi (4.17 percent). Interestingly, the lowest percentage occurred in Papua (1.10 percent), followed by West Papua (2.22 percent), both of which are in eastern Indonesia. Next came two Javanese provinces, Central Java and Yogyakarta, at 2.13 percent and 2.28 percent, respectively.

The pattern differed for individuals who were aged thirty and older.[4] The highest percentages (above 7.0 percent) still occurred in all provinces of Sulawesi. However, they were joined by Aceh and West Sumatra and by Eastern Nusa Tenggara in eastern Indonesia. West Papua scored the lowest (2.10 percent), followed by Central Java (3.38 percent) and Yogyakarta (3.45 percent). For this age group, Papua no longer scored the lowest.

Visual Disability by Age Group
As shown in Figure 9.1, the degree of visual difficulty depends on age. The percentage of Indonesians who experienced some difficulty rose with age,

FIGURE 9.1

Visual disability by age and degree of difficulty, Indonesia, 2010

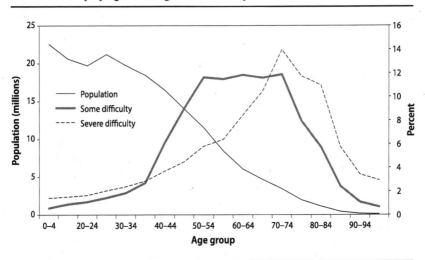

Source: Compiled from BPS (n.d.).

reaching a plateau between ages fifty and seventy-four, forming about 58.0 percent (about 3.1 million) of all people with vision problems. This significant portion may have implications for productivity in the labour market and for dignity in the community.

Among those with severe visual problems, the peak came at ages seventy to seventy-four. Many may have stopped working, so curing them may not increase their productivity in the labour market, but it may raise their dignity in society and improve their well-being.

Yet, as indicated in Table 9.1, in each age group, Indonesians with severe visual difficulty were always much fewer in number than those with some difficulty.

When the sample was separated into residents of urban and rural areas, different distribution patterns arose (Figure 9.2). The percentage of urban residents with some difficulty reached its peak at ages fifty to fifty-four, whereas it was seventy to seventy-four for people who lived in the countryside. The percentages for Indonesians with severe difficulty rose consistently until ages seventy to seventy-four, regardless of whether they lived in urban or rural areas.

As indicated in Figure 9.1, though the magnitude is much smaller, the percentage of those with severe difficulty was larger than those with some

FIGURE 9.2

Visual disability by age and place of residence, Indonesia, 2010 (%)

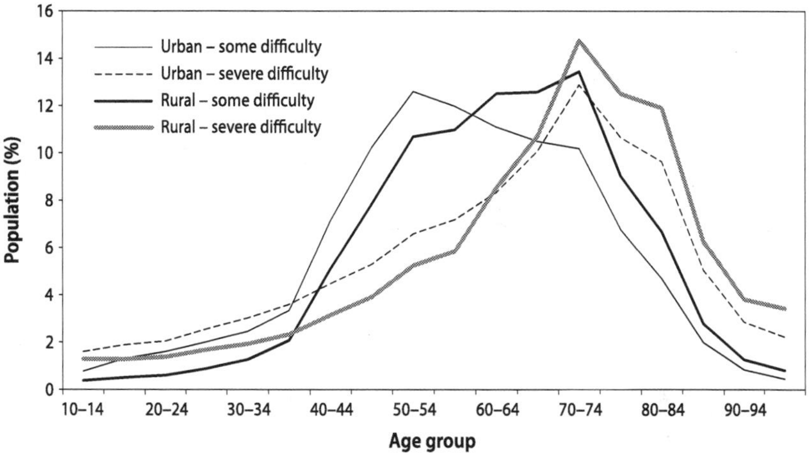

Source: Calculated based on 2010 census data (BPS, n.d.).

difficulty for Indonesians who were younger than thirty-five. After that age, the percentage with some difficulty quickly exceeded those with severe difficulty. Another turning point occurred at ages seventy to seventy-four, where the percentages for severe difficulty surpassed those with some difficulty. As shown in Figure 9.2, this pattern did not change when controlled for rural/urban location.

Though there are peaks in terms of population distribution, the prevalence rate for visual difficulties slopes upward by age,[5] except for a flat line among people aged 90–94 years old and those above 94 years old with some difficulty (Figure 9.3). This may occur because the information regarding the very old is inaccurate or because most of the "some difficulty" had become "severe difficulty."

As shown in Figure 9.3, the prevalence among those with some difficulty began to rise at the young age of twenty-five, whereas severe difficulty started at age fifty and accelerated after age seventy. In some instances, "some difficulty" may have turned into "severe difficulty." If this pattern persists during the next few decades, reducing vision problems will become increasingly challenging as the population ages.

Figure 9.4 shows that the age prevalence rate did not change when urban/rural residence was controlled for. Almost half (47.8 percent) of Indonesians

FIGURE 9.3

Age-specific prevalence of visual difficulty, Indonesia, 2010 (%)

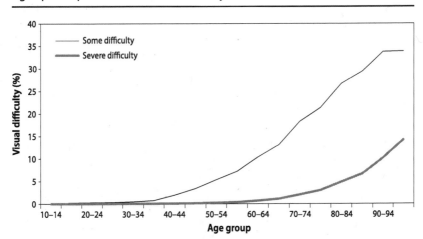

Source: Calculated based on 2010 census data (BPS, n.d.).

who had vision problems lived in urban centres, reflecting the national urbanization rate of 49.8 percent. The age prevalence was similar for rural and
urban areas, except at very advanced ages. Discrepancies crept in at age
eighty, with rural areas having greater prevalence, a gap that widened as
people grew older. Furthermore, at the very advanced ages (ninety years and
more), the prevalence of some difficulty continued to rise in rural areas,
though at a slower pace; however, in urban areas, it declined. The prevalence
for severe difficulty rose even faster in both the urban and rural areas.

Prevalence in the "some difficulty" category began to escalate as young as
thirty-five to thirty-nine. For this age cohort, the inability to see well may
reduce productivity in the labour market, especially with the rise of digitiz-
ation. On the other hand, the prevalence of "severe difficulty" started with
the pre-elderly. Government policy that reduces or postpones this prevalence may not amplify labour productivity, but it will improve the happiness
of the pre-elderly and the elderly, thus bettering their health and ultimately
lessening the cost of their care. Success in diminishing some difficulty at
young ages may prevent the rapid rise in severe difficulty at later ages.

Socio-Economic Circumstances of People with Vision Problems

We focus on two types of socio-economic circumstances. The first is economic circumstances, measured by the poverty rate (the headcount ratio),

FIGURE 9.4

Age-specific prevalence of visual difficulty by degree and residence,
Indonesia, 2010 (%)

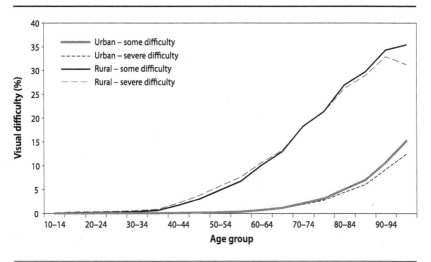

Source: Calculated based on 2010 census data (BPS, n.d.).

GDP per capita, overcrowding (in houses of less than eight square metres per capita), urbanization, and economic inequality (measured with the Gini ratio). Second is human capital. This uses three indicators: the human development index (which combines education, health, and purchasing power), education (percentage of population with at least senior high school education), infant mortality rate, and adult health (measured by self-rated health status). Our analysis deals with Indonesians aged ten and above who had visual disabilities, in thirty-three provinces in 2010, as presented in Table 9.2.

Readers should be aware that our analysis merely shows correlation and does not necessarily imply a causal relationship.[6] Further studies should be conducted to uncover possible two-way connections: from visual disability to socio-economic circumstances and/or from socio-economic circumstances to visual disability. For example, Jaggernath et al. (2014) argue that the association between the poverty rate and vision problems can be two-way: poverty can heighten the risk of visual difficulty, and visual difficulty can lead to poverty and even deepen it.

Figure 9.5 shows a significant quadratic form, at p-value < 0.5 percent, of association between visual difficulty and the poverty rate. Poverty is related to visual disability with an inverted U-curve. If the poverty rate is below

20 percent, the relationship between poverty and visual disability is positive. However, after its peak, the relationship between poverty and visual disability turns in the opposite direction: As the poverty rate increases, the percentage of visual difficulty declines. The part with the negative association

FIGURE 9.5
Association between visual difficulty and the poverty rate

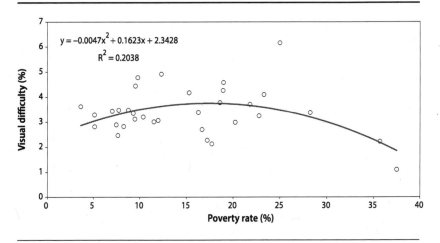

FIGURE 9.6
Association between visual difficulty and the poverty rate (West Papua, Papua, and Maluku removed)

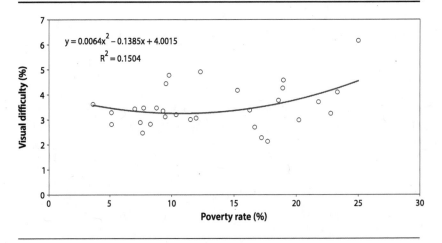

seems to be contributed by three provinces only: West Papua, Papua, and Maluku. Papua has the worst poverty rate but is the "most able" province in terms of visual difficulty. West Papua is the second-poorest province, with low prevalence of vision problems, and Maluku is the third-poorest. In other words, if these three provinces are not taken into account, the correlation between visual difficulty and the poverty rate is positive, suggesting that as the poverty rate worsens, the likelihood of experiencing vision problems intensifies. Compare Figures 9.5 and 9.6.

As poverty has many dimensions, we also examine overcrowded houses, which can pose mobility challenges for people who do not see well. Figure 9.7 depicts a positive linear relationship between visual difficulty and overcrowding. This implies that many people with vision problems are more likely to live in overcrowded houses. There was one exception to this pattern, Papua, which has the lowest percentage of people with visual difficulty and yet has the highest percentage of population living in overcrowded houses. Including Papua in the analysis turns the relationship into a quadratic form (figure not shown). This pattern is consistent with the previous analysis on the poverty rate measured with headcount ratio.

Furthermore, the association between GDP per capita and visual difficulty follows a U-curve (Figure 9.8). As GDP per capita increases, the percentage of visual difficulty decreases until it reaches its lowest point, but it slopes upward again as GDP per capita rises further. The richest provinces

FIGURE 9.7
Association between visual difficulty and overcrowded living areas

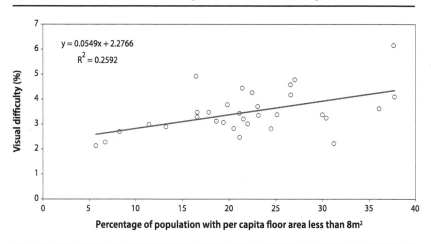

FIGURE 9.8

Association between visual difficulty and GDP per capita

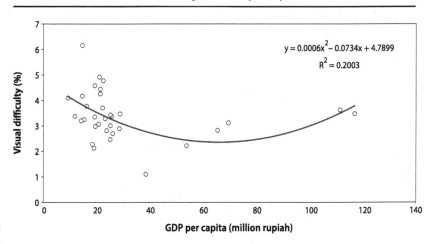

$$y = 0.0006x^2 - 0.0734x + 4.7899$$
$$R^2 = 0.2003$$

are East Kalimantan and Jakarta, but they do not have the lowest percentage of visual disability. Papua is the sixth-richest province.

The association with human development is mixed. There is no significant correlation between the human development index and visual disability. Education does not seem to be correlated with visual disability. Two opposing channels may explain this association: the first suggests that rising education is accompanied by rising GDP per capita and therefore with declining prevalence of visual disability. The second posits that higher education is associated with a higher prevalence of vision problems, either because they spend more time reading, or they are more likely to observe visual difficulty.

On the other hand, improvement in health status seems to be associated with a lower prevalence of visual disabilities. Figure 9.9 reveals that a higher percentage of health problems is linked with a higher prevalence of visual disability. Similarly, Figure 9.10 shows that provinces with higher infant mortality rates (which may crudely indicate the overall health status of the province) typically have a higher prevalence of visual disabilities.

Concluding Remarks

In a globalized world with an increasingly digitized labour market, Indonesia may face great challenges as it attempts to raise its human capital. Its prevalence of visual difficulties rises rapidly after ages thirty-five to thirty-nine,

FIGURE 9.9
Association between visual difficulty and health status

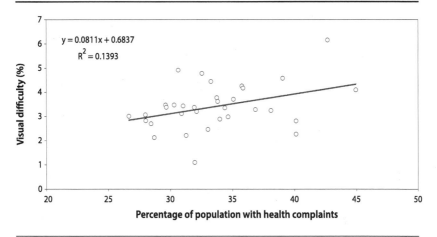

FIGURE 9.10
Association between visual difficulty and infant mortality rate

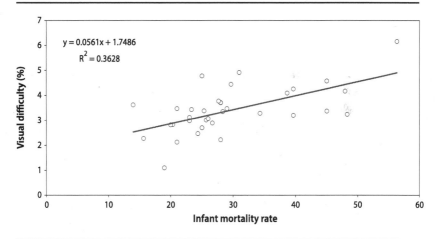

when individuals are expected to make a major contribution to the economy. At the same time, Indonesia also anticipates an aging population, bringing a new challenge: the prevalence of severe vision problems rises rapidly after age fifty-five, the pre-elderly ages. For this age cohort, untreated visual disability may reduce participation and the right to sight in the economy and society; it can diminish their dignity and increase the burden of their care. Furthermore, the statistics show that visual disabilities may rise quickly in urban areas. Worse, the peak of suffering in the urban areas occurred among those aged 50–54, supposedly at the peak of people's careers. Without proper prevention and treatment, this phenomenon could result in a huge capability deprivation and hence a productivity loss, as well as a violation of human rights.

Economic circumstances (measured by declining poverty, rising GDP per capita, and increasing per capita floor areas) seemed to have a favourable association with the prevalence of visual disability. Economic inequality and urbanization were not associated with it. Nevertheless, we also found that rural/urban differences in visual disability rates become larger among Indonesians who were seventy-five and over, with those in the countryside having a larger percentage and prevalence than those in urban areas.

Our findings on the relationship between human capital development and visual disability are mixed. Education may not be associated with impaired sight, but improvement in the infant mortality rate and self-reported health status was correlated with declining prevalence of vision problems. A different measurement, using the human development index, which combines education, health, and purchasing power is not correlated with visual disability rates.

Fortunately, many vision problems can be avoided or can be treated with relative ease and at low cost, especially if they spring from uncorrected refractive errors and/or cataracts. Therefore, at a relatively low cost, Indonesia could reduce much of its capability deprivation from visual disability. The government could intervene directly by treating those with poor eyesight or by improving economic circumstances, including promoting urbanization and raising the quality of infant and adult health. In turn, the success of these policies will raise human capital and fulfil the right to dignity of the labour force and the elderly.

Indonesia's level of visual disability is worse than the global average, particularly among persons aged sixty and over. In Indonesia, older people constitute 67.7 percent of people with severe visual difficulty. On the other hand, globally, older people make up only 58 percent of the total number of people who are blind. Although the prevalence of severe impairment in Indonesia is comparable to that of the United States, Indonesia's prevalence of "some difficulty" is much higher than in the United States (World Health Organization 2012b). Therefore, Indonesia has plenty of room for improvement on this score.

In short, the case of visual disability in Indonesia illustrates that a trade-off between development and global human rights does not necessarily exist. Improving eyesight can promote development by minimizing visual capability deprivation in the labour market and can protect global human rights by enhancing the dignity of citizens, particularly the elderly. Even the two major causes of visual disability – uncorrected refractive error and cataracts – can be addressed relatively easily at affordable cost.

Notes

1 The meaning of "human rights" is sometimes opaque, and people often have their own interpretations of what human rights are and which ones they possess. Indeed, human rights cover many concepts and issues of the human condition. Yet, they can essentially be defined as "those rights, which are inherent in our culture and without which we cannot live as human beings. Human rights and fundamental freedoms allow us to fully develop and use our human qualities, our intelligence, our talents and our conscience and to satisfy our spiritual and other needs. Human rights are based on mankind's increasing demand for a life in which the inherent dignity and worth of each human being will receive respect and protection" (United Nations 1987, 4).
2 This index of globalization consists of three dimensions: economic, social, and political.
3 Earlier data on disability were collected in the 2006 and 2009 SUSENAS (the National Socio-Economic Household Survey).
4 In the remainder of this discussion, the population aged ten and over is used as the base.
5 "Prevalence rate" refers to the ratio of people with visual difficulty in a certain age group to the total number of people in that group.
6 It is beyond the scope of the present discussion to analyze the possible causal relationship between disability and socio-economic conditions.

References

Arfat, Shabina. 2013. "Globalisation and Human Rights: An Overview of Its Impact." *American Journal of Humanities and Social Sciences* 1, 1: 18–24.
Arifin, Evi Nurvidya, and Aris Ananta. 2016. "The Past Three Population Censuses: A Deepening Ageing Population in Indonesia." In *Contemporary Demographic Transformations in China, India and Indonesia,* ed. Christophe Z. Guilmoto and Gavin W. Jones, 309–23. New York: Springer.
Badan Pusat Statistik (BPS) (Statistics Indonesia). n.d. "Penduduk Menurut Kelompok Umur dan Tingkat Kesulitan [Population by Age Group and Visual Difficulty]." Melihathttps://sp2010.bps.go.id/index.php/site/tabel?tid=273&wid=0.
–. 2011. *Kesulitan Fungsional Penduduk Indonesia: Hasil Sensus Penduduk 2010* [Functional difficulties of the Indonesian population: Results of the 2010 population census]. Jakarta: Badan Pusat Statistik.

Dineen, B.P., R.R.A. Bourne, S.M. Ali, D.M. Noorul Huq, and G.J. Johnson. 2003. "Prevalence and Causes of Blindness and Visual Impairment in Bangladeshi Adults: Results of the National Blindness and Low Vision Survey of Bangladesh." *British Journal of Ophthalmology* 87, 7: 820–28.

Donnelly, Jack. 2013. *Universal Human Rights: In Theory and Practice.* 3rd ed. Ithaca, NY: Cornell University Press.

Gopinath, Bamini, Julie Schneider, Catherine M. McMahon, George Burlutsky, Stephen R. Leeder, and Paul Mitchell. 2013. "Dual Sensory Impairment in Older Adults Increases the Risk of Mortality: A Population-Based Study." *PLOS ONE* 8, 3 (March): e55054. https://www.ncbi.nlm.nih.gov/pmc/articles/PMC3587637/pdf/pone.0055054.pdf.

Howard-Hassmann, Rhoda E. 2010. *Can Globalization Promote Human Rights?* University Park: Penn State University Press.

International Agency for the Prevention of Blindness (IAPB). 2018. *A Road Map of Indonesia's Visual Impairment Control Programme.* IAPB, 26 June https://www.iapb.org/news/a-road-map-of-indonesias-visual-impairment-control-programme/.

Jack, C.I.A., T. Smith, C. Neoh, M. Lye, and J.N. McGalliard. 1995. "Prevalence of Low Vision in Elderly Patients Admitted to an Acute Geriatric Unit in Liverpool: Elderly People Who Fall Are More Likely to Have Low Vision." *Gerontology* 41, 5: 280–85.

Jaggernath, Jyoti, Lene Øverland, Prasidh Ramson, Vilas Kovai, Ving Fai Chan, and Kovin S. Naidool. 2014. "Poverty and Eye Health." *Health* 6, 4: 1849–60.

Kementrian Kesehatan. 2014. *Situasi Gangguan Penglihatan dan Kebutaan.* Jakarta: Pusat Data and Informasi Kementrian Kesehatan.

Liljas, A.E.M., S.G. Wannamethee, P.H. Whincup, O. Papacosta, K. Walters, S. Ilife, L.T. Lennon, L.A. Carvalho, and S.E. Ramsay. 2015. "Socio-Demographic Characteristics, Lifestyle Factors and Burden of Morbidity Associated with Self-Reported Hearing and Vision Impairment in Older British Community-Dwelling Men: A Cross-Sectional Study." *Journal of Public Health* 38, 2: 21–28.

Lamoreux, Ecosse L., Elaine Chong, Jie Jin Wang, Seang Mei Saw, Tin Aung, Paul Mitchell, and Tien Yin Wong. 2008. "Visual Impairment, Causes of Vision Loss, and Falls: The Singapore Malay Eye Study." *Investigative Ophthalmology and Visual Science* 49, 2: 528–33.

Loh, K.Y., and J. Ogle. 2004. "Age Related Visual Impairment in the Elderly." *Medical Journal of Malaysia* 59, 4: 562–68.

Loskutova, E., C. O'Brien, I. Loskutov, and J. Loughman. 2019. "Nutritional Supplementation in Treatment of Glaucoma: A systematic Review." *Survey of Opthalmology,* 64: 195–216.

Mukherjee, Nisha, and Jonathan Krieckhaus. 2012. "Globalization and Human Well-Being." *International Political Science Review* 33, 2: 150–70.

National Federation of the Blind. 2018. "Statistical Facts about Blindness in the United States." Accessed August 19, 2018. https://nfb.org/blindness-statistics.

Osmani, Siddiqur Rahman. 2005. "Poverty and Human Rights: Building on the Capability Approach." *Journal of Human Development* 6, 2: 205–19.

Rius, Anna Ulldemolins, Van C. Lansingh, Laura Guisasola Valencia, Marissa J. Carter, and Kristen A. Eckert. 2012. "Social Inequalities in Blindness and Visual Impairment: A Review of Social Determinants." *Indian Journal of Ophthalmology* 60, 5: 368–75.

Rudberg, Mark A., Sylvia E. Furner, Julie E. Dunn, and Christine K. Cassel. 1993. "The Relationship of Visual and Hearing Impairments to Disability: An Analysis Using the Longitudinal Study of Aging." *Journal of Gerontology* 48, 6: M261–M265. https://doi.org/10.1093/geronj/48.6.M261.

Saw, S.-M., R. Husain, G.M. Gazzard, D. Koh, D. Widjaja, and D.T.H. Tan. 2003. "Causes of Low Vision and Blindness in Rural Indonesia." *British Journal of Ophthalmology* 87, 9: 1075–78.

Sen, Amartya. 2009. *The Idea of Justice.* Cambridge, MA: Belknap Press.

Singh, Pooja. 2014. "Persons with Disabilities and Economic Inequalities in India." *Indian Anthropologist* 44, 2: 65–80.

Szymanski, Charles F., and Mindaugas Bilius. 2011. "A Case Study with Globalization of Disability Rights: The Compatibility of Lithuania's Process for Determining the Legal Incapacity of Disabled Persons with International Legal Systems." *Baltic Journal of Law and Politics* 4, 1: 83–105.

Tausch, Arno. 2016. "Is Globalization Really Good for Public Health?" *International Journal of Health Planning and Management* 31, 4: 511–36.

Taylor, Hugh R., M. Lynne Pezzullo, Sarah J. Nesbitt, and Jill E. Keeffe. 2007. "Costs of Interventions for Visual Impairment." *American Journal of Ophthalmology* 145: 561–65.

Tsai, Su-Ying, Ching-Yu Cheng, Wen-Ming Hsu, Tung-Ping Tom Su, Jorn-Hon Liu, and Pesus Chou. 2003. "Association between Visual Impairment and Depression in the Elderly." *Journal of the Formosan Medical Association* 102, 2: 86–90.

United Nations. 1987. *Human Rights: Questions and Answers.* New York: United Nations.

Vizard, Polly, Sakiko Fukuda-Parr, and Daniel Elson. 2011. "Introduction: The Capability Approach and Human Rights." *Journal of Human Development* 12, 1: 1–22.

West, Sheila K., Beatriz Munoz, Gary S. Rubin, Oliver D. Schein, Karen Bandeen-Roche, Scott Zeger, Pearl S. German, Linda P. Fried, and the SEE Project Team. 1997. "Function and Visual Impairment in a Population-Based Study of Older Adults: The SEE Project." *Investigative Ophthalmology and Visual Science* 38, 1: 72–82.

World Health Organization. 2012a. "Disability: Report by the Secretariat." March 11. http://apps.who.int/gb/ebwha/pdf_files/WHA66/A66_12-en.pdf.

–. 2012b. *Global Data on Visual Impairment, 2010.* Geneva: World Health Organization.

–. 2013. *Universal Eye Health: A Global Action Plan, 2014–2019.* Geneva: World Health Organization.

World Health Organization and World Bank. 2011. *World Report on Disability.* Geneva: World Health Organization.

10

Urban Property Rights

————————   A View from Jakarta

MICHAEL LEAF

The popular understanding of globalization often presumes a tendency toward convergence. This is largely because globalization is seen as the transborder integration of markets (and economies more broadly), implying a teleology of the global expansion of capitalism as the dominant system of economic production and distribution. Such globalizing trends, however, are reinforced, or at least contextualized, by other social processes, including the world's ongoing demographic and urban transitions – processes that shape the global inequities that are the core concern of development practice and that are addressed in the foregoing chapters in this volume.

The policy component of globalization may be described, broadly speaking, as working to get the institutions right – including institutions in support of international trade and investment, though presumably also with safeguards in the interests of such things as consumer protection, labour rights, environmental betterment, and the maintenance of national sovereignty. With regard to property rights in land, the subject of this chapter, getting the institutions right has come to mean working toward establishing some form of freehold ownership, as its implicit tenure security is seen as a necessary incentive for investment in local economies, especially for international investors.

Actual conditions on the ground, however, belie the simplicity of this view of globalization. All societies carry with them histories of their development and change, path dependencies in their institutional make-up that may contradict global trends of convergence. In the case of Jakarta, Indonesia, such local particularities derive, on the one hand, from the complexities of land-law dualism inherited from the late colonial period and reproduced through current administrative practices. On the other hand, the Indonesian constitution contains an ideologically based stipulation that ultimately reserves all claims to the land and water of the nation to the state itself. This role of the state as the fundamental controller of the nation's territory is derived from the analysis of traditional (*adat*) land allocation, which despite the diversity of practices across the archipelago consistently included the practice of reverting under-utilized lands to the community (*hak ulayat*, or "right of avail").

Under these conditions, tensions persist in Jakarta because of the uneven resolution of land-law dualism and the possibility that this holds for perpetuating informal practices of local administration (i.e., the vested interests associated with informality or regulatory flexibility). Ultimately, though, one finds a disjuncture between the trend toward individualization in property rights, as advanced through the mechanisms that promote a globalized view of the world, and the understanding of territorial claims as a collective right. Thus, one could argue that there are presently two ways to claim a right to the city: as an individual right to the exclusive use of property, and as a collective, political right to the city. The latter will become increasingly relevant for those who are excluded by the ongoing growth of the city's formal capitalist economy.

Property Rights, Globalization, and Local Contexts

The essence of theory is simplification. The world, with its diversity of social, economic, and political relations, is undeniably too complex to be fully encapsulated by theory, even if sliced thinly by the narrow parameters of one or another interpretive discipline. Yet we persist in our practices of simplification, as these are the only means at hand to interpret complex worldly phenomena. What I am concerned with here are the simplifications that underpin assumptions regarding neoliberal globalization, both as an interpretive framework and as the basis for policy formulation.

There is an implicit assumption in much popular and academic thinking regarding our current phase of globalization, that through the ongoing transboundary expansion of capitalist relations and practices – or perhaps more specifically, through the reproduction of institutional structures under the aegis of the modern state system – one may identify various (and seemingly increasing the numbers of) points of convergence across the globe.

And, as argued by some, such a trend leads to systemic unification, or at least institutional alignment. Of relevance here is the apparently global trend toward clarification, formalization, and, ultimately, privatization of property rights under one or another variant of freehold ownership. In this, we may discern the development of a particular form of property rights regime taken to be a "natural end-point" of institutional evolution under neoliberal thinking.[1] With regard to urbanizing territories in developing countries, this shift away from a world of highly diverse and locally grounded forms of tenure claim and toward a seemingly singular global standard of freehold ownership has been anticipated for decades.[2]

In the case of Indonesia, "the rise of capital," which is inherent to the understanding of globalization, may be seen as dating from the early years of the Soeharto new order period and the transition away from the statist policies of the Sukarno presidency (Robison 1986). Socio-economic trends over the subsequent decades – especially the growth and consolidation of domestic capital and the rise of a significant consumption-oriented urban middle class (van Leeuwen 2011) – have created constituencies within Indonesia that favour such narrowing in the conceptualization of the nation's property rights regime.

Such perceived tendencies toward convergence are therefore occurring not merely because of globalization per se, meaning the increase in transborder economic connectivity. This is not narrowly a tale of the geographic spread of neoliberal ideology to every corner of the earth. Of concern here are other, more local factors that contextualize the effects of globalization, in particular the demographic, institutional, and cultural shifts associated with the ongoing urban transitions in the world today. By "urban transitions," I am referring to the historically unprecedented shifts of national societies from their historical norms of being predominantly rural (on the order of 10–15 percent urban) to becoming overwhelmingly urban (Jones 1997). And by "ongoing," I mean the second wave of the global urban transition, the current phase of rapid urban growth in the ostensibly developing, post-colonial world, following on the urbanization since the nineteenth century of what are now considered as developed countries. It is the global unevenness of these transitions – the urban transition and the demographic transition with which it is associated – that creates the impetus for development practice in the world today. While what are now the rich world countries were undergoing rapid industrially led urban growth, the colonies of the time had their urbanization suppressed, as labour was concentrated in rural, primary production to provide the inputs for European industrial development. The big unknown in this presumption of convergence – whereby developing (and urbanizing) societies become developed (and urbanized) – lies in the teleology of urban growth and development, and the overall modernization of society of which it is a constituent part.

Such a narrowing of perspective under the banner of modernization – and the one-size-fits-all policy stipulations that flow from it – rests on a particular understanding of what constitutes a state as a political entity and a Lockean interpretation of the function of the state as fundamentally the guarantor of property rights. In short, there are assumptions here, not only about an idealized relationship between state and society, but as well about the more or less linearly progressive development of property rights globally, an unfolding of private property regimes across the world's nations as an obvious outcome of the international institutional alignments of globalization. Such assumptions, however, are quickly refuted by the careful consideration of structures of real, existing property rights and what they imply about the nature of state-society relations on the ground.

One should also be careful not to assume that there is an immutable condition known as individual property rights, or more specifically what is referred to in English as the freehold ownership of land. The point to keep in mind is that this, like all other ways in which territory is occupied or claimed by human beings, is due to social convention. In other words, property rights are socially constructed; they are an institution. What is most important to understand is that such rights are not just about the relationship between the "owner" and the territory he or she claims, but also the relationship between that owner and other potential claimants (or really, about all other members of society in that they are excluded by virtue of that right of "ownership").

The other important relationship to consider is between these various sets of people and the state, in that the state provides the means by which rights claims are clarified and enforced. It is a common assumption that freehold ownership represents some sort of default category; in actuality, it is a fairly new form of rights claim on land, historically speaking. And it is so important at this point in human history, however, because of its critical role in the establishment and expansion of capitalism.[3] The exclusivity of such property rights, or to be precise, their inherent exclusionary nature, is absolutely central to how capitalism works as a system (Neale, 1985). Thus, unsurprisingly, one of the major effects of globalization has been the promotion of private, freehold ownership as a sort of global standard. Foreign investment will not flow into a country unless investors are confident that their "right" to exclusive control of property (or territory) will be respected and that their land will not be nationalized or otherwise shared with others. In practical terms, one need not invoke the bogeyman of neoliberalism as some sort of ideological undercurrent to explain the global expansion of freehold as the ideal standard. From the perspective of a state that has bought into a strategy of development through modernization, this is simple pragmatism. If you want rich foreigners to invest in your country, create jobs, gain foreign exchange, and so forth, you must show them that their property rights are secure and their investments are not at risk.

The idea that one may perceive convergence across multiple and diverse jurisdictions also prompts the question of the means by which such legal transfers occur. In his illustrative case study of the formulation and adoption of commercial law in support of economic reforms in Vietnam, for example, Gillespie (2008) details the give-and-take between relevant ministries and agencies, and shows how a particular "interpretive community" developed among certain Vietnamese analysts and policy makers and their foreign advisers. This in turn provided the basis for negotiating neoliberal reforms in exchange for trade-offs regarding the continued state oversight of commercial activities. Gillespie's use of discursive analysis emphasizes how the transborder (or cross-cultural) transfer of particular laws, if not also the legal principles behind them, is not a straightforward undertaking but is highly coloured by the institutional – and thus cultural – specificities of the societies from which these laws originate. He refers to this tendency as being "Country and Western," in that the imported laws tend to be labelled as either originating from a Western *country* or as being generically *Western.* Although such legal transfers can thus be viewed as an aspect of the Westernization of legal practices around the globe, it is perhaps more helpful to see them as less about the adoption of Western practices per se than they are about the global expansion of capitalism, as it was the legal guarantees of property by Western nation-states that undergirded the initial growth of capitalism in the West.

Reinventing Land-Law Dualism in Jakarta

For what is now the post-colonial nation of Indonesia, one particularly consequential encounter of the Country and Western sort occurred in the late nineteenth century, with the shift in Dutch policy to encourage investment in the colony by European private investors. This policy shift, as reflected in the Agrarian Law (Wet Agraria) of 1870, had two major effects. For Europeans, it meant that the precepts and categories of Dutch land law were put into place in the colony, essentially providing both familiarity and guarantees of protection of these rights by the Dutch colonial state. For native Indonesians, the law provided partial amelioration from the most exploitative excesses of the previous policy, known as the Cultivation System (Cultuurstelsel), which mandated that a portion of agricultural production be given over to the state in lieu of taxes. This policy essentially turned the farmers into sharecroppers on lands that in many cases they had worked for generations. With the advent of the Agrarian Law, farmers were once again able to maintain control of their lands in perpetuity, though their claims were now layered onto the Dutch categories of land rights that had been introduced with the Agrarian Law.[4] Thus, in and around what was then the colonial capital of Batavia (now Jakarta), swaths of land were designated for establishing plantations under European and other foreign ownership and control. Such lands were not some form of *terra nullius*, however, as they were occupied and used by local farmers whose claims predated those of the Dutch colonial masters yet which, under the Cultivation System, had become subservient to the claims of European colonists. Thus, the specific nature of late colonial legal dualism – with a layering of Dutch legal designations on top of pre-existing Indigenous claims – became a characteristic that land law in the newly independent Republic of Indonesia needed to address, one of Jakarta's own local conditions.

A second particularity of indonesian land law that shapes categories of rights in the Jakarta region is the indigenous practice of collective control at the community or village level. This practice, referred to in Indonesian as hak ulayat, or somewhat awkwardly in English as "right of avail," was identified as a key aspect of traditional land rights by the progressive Dutch legal scholar, Cornelis van Vollenhoven, who undertook at the beginning of the twentieth century to study and categorize indigenous practices of land tenure and control in what is now Indonesia. His interest was to codify indigenous legal practices so that Indonesians would have a basis for resisting the imposition of a European legal system. Through this work, he was able to identify nineteen zones of traditional (adat) practice corresponding largely to linguistic groupings, with hak ulayat a consistent feature across all of them.

When Indonesia achieved independence at the end of the 1940s, it thus inherited a complex, multifaceted, and expressly dualistic legal system, and the government set about devising a unified code for land rights, resulting in the promulgation of the Basic Agrarian Law (Undang-undang Pokok Agraria, or UUPA) of 1960. This law was, of course, based on the Indonesian constitution of 1945, whose article 33(3) stated that "the land, the waters and the natural resources within shall be under the powers of the State and shall be used to the greatest benefit of the people," a stipulation that can be interpreted as the articulation of hak ulayat at the level of the nation-state. This condition, which is distinguished from outright state ownership, nonetheless gives the state a much stronger position from which to take back the land from individual owners when compared to most Western systems.

Thus, Indonesian land law was grounded in two characteristics – a strong state role in the disposition of land rights under the formal system of the UUPA and a history of local state recognition of traditional claims on the land (or technically, *bekas adat*, "former traditional," once the UUPA came into effect). By the late 1980s, this led to the situation whereby those with bekas adat claims to their land had a fairly strong sense of their security of tenure, whereas those whose claims were properly registered under the UUPA nonetheless felt that the state could intercede to take their land at any time (Struyk, Hoffman, and Katsura 1990). The gap in the sense of tenure security was not as great as might be typically assumed in developing country contexts, a situation that in relative terms provided little impetus for informal landowners to legally register their properties.

Incentives for individuals to register lands under the UUPA have been weak, and even with repeated programs to accelerate the process, supported by the World Bank and other foreign or supranational agencies, the head of the National Land Agency (BPN) recently admitted that only 45 percent of parcels nationwide had been registered in the more than half-century since the promulgation of the Land Law,[5] though another recent estimate from legal scholar Daryono (2010) puts this at only 21 percent. One might presume that urban lands would have a higher rate of registration, as any modicum of improved stability would be deemed beneficial in volatile urban land markets.[6] Nonetheless, even in the highly urbanized territory of East Jakarta, registered real estate currently accounts for little more than two-thirds of the land.[7]

As I have argued elsewhere (Leaf 1994), it is seemingly ironic that the promulgation of a law that was intended to do away with land-law dualism has instead led to the establishment of a new form of dualism. The previous dichotomy between indigenous tenure rights and those imported from Europe during the colonial period has, in effect, been replaced by the persistent distinction between lands that are registered with the National Land Agency (referred to as *bersertipikat*) and those that have not yet been registered.

Two points to bear in mind when examining this dualism are that, first, most "not yet registered" lands are those territories on which the city's burgeoning informal housing is built, and, second, a principal means by which they are added to the official registry is through the actions of Jakarta's formal real estate development industry. Regarding this first point, although the international literature on informal urbanism sometimes conflates such categories as "slum" and "squatter" housing, the word "slum" typically refers to poorly built structures, whereas "squatter" designates unauthorized occupation and is thus a legal distinction. Due perhaps to the legacy of colonial-era legal dualism, Jakarta has relatively few true squatters, as most informally developed housing is on former plantation lands, leaving only 3–5 percent of the city's housing stock, mostly along river banks and railroad rights-of-way, as unambiguously squatter housing (Struyk, Hoffman, and Katsura 1990).

As for the second point, the city's real estate industry cannot legally sell properties that are not officially registered under conditions established by the UUPA. In acquiring land for their projects, however, developers prefer to purchase unregistered parcels. Not only are they consistently cheaper than registered lands, but more importantly, at the beginning of the land development process developers are issued a location permit (*izin lokasi*), which grants them the exclusive development rights for any particular territory. This equates with designating monopsonistic purchasing rights to developers, as once the permit has been issued, the land is essentially taken out of the open market.

In this regard, one can readily identify a set of vested interests in maintaining Jakarta's land-law dualism and thus perpetuating its market in informal lands and housing. From the perspective of the real estate development industry, the informal neighbourhoods constitute a large and low-cost land bank for development into the future; all that is needed for a developer to secure such lands are location permits. These permits tend to be renewed on a regular basis and thus can be maintained in perpetuity despite periodic government announcements that such abuses of the development process will be curbed. From the normative position of urban governance, one might expect that the local state would defend the interests of small landowners over those of the more powerful real estate developers. This may be especially so in cases where land-law unification is being attempted, since, as Daryono points out, unification perforce "also involves an extension and deepening of the government's role in land affairs." Rather than helping to resolve land-law dualism, this may further complicate matters, as the "extension of government involvement in land administration, a consequence of these attempts at transforming land law, has created further complexity as bureaucratic capacity itself is highly limited and responds in an unsatisfactory manner to local circumstances and needs" (Daryono 2010, 10).

Informality and Governance

The somewhat benign assumption of insufficient administrative capacity, however, obscures the possibility of another set of vested interests in maintaining the status quo, those of the government itself. The implication here is that of the moral hazard created by the expansion of local regulatory powers with limited resources for enforcement. One might readily label the resulting informal practices as a type of administrative corruption, and indeed this system does not work as it was ostensibly intended, and undoubtedly payoffs and kickbacks from the development industry and its associated middlemen are rife at every level of the state regulatory system. Applying the label of corruption, however, tends to end discussion by implying ultimately a failure in the rule of law or alternatively a pervasive moral failure on the part of those who are entrusted to uphold the law. Such an analysis, however, is insufficient for fully understanding the implications of Jakarta's land law dualism for the city's spatial development.

My point here is that this is a situation whereby we can interpret the informal practices within the state's local regulatory machinery not as an aberration or as a misapplication of the formal rule system,[8] as is implied by the use of the word "corruption." Instead, we can see informality as a mode of governance in and of itself. One very useful contribution to this manner of understanding informality at the level of the local state comes from Alan Gilbert (1990) in his interpretation of "the costs and benefits of illegality and irregularity" in urban land development. Gilbert asks why governments establish laws that they seemingly have no interest in enforcing and answers his question with the straightforward application of cost-benefit analysis: if the costs of enforcing a law outweigh its benefits, it tends to go unenforced. And it should be mentioned here that such a calculus is not limited solely to monetary costs and benefits, as political costs and benefits may weigh heavily in the decision-making of local officials as well.

The obvious rejoinder to this interpretation is to ask: Why have such laws in the first place if the government is not serious about their enforcement? Here, it is helpful to think about the nature of constituencies to which a local state is beholden and to consider that such a cost-benefit interpretation for one constituency, or one component of urban society, may be very different for another. In this case, proper registration of land under the UUPA serves to benefit buyers in the so-called formal market, those who purchase their homes from the city's burgeoning development industry and who desire full legality as part of the "bundle of attributes" associated with their new acquisition. Adhering not only to the stipulations of the UUPA, but also to various building and planning codes, such as minimum lot size, engineering specifications, and land-use restrictions, is important for gaining access to formal housing finance and the potential future use of the property as collateral. Such considerations, however, do not apply to those whose properties are obtained or maintained through informal practices, as they are unlikely to benefit from a property's full legality.

The idea that there are varying sets of costs and benefits according to different constituencies is paralleled in certain respects by the observation that differing sets of costs and benefits may be important at different levels in the city's administrative hierarchy as well. For one thing, whereas records of formally registered lands are maintained at the municipal and borough-level offices of the National Land Agency (BPN), lands claimed under informal or former traditional categories are recorded and maintained at the lowest level of the official administrative hierarchy, the *kelurahan* (sometimes translated as sub-district). This, in a sense, keeps local knowledge at the most local of levels, an ostensibly informal practice that could be seen as accommodating the interests of officials at the lowest echelon of the administrative system by their superiors at the municipal level. One could interpret this through the lens of subsidiarity in that the detailed information on landownership, transfers, and taxation of informally registered lands is kept at the administrative level closest to the citizenry. Considering the pervasive kickbacks and side-payments associated with transactions on these lands, one might wonder if this could also be interpreted as the subsidiarity of corruption.

State authorities have three possible responses when confronted with informality (and here I refer to informal practices by citizens and lower-level government officials): they may be supportive, tolerant, or repressive. A supportive response would be the recognition by local officials of informal agricultural practices on empty lots and the establishment of a local community organization to oversee this. An example of repression would be a crackdown on street vendors in particular shopping districts and the confiscation of their wares. Tolerance lies somewhere between support and repression. Unlike active support, it confers no recognition and thus establishes no precedent. One relevant example of tolerance would be with respect to the minimum lot size for residential construction. This standard, established during the Dutch colonial period, effectively differentiated the permanent housing of the European and wealthier Asian populations from the comparatively makeshift construction of village (*kampung*) housing by native Indonesians. It has been maintained in Jakarta ever since, despite the fact that the majority of residential properties in the city are now below the minimum. Rather than lowering the standard to reflect reality, maintaining it and yet tolerating its abuse allows local officials a degree of leverage over the populace that they would not otherwise enjoy. If most Jakartans live in technically illegal housing, according to the letter of an unenforced law, there is always the possibility that the state might choose to apply the rules and demolish substandard examples.

Thus, tolerating informal practices confers greater power to local officials. As a generalization, the under-specification of rules permits greater discretion in their application, though it also results in more ambiguity. And within the administrative hierarchy, tolerance of informality at lower levels by those higher up in the administrative pyramid creates sets of mutual obligations and likewise establishes an additional means of control by higher-level officials.

The field of informality studies has become increasingly complex and multifaceted in recent years, and has provided useful insights into practices of governance and state-society relations in many contexts around the world. The idea that not just agents of the state, but the state itself, would have a vested interest in maintaining informal practices may seem counterintuitive. After all, definitions of the concept of formality or formal practices typically emphasize adherence to established laws and regulations, with informality therefore seen as an abrogation of expected state practices. This idea of informality as a particular mode or strategy of governance is by no means unique to Jakarta. For example, the legal scholar Peter Ho (2001) advances similar arguments in his analysis of landownership and control in China. He emphasizes that the "institutional ambiguity" surrounding rural land rights is a deliberate strategy on the part of the Chinese government, in order to maintain greater fluidity in its relations with lower-level officials.

Conclusions: Property Rights and the Right to the City
The situation with land and property rights in Jakarta gives us one indication of the caution that should be exercised in thinking about the ostensibly

homogenizing effects of globalization. On the face of it, Indonesia is part of the global trend toward the normalization of freehold ownership as the prevailing global standard in land rights, a trend that is consistent with the global expansion of capitalist relations and that is seen to benefit capitalists and consumers alike. Yet, in the context of Jakarta's post-colonial governance, things are not always as they first appear. As I have emphasized here, such seemingly path-dependent factors as the rearticulation of colonial-era land-law dualism (which underpins the so-called informal market in land) and the persistence of personalistic relations across the city's hierarchical administrative structures belies the potential for true global convergence of practices pertaining to land rights and land markets. Although institutional forms may appear to be increasingly similar between one or another national or local context, the embedded norms by which they function may nonetheless diverge.

The resulting persistence, if not growth, of what is known in the academic literature as informality, or the prevalence of informal practices, can be expected to continue for some time, though not only because they are so socially embedded. This is not just a case of path dependence, but also of new paths opening up, new pressures, and new possibilities that will shape Indonesian society into the future. Most importantly, persistent informality and the resulting segmentation of urban property markets (and the urban spatial economy in general) are occurring in the overall context of the ongoing urban transition, an unprecedented shift in society from the rural agrarian past and into a largely unknown urban future.

Indonesia's urban transition, however, is not just a story of continuing urban growth, but also of the class formation that accompanies it. The principal segmentation of traditional Indonesian society, with elites and middle classes in the cities while the "floating mass" of peasant farmers remained in the countryside, is quickly becoming a thing of the past. In its place, one finds an increasingly bifurcated society in the expanding urban setting, with both the burgeoning middle classes who are so attractive to capitalist investors and a perhaps even more burgeoning urban underclass, those of post-peasant background who are young, poor, and disaffected, and who will never have the experience of private ownership in the city's property markets. For them, their only claim to a right to the city will be that of a collective right, expressed not through individual property ownership but through their overall presence in the city as a constituency that cannot be ignored or suppressed.

Notes

1 For an elaboration of this point, though primarily with reference to trends in agrarian lands, see Hall, Hirsch, and Li (2011), Chapter 2 in particular.
2 See Baross (1983) for one such observation along these lines from the early 1980s.
3 See Polanyi (1944) for an analysis of the historical development of freehold ownership and its importance in the evolution of capitalism.
4 See Leaf (1993) for a more detailed analysis of this point.
5 "Only 45 Percent of Land in Indonesia Has Certificates: BPN Head," Tempo.co, September 22, 2016, http://en.tempo.co/read/news/2016/08/16/056796370/Only -45-Percent-of-Land-in-Indonesia-has-Certificates-BPN-Head.
6 And one may identify a price differential between formally registered and not-yet registered properties in Jakarta (Dowall and Leaf 1991).
7 "30 Percent of Land in E. Jakarta Not Yet Certified," Nurito, *Berita Jakarta,* May 12, 2016, https://www.beritajakarta.id/en/read/14504/30-percent-of-land-in-e-jakarta -not-yet-certified#.YCmScndKhSx.
8 Various interpretations of informality have been put forward since the 1970s, when the term first emerged in the academic literature. My own overview and analysis of this literature may be found in Leaf (2005).

References

Baross, P. 1983. "The Articulation of Land Supply for Popular Settlements in Third World Cities." In *Land for Housing the Poor,* ed. Shlomo Angel, Raymon W. Archer, Sidhijai Tanphiphat, and Emiel A. Wegelin, 180–210. Singapore: Select Books.

Daryono. 2010. "The Transformation of Land Law in Indonesia: The Persistence of Pluralism." *Asian Journal of Comparative Law* 5, 1: Article 1.

Dowall, D., and M. Leaf. 1991. "The Price of Land for Housing in Jakarta." *Urban Studies* 28, 5: 707–22.

Gilbert, A. 1990. "The Costs and Benefits of Illegality and Irregularity in the Supply of Land." In *The Transformation of Land Supply Systems in Third World Cities,* ed. P. Baross and J. van der Linden, 17–36. Aldershot, UK: Gower.

Gillespie, John. 2008. "Towards a Discursive Analysis of Legal Transfers into Developing East Asia." *New York University Journal of International Law and Politics* 40, 3: 657–722.

Hall, Derek, Phillip Hirsch, and Tania Li. 2011. *Powers of Exclusion: Land Dilemmas in Southeast Asia.* Singapore: NUS Press.

Ho, Peter. 2001. "Who Owns China's Land? Policies, Property Rights and Deliberate Institutional Ambiguity." *China Quarterly* 166: 394–421. DOI: https://doi.org/ 10.1017/S0009443901000195.

Jones, Gavin W. 1997. "The Thoroughgoing Urbanization of East and Southeast Asia." *Asia Pacific Viewpoint* 38, 3: 237–49.

Leaf, M.L. 1993. "Land Rights for Residential Development in Jakarta, Indonesia: The Colonial Roots of Contemporary Urban Dualism." *International Journal of Urban and Regional Research* 17, 4: 477–91.

–. 1994. "Legal Authority in an Extralegal Setting: The Case of Land Rights in Jakarta, Indonesia." *Journal of Planning Education and Research* 14, 1: 12–18.

–. 2005. "The Bazaar and the Normal: Informalization and Tertiarization in Urban Asia." In *Service Industries, Cities and Development Trajectories in the Asia-Pacific*, ed. Peter Daniels, Kong Chong Ho, and Thomas Hutton, 110–28. London: Routledge.

Neale, Walter C. 1985. "Property in Land as Cultural Imperialism: Or, Why Ethnocentric Ideas Won't Work in India and Africa." *Journal of Economic Issues* 19, 4: 951–58.

Polanyi, Karl. 1944. *The Great Transformation*. New York: Farrar and Rinehart.

Robison, Richard. 1986. *Indonesia: The Rise of Capital*. London: Allen and Unwin.

Struyk, R.J., M.L. Hoffman, and H.M. Katsura. 1990. *The Market for Shelter in Indonesian Cities*. Washington, DC: Urban Institute Press.

van Leeuwen, Lizzy. 2011. *Lost in Mall: An Ethnography of Middle-Class Jakarta in the 1990s*. Leiden: KITLV Press.

11

Indonesia

──────────

The Links between Globalization, Poverty, and Income Inequality

RICHARD SCHWINDT

As noted in the Foreword, this volume is one of five that focus on the interface of globalization, in particular trade expansion, and compliance with international human rights standards, especially socio-economic standards. In many cases, the research question is fairly clear-cut: Is trade expansion compatible with enhanced access to health care, adequate housing, and education, increased food security, creation of employment characterized by acceptable working conditions, security in old age and during periods of unemployment, and so forth? Further, there is little debate that these types of socio-economic rights are well founded. Most would accept that the collective, as represented by the state, has a duty to provide care for those with physical and mental infirmities and to attenuate hunger, homelessness, lack of access to education, insecurity during old age and periods of economic distress, and unfair employment practices. This, of course, is all subject to a very strong binding constraint, the availability of adequate economic resources (land, labour, capital, and entrepreneurial talent) to undertake the task.

This volume is concerned with less straightforward human rights. It deals with poverty and economic inequality. Poverty, especially extreme poverty, is linked to human rights in two ways. First, it can result *in* the failure to enjoy accepted rights, and second, it can result *from* the failure to enjoy such rights. For example, in jurisdictions with weak social safety nets, the very poor commonly cannot afford adequate health care, housing, nutrition, and education. On the other hand, denial of access to food, health care, employment, and education can result in extreme poverty for those denied. Broadly speaking, globalization can have a salutary effect on poverty levels via two paths. First, increased trade will amplify the demand for certain inputs, often labour, which will result in higher returns to those factors. Second, international integration can bring with it adherence to human rights standards, such as in employment, that facilitate the movement out of poverty. These salutary impacts are not, of course, guaranteed.

The link between economic inequality and human rights is more complex. The human rights literature makes a distinction between horizontal and vertical inequality that resembles economists' notions of vertical and horizontal fairness or equity. For the economist, horizontal fairness implies that people in the same position should be treated in the same way. Students of human rights James Heintz, Diane Elson, and Radhika Balakrishnan (2015, 5) take a parallel view: "Horizontal inequality is defined as inequality between culturally defined or socially constructed groups. Inequalities with respect to gender, race, ethnicity, religion, caste, and sexuality are all examples of horizontal inequalities."

The concept is similar across disciplines. For the economist, horizontal fairness requires equal pay for equal work (i.e., output) regardless of gender, race, religion, age, or sexual preference. For the human rights community, horizontal inequality would exist when, for example, women were paid less than men for an identical job. Indeed, much of the focus of the human rights movement is on horizontal inequality. Discrimination on the basis of culturally defined or socially constructed groups in the context of voting rights, freedom of movement, religious worship, employment opportunities, wages, public office holding, landholding, and so on has long been a target of human rights activists. Importantly, economists generally agree that horizontal fairness is efficiency enhancing. For instance, if an employer hires on the basis of race, gender, or religion rather than productivity, output will ultimately suffer.

However, vertical inequality is viewed differently across disciplines. For the economist, vertical fairness requires not taking from the poor to give to the rich. An application here would be the progressive income tax. For the human rights community, there appears to be no clear definition of when vertical inequality becomes an abuse of human rights. At the outset, it must be recognized that economic inequality, whether measured in terms of income or wealth, is not synonymous with poverty. There are wealthy countries with an unequal distribution of income that do not suffer serious poverty, and poor countries with relatively equal incomes and high levels of serious poverty. At issue is whether economic inequality has an independent (i.e., independent of its association with poverty) negative impact on the enjoyment of human rights.

Two lines of argument link economic inequality to human rights concerns. First, economic inequality can negatively affect social cohesion, which in turn can compromise the enjoyment of specific rights. Second, economic inequality can impede economic growth, which can exacerbate the problem of poverty (a falling tide sinks all boats).

Numerous studies find a correlation between economic inequality and social ills, many of which could be viewed as an impairment of human rights. For example, in Chapter 2 of this volume, James Dean and Colin McLean refer to the work of Richard Wilkinson and Kate Pickett (2009), who argue that income inequality has pernicious effects on societies. The authors isolate a set of eleven indicators of well-being – physical health, mental health, drug abuse, education, imprisonment, obesity, social mobility, trust and community life, violence, teenage pregnancy, and child well-being. They claim that performance on these indicators was worse in countries with more unequal income distributions, regardless of whether they were rich or poor. These indicators can be matched to specific human rights. For example, the right to safety is compromised in a society plagued by violence. The right to education is impaired when educational performance is poor.

There is also an argument that economic inequality impedes economic growth, which is an essential component of economic development. Perhaps the best-known advocate of this view is Nobel laureate Joseph Stiglitz (2012):

> Inequality leads to lower growth and less efficiency. Lack of opportunity means that its [America's] most valuable asset – its people – is not being fully used. Many at the bottom, or even in the middle, are not living up to their potential, because the rich, needing few public services and worried that a strong government might redistribute income, use their political influence to cut taxes and curtail government spending. This leads to underinvestment in infrastructure, education, and technology, impeding the engines of growth.

Stiglitz's position is echoed in a recent OECD (2015) study on economic inequality:

Some may consider that the social and political costs of high and rising inequality are in and of themselves sufficient to justify action. The central argument of this publication is different. It is that, beyond its serious impact on social cohesion, high and often growing inequality raises major *economic concerns*, not just for the low earners themselves but for the wider health and sustainability of our economies. Put simply: *rising inequality is bad for long-term growth* (emphasis in original).

Interestingly, though economic inequality has become a centre-stage issue for economists, politicians, and social activists, it has only recently drawn significant attention from the human rights community. In 2015, the United Nations Human Rights Council's special rapporteur on extreme poverty and human rights, Philip Alston (2015), wrote:

> To date, however, the debate over inequality, which has assumed a new vibrancy in the wake of the publication of Thomas Piketty's book *Capital in the Twenty-First Century*, has paid very little attention to the relevance of human rights and much of the discussion that has taken place has been far more concerned with the plight of the middle classes than of those living in extreme poverty.
>
> The international human rights community has largely reciprocated the economists' neglect by ignoring the consequences of extreme inequality in the vast majority of its advocacy and analytical work. It does so at its peril, however, since a human rights framework that does not address extreme inequality as one of the drivers of extreme poverty and as one of the reasons why over one quarter of humanity cannot properly enjoy human rights is doomed to fail.

The reason for this neglect is not altogether clear. Samuel Moyn (2015) argues that, conceptually, human rights are compatible with inequality, even radical inequality. He goes on to claim that human rights advocates, when focusing on socio-economic rights, have emphasized a floor (the right to live above an absolute poverty line), not a ceiling. This in turn was consistent with the workings of largely unfettered markets. Human rights followed economic globalization. Activists no longer stressed the role of the state to manage welfare, but rather concentrated on the rights of individuals to be free from harm and to enjoy a limited government that protected them from disaster and abjection. Moyn concludes that the human rights movement abandoned postwar egalitarianism in theory and practice in its pursuit of cosmopolitanism.

In summary, freedom from abject poverty is recognized as a human right. Economic equality is not viewed as a human right. However, it is understood that extreme economic inequality can impair economic growth and thereby impair the attenuation of poverty. Further, extreme economic inequality, insofar as it plays a causal role in social debilities such as violence, crime, drug use, and lack of community, can be viewed as compromising the enjoyment of basic human rights. At issue is the relationship between globalization and both poverty and economic inequality.

The Volume

The chapters in this book focus on the nexus between globalization and both poverty and economic inequality in a single country, Indonesia. Although globalization encompasses many elements, such as international trade in goods and services, direct foreign investment, migration, and standards, including property rights, the emphasis here is on trade openness, albeit other elements are considered.

In Chapter 2, James Dean and Colin McLean provide a broad review of the academic literature on the relationships between globalization and economic growth, poverty levels, and economic inequality. As they point out, the literature tends to agree that trade openness has a positive effect on economic growth and poverty reduction but disagree regarding its impact on economic inequality. Arguably, inequality ranks among the most contentious issues across academic disciplines dealing with globalization. It has also become a flashpoint in recent important political contests and is the focus of some of the most widespread popular movements of our day (the international Occupy movement is a case in point). And, as noted earlier, there is some ambiguity over the link between human rights and economic inequality. This volume contributes to the debate by documenting Indonesia's experience with opening its economy to increased international trade and the subsequent impacts on economic growth, poverty levels, and income distribution.

Chapters 3 and 4 provide original empirical research bearing on the trade, poverty, and inequality interconnections in Indonesia. Chapter 3, authored by Teguh Dartanto, Yusuf Sofiyandi, and Nia Kurnia Sholihah, deals with the impact of increased trade openness on economic growth, poverty levels, and income inequality at the provincial level over the period 2000–13. Their results show that this element of globalization has a salutary effect on growth and poverty alleviation but has resulted in greater income inequality. Interestingly, they find that another core component of globalization, foreign direct investment, does not play an important role in explaining growth, poverty levels, or income inequality.

In Chapter 4, Yessi Vadila and Budy Resosudarmo examine the relationship between two core components of globalization (foreign direct investment and trade openness) and income inequality. Their analysis is carried out at the subnational level (employing data from twenty-two of Indonesia's thirty-three provinces) and provides interesting results. One component of globalization, foreign direct investment, is associated with greater equality, whereas the other, trade, is linked to greater inequality. The authors explain that foreign investment targeted sectors that relied on the intensive use of unskilled labour, which in turn benefitted the poor. Trade, on the other hand, generated greater benefits for the rich.

Chapters 6 and 7 discuss the ramifications of thwarting globalization, specifically how the government policy of impeding rice imports affected poverty and inequality. Pursuing a "pro-poor" trade policy, Indonesia erected barriers to the importation of rice, with the intent of assisting farmers and attenuating rural poverty. The policy did not work. In Chapter 6, Richard Barichello and Faisal Harahap scrutinize barriers to rice imports from 1983 to 2009 and note that they had very modest positive effects on rural wage rates in the provinces of East, West, and Central Java, which account for nearly half the country's population. Moreover, there were obvious unintended consequences. Rice is a basic foodstuff in Indonesia, and increases in its price due to trade restrictions have a regressive impact – when rice prices go up, the poor suffer more than the rich. The authors also find that increases in manufacturing wages had a much more salutary effect on rural wages than trade constraints. The explanation is that expansion of the manufacturing sector drew labour away from agriculture through rural-to-urban migration, with a resultant positive effect on rural wages.

Dealing with the same issue in Chapter 7, Arianto Patunru reaches a simple conclusion using detailed, disaggregated data. Increases in rice prices, the goal of import restrictions, provide very little benefit to poor rice producers and impose very large costs on rice consumers, particularly the poor. The author explains why this protectionism persists, given its clearly deleterious effects on the poor and an avowed public policy to mitigate poverty. The usual suspects emerge: effective rent-seekers (richer farmers and traders), calls for food self-sufficiency, anxiety about a lack of competitiveness, and fear of dependence on unstable, thin markets for traded rice. The policy recommendation, education of the population as to the distributional effects of protectionism, could be expanded to education as to the distributional impact of all trade policy, both protectionism and liberalization.

Three chapters present case studies of the effects of globalization on specific groups – children, coffee producers, and the visually disabled. Their common thread is that globalization generally has had positive but uneven consequences for the poor. The lesson is that policy makers must be alert and sensitive to these consequences if they wish to mitigate negative impacts on the vulnerable.

In Chapter 5, Santi Kusumaningrum and her colleagues focus on child poverty. Using extensive descriptive statistics, they show that whereas child poverty rates as measured by income levels declined during the period of trade expansion, a closer examination of the multiple dimensions of child poverty indicates that Indonesia has a considerable way to go. There remain serious deficiencies in the provision of health services, adequate nutrition, and education to impoverished children. Further, these deficiencies vary markedly across regions. The authors argue that if they are not corrected by government policy, Indonesia will fail to fully exploit anticipated changes in its demography. Succinctly, Indonesia is predicted to benefit from an increase in the proportion of working-age individuals in the near future, the so-called demographic dividend. This will be fully realized only if that cohort is healthy and educated.

In Chapter 8, Bustanul Arifin examines a change in international consumer tastes – eco-certification – that might be expected to benefit poor Indonesian coffee growers but in fact has not. The demand in developed countries for agricultural products that are created by sustainable, environmentally friendly methods seems benign and in line with human rights focused on environmental integrity and freedom from poverty. There is a perception that sustainable agriculture favours smaller producers who are more attuned to their holdings than large, corporate operators. However, this study, based in part on extensive field work, shows that eco-certification has had little effect on the farm-gate price of coffee. This has to do with the insensitivity of Indonesian farm-gate prices to global coffee prices. However, the author ends on a more hopeful note, with the observation that eco-certification necessitates the establishment of farmers' organizations, which could play a positive role with regard to information collection and dissemination, negotiation, and conflict resolution.

In Chapter 9, Evi Arifin and Aris Ananta identify an interesting and representative paradox of globalization. On the one hand, the integration of markets has generated a dependence on digital technologies, which has disadvantaged the visually disabled, particularly the poor. On the other hand, trade facilitates the dissemination of knowledge with respect to treatment of vision problems and the availability of corrective technologies. It simultaneously exacerbates the problem and provides a solution. The authors supply detailed data with regard to the prevalence of visual disabilities in Indonesia and conclude that a strong correlation exists between uncorrected vision issues and poverty. They point to a clear conclusion: globalization will further disadvantage the visually impaired. In many instances, corrective measures are available and not inordinately costly; policy makers should address the issue.

In Chapter 10, the final essay in the volume, Michael Leaf discusses property rights. He notes the presumption that globalization will lead to a homogenization of basic conditions critical to market economies. One of these conditions is the existence of well-defined and effectively enforced private rights to real property. This presumption does not hold with respect to Indonesia. In effect, the country has a dual system of rights to land – formal and informal, or traditional. The systems continue to co-exist because they are of benefit to both private and public interests, and because eradicating either one would incur costs. This duality is of particular interest in the context of urbanization. There is a positive correlation between urbanization and economic growth, and between growth and poverty reduction. Indonesia has experienced rapid urbanization, and this has been accompanied, according to Leaf, by a division within urban society between a middle and upper class who exercise formal rights to real property and an urban underclass who enjoy only an informal right to live in the city.

Lessons

The research presented in this book adds to our knowledge of the interconnections between globalization and two human rights areas of concern, poverty and income inequality. The results of the empirical studies are consistent with the economics literature on the subject. International trade has a positive effect on economic growth and the attenuation of poverty. Though claimed to be "pro-poor," trade restrictions have not had a meaningfully positive impact on poverty levels. And, in the case of Indonesia, trade openness has an unclear influence on income inequality.

In-depth examination of how certain groups have fared as Indonesia enlarges its engagement with the world economy shows that effects are uneven and that policy makers must be sensitive to this.

References

Alston, Philip. 2015. "Report of the Special Rapporteur on Extreme Poverty and Human Rights." Human Rights Council, United Nations. https://www.ohchr. org/EN/HRBodies/HRC/RegularSessions/Session29/Documents/A_HRC_29_ 31_en.doc.

Heintz, James, Diane Elson, and Radhika Balakrishnan. 2015. "What Does Inequality Have to Do with Human Rights?" Political Economy Research Institute Working Paper Series, University of Massachusetts, Amherst. https://www.peri.umass. edu/publication/item/687-what-does-inequality-have-to-do-with-human -rights.

Moyn, Samuel. 2015. "Do Human Rights Increase Inequality?" *Chronicle of Higher Education* (May 26). https://www.chronicle.com/article/Do-Human-Rights -Increase/230297/.

OECD. 2015. *In It Together: Why Less Inequality Benefits All.* Paris: OECD. http:// dx.doi.org/10.1787/9789264235120-en.

Stiglitz, Joseph. 2012. "The Price of Inequality and the Myth of Opportunity." Project Syndicate, June 6. https://www.commondreams.org/views/2012/06/06/ price-inequality-and-myth-opportunity.

Wilkinson, Richard G., and Kate Pickett. 2009. *The Spirit Level: Why More Equal Societies Almost Always Do Better.* New York: Bloomsbury Press.

Contributors

Aris Ananta is a professor of population economics at the Faculty of Economics and Business, Universitas Indonesia. A demographer-economist with an interdisciplinary perspective, he earned his PhD in economics at Duke University, specializing in population economics. He also taught at the Department of Economics, National University of Singapore, and was a senior research fellow at the Institute of Southeast Asian Studies, Singapore. His publication topics include population aging, migration, ethnicity and religion, population and development, environment, poverty, economic development, and politics. His research covers much of Asia, with Indonesia as his core area. Currently, he is also president of the Asian Population Association.

Bustanul Arifin is a professor of agricultural economics at the University of Lampung. He is also a senior economist at the Institute for Development Economics and Finance and a professorial fellow at the School of Business at IPB University. He has over thirty years of professional experience in the field of food and agricultural policy, institutional change, and sustainable development strategies. He earned his PhD in resource economics from the University of Wisconsin-Madison in 1995. His professional service in Indonesia includes appointments as chairman of the Forum of Statistic Society, food policy adviser at the Coordinating Ministry of Economic

Affairs, Government of Indonesia, and vice president of the Indonesian Society of Agricultural Economics.

Evi Nurvidya Arifin is a statistician-demographer with a multi-disciplinary interest. She is a senior assistant professor at Universiti Brunei Darussalam (UBD). Her research publications encompass various areas such as functional disability, the aging population, population mobility, fertility and family planning, health, and culture (ethnicity, religion, and language). She earned her PhD in social statistics, specializing in demography, from the University of Southampton. Prior to teaching at UBD, she taught at Universitas Indonesia and was a visiting research fellow at the Institute of Southeast Asian Studies, Singapore, a post-doctoral fellow at the Asian MetaCentre for Population and Sustainable Development Analysis, and at the Asia Research Institute, National University of Singapore.

Richard Barichello is a professor in food and resource economics at the University of British Columbia. He earned his PhD from the University of Chicago and is director of the Centre for Southeast Asia Research at UBC. He has taught in China, Ethiopia, Indonesia, Myanmar, Poland, Thailand, and Vietnam. He was president of the Canadian Agricultural Economics Society in the late 1990s and became chair of the International Agricultural Trade Research Consortium in 2015. His research has focused on the analysis of trade, agricultural policies, and institutions, Canadian dairy quota markets, Southeast Asian rural labour markets, issues related to agricultural productivity in Asian countries, and investment projects.

Cyril Bennouna is senior adviser for research at the Center on Child Protection and Wellbeing (PUSKAPA) at Universitas Indonesia. He has also served as a senior researcher for the Program on Forced Migration and Health at Columbia's Mailman School of Public Health, the CPC Learning Network, and the International Trauma Studies Program. He has completed projects for a variety of partners, including the World Bank, United States Agency for International Development, Australian Department of Foreign Affairs and Trade, the Centers for Disease Control and Prevention, and the United Nations Children's Fund. He has a master's degree in public health from Columbia University and is currently a political science PhD candidate at Brown University.

Teguh Dartanto is the vice dean of academic affairs at the Faculty of Economics and Business and a senior researcher at the Institute for Economic and Social Research, Universitas Indonesia. His interests include poverty, social protection, development economics, health economics, and micro-econometrics. He has published in the *Lancet, World Development Perspectives, Economic Modelling, Energy Policy, Bulletin of Indonesian Economic Studies, Singapore Economic Review,* and *Economics Bulletin.* He has been a consultant to Japan International Cooperation Agency, Asian Development Bank, United Nations Development Programme, and the Organisation for Economic Co-operation and Development. A member of the Indonesian Young Academy of Sciences and a 2017 Eisenhower fellow, he has a PhD in international development from Nagoya University.

James W. Dean (deceased) was emeritus professor of economics at Simon Fraser University. He held a bachelor's degree in mathematics from Carleton University and master's and PhD degrees in economics from Harvard. During his tenure at Simon Fraser, he held visiting appointments at twenty-seven universities and research institutes in the United States, South America, England, Western and Eastern Europe, Africa, Asia, and Australia. He published widely, with a focus on international macro-economics, specifically financial crises and sovereign debt relief. He played jazz tenor saxophone with the Vancouver-based James Dean Trio (modestly describing his skill level as "merely mediocre").

Faisal Harahap is an economics PhD candidate in the Resource Management and Environmental Studies program at the University of British Columbia. He has worked as a senior research fellow for the Indonesian finance minister, Dr. Radius Prawiro, as a financial analyst with ING Barings Hong Kong, as a research fellow at the Institute for Southeast Asian Studies, Singapore, and as a senior associate at InterSource Health Systems in Phoenix and Jakarta. He has obtained two graduate economics degrees, a master's degree from the University of Oklahoma and a master's degree in agricultural economics from UBC.

Santi Kusumaningrum is the co-founder and director of the Center on Child Protection and Wellbeing (PUSKAPA) at Universitas Indonesia. Her work focuses on making systems and services enable social inclusion, child well-being, and resilience; solving the barriers to legal identity to facilitate access to public services, justice, and opportunities; and mastering the politics of policy transformations. She was trained in criminology and social policy at Universitas Indonesia and got her doctorate in public health from Columbia University. She received Columbia University's Award of Excellence in Global Health twice and has published in such journals as the *Lancet, PLOS ONE,* and *BMC International Health and Human Rights.*

Michael Leaf is an associate professor in the School of Community and Regional Planning at the University of British Columbia, a research associate of the UBC Centre for Human Settlements, and formerly the director of the Centre for Southeast Asia Research in UBC's Institute of Asian Research. His work focuses on urbanization and planning in cities of developing countries, with particular emphasis on Asian cities. Since the time of his doctoral research on land development in Jakarta, he has been extensively involved in urbanization research and capacity-building projects in Indonesia, Vietnam, China, Thailand, and Sri Lanka.

Colin McLean is a PhD candidate in philosophy at the University of St. Andrews. His research concerns the normative limits of public policy in liberal-democratic societies, touching on a variety of topics in moral and political philosophy such as value pluralism, political legitimacy, and the nature and value of freedom. Before embarking on his doctoral studies, he completed a master's degree in public policy at Simon Fraser University, after which he worked as a policy analyst at the Canada Deposit Insurance Corporation and consulted for BC Hydro on regulatory frameworks for the management of catastrophic risk.

Arianto Patunru is a fellow at the Arndt-Corden Department of Economics, Crawford School of Public Policy, at the Australian National University (ANU). He is a member of the ANU Indonesia Project. Prior to moving to Australia, he was the director of the Institute for Economic and Social Research at Universitas Indonesia. He is a co-editor of the *Bulletin of Indonesian Economic Studies,* and he has a PhD from the University of Illinois at Urbana-Champaign. His research has focused on environmental and resource economics and, more recently, trade and industry in developing countries. His publications include papers in the *American Journal of Agricultural Economics, Journal of Development Studies,* and *Contemporary Economic Policy.*

Budy P. Resosudarmo is a professor at the Arndt-Corden Department of Economics, Crawford School of Public Policy, at the Australian National University. His research areas are development and environmental economics. He has been working on the economy-wide impact of economic and environmental policies and resource utilisation. He was president of the Regional Science Association International and of the Pacific Regional Science Conference Organization. He is also a member of the board of directors of the East Asian Association of Environmental and Resource Economics.

Richard Schwindt is emeritus professor of economics at Simon Fraser University. He received his PhD from the University of California (Berkeley) in industrial organization and anti-trust policy. His research continued this specialization and was broadened to the industrial economics of, and public policy toward, agriculture, forestry, and the Pacific salmon fishery. This interest in anti-trust economics and policy led to teaching micro-economic policy courses and providing litigation support for both anti-trust authorities and private-sector stakeholders. He observed, interpreted for his students, and played a modest part in the evolution of Canadian competition policy from an ineffectual to a world-class anti-trust regime.

Nia Kurnia Sholihah is a researcher at the Institute for Economic and Social Research, Faculty of Economics and Business, and an assistant lecturer of economics at Universitas Indonesia. She has an undergraduate degree in economics from Universitas Indonesia. Her interests include development economics, social protection, and health economics, as well as environmental economics. She has been involved in consulting projects for the Indonesian Ministry of Finance and the Coordinating Ministry for Economic Affairs, as well as international organizations such as the Asian Development Bank.

Clara Siagian is a senior researcher at the Center on Child Protection and Wellbeing (PUSKAPA) at Universitas Indonesia. Prior to joining PUSKAPA, she worked with World Bank Indonesia on disability and with a Global Fund HIV-AIDS project in the Southeast Asia region. She was the lead local researcher for an ARC-funded project on childhood poverty in Indonesia with the Australian National University. She holds a master's degree from the Australian National University and is pursuing her doctorate on eviction and social housing policy at the same university.

Yusuf Sofiyandi is a junior research associate at the Institute for Economic and Social Research in the Faculty of Economics and Business, a co-lecturer in the Master of Public Policy and Planning Program, and a member of the Centre for Urban and Transport Economics, at Universitas Indonesia. He has a master's degree in spatial, transportation, and environmental economics from Vrije Universiteit, Amsterdam. His interests include spatial economics and urban and transportation economics, as well as the economic impact of infrastructure investment.

Yessi Vadila works as a trade analyst at the Ministry of Trade, Republic of Indonesia. She first joined the ministry in 2006, after completing a bachelor's degree in chemical engineering at Universitas Indonesia, where she also went on to study economics and earn a master's degree cum laude in international trade. Finally, she received her economics PhD from the Australian National University. Her research focuses on the socio-economic, environmental, and health impacts of trade liberalization in Indonesia. She was the assistant to the Ministry of Trade's Lead Adviser on International Trade from 2017 to 2019.

Index